Biology of Dogs

From Gonads through Guts to Ganglia

Tim Lewis, PhD

Publishing

Wenatchee, Washington U.S.A.

Biology of Dogs
From Gonads through Guts to Ganglia

Tim Lewis, PhD

Dogwise Publishing
A Division of Direct Book Service, Inc.
403 South Mission Street, Wenatchee, Washington 98801
1-509-663-9115, 1-800-776-2665
www.dogwisepublishing.com / info@dogwisepublishing.com

Art director: Jon Luke
Chapter introduction illustrations: Brad Palm
Illustrations and photos: Tim Lewis
Interior: Lindsay Davisson
Cover design: Brad Palm and Jesus Cordero

Library of Congress Cataloging-in-Publication Data

Names: Lewis, Tim, 1962- author.
Title: Biology of dogs : from gonads through guts to ganglia / Tim Lewis, PhD.
Description: Wenatchee, Washington : Dogwise Publishing, 2021. | Includes bibliographical references and index. | Summary: "You may be thinking, how can I take a book seriously when the subtitle starts with the word "gonads?" Well, you have probably not met Tim Lewis yet and only know the slang definition of the word. But seriously, gonads (testicles and ovaries) are what biology is all about, they are the mechanisms that allow living beings to reproduce - and without reproduction - and without reproduction, no life. Of course, there is way more to the biology of dogs than just that. Biology of Dogs takes you on a series of tours through the inside of the dog leading you through all the major biological systems - reproductive, nervous, musculoskeletal, digestive and more. Tim will lead your tours in a fun and irreverent manner to provide you - the dog enthusiast - what you need to know to enhance your dog-human relationships such that you abandon all of your human friends and spend more time with your dog!"-- Provided by publisher.
Identifiers: LCCN 2020042288 | ISBN 9781617812767 (paperback) | ISBN 9781617812774 (ebook)
Subjects: LCSH: Dogs--Physiology.
Classification: LCC SF768.2.D6 L49 2021 | DDC 636.7--dc23
LC record available at https://lccn.loc.gov/2020042288

ISBN: 978-1-61781-276-7
Printed in the U.S.A.

What Other Geeks, Nerds and Dog Enthusiasts Are Saying About Biology of Dogs

Biology of Dogs is the definitive guide for understanding your furry four-legged companion. Tim has translated the science with relatable analogies and a conversational style. This is one for your permanent library - you'll keep coming back to it.
Lesley Scibora, DC, PhD. Associate Professor of Health and Exercise Science, but she owed Tim a favor....

Here is the recipe for a fun and informative book about dogs. Start with an insatiable curiosity. Add a PhD in how living things work (the study of Biology). Add a dash of wit, sarcasm, and a healthy dose of irreverence. Finish it off by stirring in a few very personal stories and a strong desire to maintain his position as the best dog dad ever.
Ruth Lewis, CCFT. While forced to review the book as Tim's wife, in her own right she is a certified canine fitness trainer, a member of APDT, and an instructor of agility and canine freestyle.

When he was 3 or 4 years old, Tim drew a perfectly proportioned letter B in red pen on a velvet throw pillow. It was so stunning even our mother could not be mad. No one knew he could write. This book may prove otherwise.
Barb Lewis, MFA. Tim's favorite sister who grew up to be a professional editor, and really wants to be known as the only other woman Tim has lived with. What about Mom?

Makes the perfect bathroom book - because, let's be honest, your dog is already in there with you, biology is already on your mind, and when you emerge, you and your dog will surely be transformed, your bond deeper because you have an insider's understanding.
Sue Sternberg, Canine behavior consultant, shelter expert, and the author of a dozen books on canine behavior and training. Known locally as The Desert Rat and a lover of all things dinosaur, she made Tim review one of her books two years ago; payback can be rough.

Turns out the inside of a dog is not too dark to read - Tim is our guiding light for learning all there is to know about our dogs' biology.
Sarah Palm, Animal Assisted Interventions Specialist, University of Minnesota; Canine Sports Massage Therapist; and Team Evaluator for Pet Partners. Tim says that "One of her dogs is named Ruthie, so they hit it off well from the start, but they first met when she helped Gromit when he came up lame at AKC Nationals a decade ago. No idea what leverage I had on her!"

At least this will make a good doorstop, with the bright yellow cover you won't trip on it.
Anonymous. You can only guess who wrote that!

Dedication

For Gromit, who taught us what it means to be dog people.

Table of Contents

Acknowledgements

No work such as this stands alone. This journey reflects on all who have taught me through the years including professors, colleagues, friends, students, and the dogs who share their lives with me. I owe my deepest thanks for this volume to my mentor and dear friend Sue Sternberg, who convinced me that the topic was good, that the point of view was useful, and that I should write this. Jon Luke at Dogwise likewise encouraged me to start this even after he had heard me teach. Sam Boyd kept the rest of my work world in order while I focused on this project. I thank my reviewers, including Sue Sternberg, Barb Lewis, Ruth Lewis, Lesley Scibora, and Sarah Palm, and my editors the staff at Dogwise, including Larry Woodward, Jon Luke, and the incredibly precise and knowledgeable Adrienne Hovey, for their attention to detail and willingness improve my words and clarify my thoughts. Brad Palm listened to the book's message, created the cover design and chapter introductory art. Any errors in this work are mine alone. Ruth taught, supported, and encouraged me throughout, as she has for four decades. Thanks is not enough. It has been a most rewarding year.

Foreword
by Sue Sternberg

Dog person or not, after reading this book you will likely be different, altered. You will almost certainly never again buy a dog toy without first considering the color. Nor will you be able to look at red cars on the highway the same way. You will likely never walk into a room again and not wonder if perhaps there could be an elephant lurking somewhere you cannot see.

His friends refer to him as "Tim-i-pedia" which sounds funny at first, but then of course you realize he really is. And he does tend to come in awfully handy. Once, vacationing with relatives in Quebec City in the dead of winter, the question of how long it takes for our bodies to acclimate to this 10 degree F frigid temperature came up. *Let's call Tim!* So you learn what mitochondria are ("the powerhouse of your cells," says Tim with great reverence) and that they will begin to increase in numbers to keep up with your body's demand for more heat/energy, and how ATP molecules ("like tiny rechargeable batteries," Tim tells you with mounting excitement for the process) take whatever sugar you just ate and replicate to make more and more power to keep your body warm. And because Tim is so excited and impressed by how biological processes work, you can't help but feel passionate, too.

Now apply all this biological passion to the world of dogs and you get this book. Tim defines and describes biological terms not because you might not understand or not know some of the basics, but because he loves to teach, he loves to explain, he loves to get people to "get it" and mostly because he is a hopeless geek. His scientific mind and scientific approach to life seep into you when you hang around him, until pretty soon you're at a party listening to someone give their opinion and wondering if they have a condition called "confirmation bias," which you learned about from Tim and has something to do with red cars. Tim doesn't just give you answers to the many needling questions that sometime plague us when we are not in a position to Google search the answers, like at 2AM, or while driving, but Tim gets us to think more richly, ask better questions, to wonder better.

Getting to know Tim changed me in ways others have been trying to get me to change since the early 1990s. People have been trying to get me to think more like a scientist since as far back in my lecturing career as I can remember. I'm a dog trainer and work mostly with shelter dogs. Everything I learned about dogs I learned on the job. I began formally teaching workshops on dogs around 1993. Sometimes PhDs, animal behaviorists, and other scientists would come up to me after a presentation and challenge my content. It was suggested to me that I should be collecting data before reporting and teaching about shelter dog assessments. Some wanted me to be doing formal research on what I was saying, make the language in my dog-assessment procedures more objective and less open to interpretation. *Objective…Interpretation…*I only vaguely remember what they said, because mostly I felt criticized. I couldn't seem to grasp what they were suggesting or how they wanted me to change. I did not think like a scientist, nor even know how a scientist thinks. I had no concept that this way of seeing the world might be useful.

Fast forward to Vermont in 2007, on a grassy slope at Marlboro College, where, once a year, Camp Gone to the Dogs was held. I was an instructor, hosting my daily afternoon Come-Ask-Your-Dog-Behavior-Questions class. Enter Tim Lewis, a man I knew only as my friend Ruth's husband. Married to a dog trainer, a dog lover himself, a professor and a biologist who had studied deer and turtles, Tim sat in on my outdoor classes and started to chime in, not so much with his own dog behavior questions, but with kind and interesting questions based on my answers. He would ask questions about my answers that had to do with *knowing* something vs *believing*. He would ask me about whether I was *interpreting* something I had observed, or *observing* something I had noticed. I think because Tim wasn't himself a dog trainer, and he had such reverence for dogs and science, I heard myself start rephrasing my sentences with "In my experience…" rather than "I know the following…".

If you already approach the world like a scientist, you may not be terribly altered by this book, but you will certainly know way more about dogs. If, like me, you did not approach the world like a scientist, you will experience a transformation after meeting Tim. Tim straddles the world of science and the world of experience, field-experts and lay people—he translates so we can all understand each other. Some of the changes you will experience after reading this book may be subtle, some more powerful, but all will likely affect not only the way you think, see, interact with, and understand your dog, but also how you see the world at large. You, like me, will soon never be able to *not* have Tim in your head. You might be watching a lovely sunset, and you will hear, "You see with your brain, Sue, not your eyes," and you will wonder how might that sunset look upside down.

For most of us who have forgotten more biology than we had ever learned, Tim bridges the gap in the dog world between experience and field work (a.k.a. dog training and shelter work) and science and data. So, just when you think your relationship with your dog could not possibly get any better, along comes this book.

Introduction

Ovaries and testicles. That's pretty much all a dog is about. Biologically, that's all any of us is really about. Here's a basic truism: If your parents didn't have any kids, odds are you won't either. Things that make copies of themselves are more likely to have copies of themselves in the next generation than those that don't. Reread that. It is a deliberate tautology. But it sums up life, from viruses to white pine trees. Try it this way: Dogs who make copies of themselves (puppies) will have more copies of themselves in the next generation than dogs who do not have any puppies. Dogs who make many successful copies make more copies of themselves than those who make fewer. You can't "be fruitful and multiply" with unsuccessful offspring. Two or three, heck even one successful copy of yourself in the next generation is evolutionarily better than 100 unsuccessful copies. Doesn't matter if we are talking computer viruses or dogs. Those that don't reproduce successfully have fewer copies than those that do. Those that do, populate the world. Whatever helps make successful copies is all that matters in the evolutionary long haul. It is not "survival of the fittest" unless by "fittest" you simply mean the ability to make successful copies of oneself. What parts make those copies? Testicles and ovaries, but not by themselves.

So it's all about sex? Not really, it is all about reproduction. Successful reproduction. Reproduction is making versions of yourself in the next generation. Puppies. Sex is just one way to do that. We will see others. Which is more important, food or sex? We are not just talking about what you do on dates here. In the long run, only reproduction, not food, not sex. In the short run, enough food to give energy for reproduction. The juvenile stage is all about food, to get to the reproductive stage, which we call adulthood. Taken to extremes, juveniles are all about eating. Think of your typical teenager. Right, you'd probably rather not. Think of insect larvae gnawing away day and night. Mayfly adults don't even eat; in fact, they don't have a mouth or a digestive system. They live as adults for only one day. They have one day to find a mate and continue a species after a year or two in a stream, eating, as juveniles.

Getting ovaries and testicles together

Back to ovaries and testicles, not that we ever really left them. A chicken is just an egg's way of making another egg. A dog is just the canine way of getting testicles and ovaries together to make another set of testicles and ovaries via dog transport. So that's really all you need: ovaries and testicles. Why didn't nature just put them in the same individual and be done with it? That would certainly eliminate a lot of fuss and commotion. Some species do just that, but the short answer for now is inbreeding. Bad stuff in the long run, and I do mean long, like hundreds of generations. Avoid this at all costs. But inbreeding is also the primary technique we use to domesticate a species and bring out distinguishing attributes like high milk production in a cow or the ability to turn a flock of sheep in a domestic dog. We often do interesting things in the short run that in the long run are unwise. Inbreeding leading to domestication is a useful tool for humans in manipulating species to our goals. It just does not make them more fit for survival in the wild, so in nature it is avoided. You need to put those testicles somewhere away from any closely related ovaries to avoid inbreeding. And while we are at it, hang the testicles out in a bag because the inside of the dog is just too warm for optimal sperm growth.

A testicle running through the woods or city in pursuit of an ovary is really all you need. Except testicles can't run. Maybe they can roll a bit, if you pushed them with a stick. You need a transport system to get them around. Movement takes energy, so the transport system has to procure food and process that a bit. Enter the mouth and teeth and the digestive system, and the whole food industry and the debate about kibble versus raw, and picking up poop. Teeth and hair and claws help keep the package alive while the testicles are searching for those ovaries. Testicles and ovaries are relatively unlikely to bump into each other unless they are literally all over the place. That is a common plant sex strategy. Dump all those sperm into the air—give a few people hay fever—and hope some of it lands on waiting genitals, known as flowers. Enlist bees for transport and you get a bit more precision. Throw in a system to sense the outside world and a decision-making processor to select good mates, which you might know as a nervous system with a brain, and now those gonads can finally find each other effectively.

To be a bit more accurate, it's really not about testicles and ovaries after all, but what they make. Sperm and eggs. Actually, not even that. It is all about DNA, since sperm and eggs are living cells in their own right, just delivering genetic material for the organs that made them. FedEx for DNA. More on that later, for sure. Viruses pretty much skip the whole body experience, wrap the DNA (or RNA) in a protein shield, and let someone else's body provide the replication machinery and spread the DNA. I am reminded of that every time I have a head cold or the flu.

It is all about sex

Ultimately that is all this book is about. Successful sex. Not a how-to book for you, God knows I am no expert there. This book is about what it takes to get those two organs together in dogs. I also hope the book will provide enough other information that the average dog owner, partner, or companion gains some appreciation for the four-legged furry friends who have, in the evolutionary blink of an eye, gone from deadly predators roving in gangs to the best friend you can ever have. Along the way, we can look at enough science-y stuff to be interesting, with a mind to the practical implications for you so that you and your dog can cohabitate better, live longer, run faster, and maybe win at Westminster, or maybe just once run cleanly at the local dog sports competition.

Dogs, of course, are way more than gonads, the general term for ovaries and testicles. No one invites a pair of gonads into the house, and then falls in love enough to spend a king's ransom on collars and leashes. For at least 14 millennia, and maybe 36,000 years, we have lived with and accelerated selection for the ideal partner. Or, as my sister put it, we got tricked by the cuteness of our pets to help them reproduce successfully. Dogs have been so inseparable from humans that we started burying them with us—after we died, of course, but not always after they did. We painted them on cave walls. Today we buy drawings and photos of them for our cave walls. I can't look at any wall in my house and not see a dog-related picture, portrait, drawing, or knickknack. Sometimes a friend makes us ceramic figurines of our dogs. Or mugs with our dogs on them. Or caricatures of our dogs. Or…this really could go on quite a while. Dogs look so damn cute and there are millions of them everywhere. Millions? Globally probably 900 million. Three-quarters of those are free ranging with no fixed home. In the United States, estimates put the number of pet dogs at under 100 million, probably about 75 million distributed in 50 million homes. Or, looking at it another way, almost 40 percent of all households in the U.S. have a dog in them.

What makes them the perfect partner, therapist, or running mates? How can they pull a sled all day in the Alaskan cold for two weeks, covering 1,000 miles in the Yukon Quest, rest a few days, and do it again in the Iditarod? They are simply remarkable creatures of wonder and spirit. They are alive, thinking, and feeling beings. Their biology is not at all dissimilar from ours.

A biological tour

While I would never say this in public nor personally admit to it, I am told I am a geek. Worse, an academic geek. Even worse than that, I am a scientist geek. But wait, it gets even worse, so you probably won't be inviting me to your parties: I am a biologist. I built my career studying reptiles. But since I study turtles, and turtles are pretty cool, maybe we can still talk a bit. I also study dogs, particularly their vision, so sometimes real people put up with me. I teach ecology and evolution, but my favorite course to teach is biology for the general public. This book is for people who maybe want to know a little more about science, but might find the way science gets taught is too often dull or unrelated to their daily life. I use dogs as examples in class because people relate to them and I can teach almost any biological concept using them. I have been invited to give talks about dogs and science around the country, in universities, fairgrounds, prisons, public meetings, and as a keynote speaker. I get invited to dog groups to talk biology because I also have dogs. Worse, Border Collies. Even worse than that, up to four of them at a time.

I find most people don't really know much biology, the formal body of knowledge about life and living organisms. Yet they have dogs, or they like people with dogs, or they understand that cats are mammals so most of what we know about dogs informs us about cats, and ourselves. We all really should know a little more about biology.

Doing so will help your relationship with your dog. I so often hear that my talks rekindle a love of biology, or at least make people see that it is important. If you can excuse the baggage—you know, the fact that I actually love Border Collies and turtles and people all at once—walk with me a bit and you will learn some pretty useful stuff, and also a lot of fun facts for the parties you get invited to. One of the many things this book is not intended to be is the end-all-be-all introduction to all of the biology we know. The introductory textbook I use for college biology majors, now in its 11th edition and listing new for north of $200, has almost 1,500 information-packed small-print double-columned pages. Even a year-long college course cannot cover all of that material.

I do not intend to constantly drown you in every available detail on every aspect of canine biology. This book is more of a guided tour of the more interesting and useful areas of the canine organism and is intended to shine a light into the complex world of biology of the dog. You will be gasping for air at times, hopefully because you will be breathless at the wonderful animal at your side. You will also have some of those ah-ha moments where you finally understand why you saw something with your dog. Most importantly, you will take away ideas and knowledge that will make your life with your dog better, and increase your dog's happiness and wellbeing.

What's inside matters
Recently I heard one of the current great dog authors, an animal behaviorist, at a national professional dog trainers' conference, say that it really does not matter what goes on inside a dog's head, that neuroscience offered nothing to work with for understanding dog behavior. His point was that you don't need to know how a car runs to drive it. I am making the argument in this book that, if you do know how the car runs, you will appreciate the car (I really mean the dog here) a lot more. You won't feel as stupid when you hear a grinding sound that you can't identify, and you will give the mechanic a lot more to work with, which will save you time and money.

That's when I decided I needed to write this book that had been rattling around in my head for a decade. I have spent a good chunk of my life teaching people about the biology of dogs based on the idea that knowledge will enhance the dog-human bond. People tell me that it has helped them a lot in their relationship with dogs, whether it was learning about dichromaticism, the carnassial pair, or the amygdala. Dogs carry so much variety in size, shape, genetics, and individual variation. There is no way to include all possible details about each breed. I take the common scientific approach. I define an average dog, and calculate or extrapolate from there. The common scientific joke fits here. In discussing the physics of animals, we start with "Assume a spherical cow…." No dog is spherical, but some things have to be calculated, and one needs a baseline. I calculate some things to give you a scale of what we are looking at. Don't worry if your dog is not 30 pounds, the illustration will still give you a sense of the scale. What follows is a whirlwind tour of the dog, with enough depth to be useful, and enough fun to keep you on the tour bus. Be forewarned. You will learn a lot about yourself, too. Humans really aren't all that different from dogs.

What most people see: Cute dog asleep. Awwww.

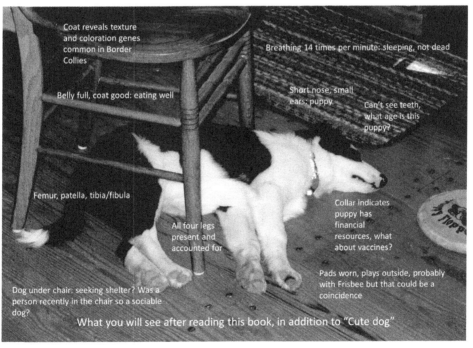

Coat reveals texture and coloration genes common in Border Collies

Breathing 14 times per minute: sleeping, not dead

Belly full, coat good: eating well

Short nose, small ears: puppy

Can't see teeth, what age is this puppy?

Femur, patella, tibia/fibula

All four legs present and accounted for

Collar indicates puppy has financial resources, what about vaccines?

Dog under chair: seeking shelter? Was a person recently in the chair so a sociable dog?

Pads worn, plays outside, probably with Frisbee but that could be a coincidence

What you will see after reading this book, in addition to "Cute dog"

How our tours will be organized

Being an ecologist (me, not you, but if you are one, all the better) I have started with a look at the wolf living in your house from an evolutionary perspective. I will explore how we (the two species, not you and your dog) got together. Then we have to define what you probably think you know: What is a dog? Turns out, that is a tougher question, at least separating wild wolf from domestic dog. That will lead us to DNA, some genetics, and a look at breeds. In subsequent chapters we will dive deep into feeding and digestion and all that gurgles inside your dog. Dogs need to move around, so we will explore the biology of the skeleton and muscles. We have to feed the cells with energy and oxygen. How does that get where it needs to go? Everything needs packaging, so we wrap that all up with skin and hair, protected by teeth and claws. All of these parts are managed by the brain, or so we like to think. I expect to change your view of a dog once you see the world through their eyes. In the end, we will look at dog health and aging, including what many vets wish you would pay more attention to.

Units of measure while on the tour

Now follows a required scientist comment about units, without which I could be decredentialed and cast into darkness. From here on, wherever I use the common U.S. units of feet, pounds, miles, etc., I put the metric (SI) conversion in parentheses. I don't deny that I am a metric snob, as virtually every scientist anywhere is. In fact, the whole world uses metric except for three countries: Liberia, Myanmar, and the United States. There are 7,800,000,000 people in the world; 331 million live in the U.S. and 53.7 million in Myanmar. Liberia adds 4.8 million. So 95% of the world's population officially uses the metric system. Both Liberia and Myanmar also dually use the metric system. Really, I should be using metric and translating that to the United States Customary System as the parenthetical aside. But I digress. And that will happen a lot in the pages ahead, but we will always tie it back to dogs. Here, the tie is more one of commonality. People around the world outside of the U.S. have most of the dogs, in fact they have 90% of the world's dogs, and I don't want our unique (archaic) use of measures to forget that or isolate us. At the very least, when you see those metric conversions, I would like you to think about dogs in other parts of the world. They share the same biology as our dogs, but live in very different cultures where dogs have high to low or no standing whatsoever.

TOUR 1

DOGS AND HUMANS

Why start here? The reason for that is the development of the modern dog is so wrapped up with humans, and with the wolf it comes from, that fully understanding dogs, both inside and out, requires knowledge of how the relationship got started and evolved over time. You might even make the argument, as some have, that you can't understand humans without knowing the influence that dogs have had on our own development.

Do you identify with this?

I'm thinking many of you will relate to my own relationship with my dog. I see a reflection of myself when I look into my dog's eyes. She looks at me longingly, hungry. It is only 4:00 and her breakfast is not until 5:00. I think she believes I forget, and that it takes an hour to get me moving. Normally I brush her off and tell her to wait. Does she understand time? This afternoon, however, I take her head into my hands, and I return the look. Part of me thinks loving thoughts because, as a 2-year-old rescue, this now 11-year-old Border Collie wormed her way into our lives with this same soft but piercing stare. Part of me sees a warm, caring, almost human animal who must ponder the expanding universe and what lies beyond the ocean's horizon. As I said, I see a reflection of me; she is a mirror of my humanity. We actively anthropomorphize, making human what is not. Science, however, is repeatedly showing that there really is not much to distinguish the biology of humans from other mammals. Another part of me sees that the reflection is because we are backlit and, indeed, I am reflected on her corneas. The light shines off her tapetum, the layer at the back of her eyes that seems to glow in dim light. I know that embryologically the cornea is derived from skin, but the retinal layer started as brain tissue. I can literally see her brain. What rattles around in there? Am I more than a food dispenser to her? Does she love me as I do her? How did we get from a feared wolf, which if it sat this close would be eating me at its next earliest convenience, to a manipulative canine who sleeps in my bed and licks my face, all of which I reward? There is a lot of biology there, in my Border Collie. She is smart, pushy, and getting a bit gray. Like I said, a reflection of me. Why does she age so fast, and not last 80 years? When she looks at me, what does she see? Not me per se, but what colors? How good is her eyesight? What is her field of view? What, when you come down to it, is a dog, anyway?

Dogs do so many things in our society, it is difficult to imagine a time before they and humans began this relationship. My dogs provide therapy when I am sad. They listen to my class lectures several times before my students hear them. Together we have run 10ks, pulled sleds over snow-packed country roads, and hiked through countless woods. I learned to herd sheep with them. We toss a Frisbee nearly every day. In the summer, I swim with them. My dogs, through my wife's skill and effort, have titled in the sport of agility and even won races at national agility championships, running obstacle courses: passing through tunnels, leaping over jumps, and weaving through closely spaced poles. These dogs titled in musical freestyle, a collaborative dance with a person and a dog set to a song. Our dogs play at the sport of nose work, sniffing for hidden scent odors. Did you catch that pronoun shift? "My dogs." "Our dogs." Both are possessive terms. We are their humans. That gets the possession more correct, I believe.

Anyway, my dogs have taken wilderness canoe trips and helped me find agate rocks in trackless areas of Utah and the North Shore of Lake Superior. With teams of professional dogs, I have gone sledding on multi-day trips in the wilderness. Our dogs ride cross-country with us in our car, so far never having flown. I like to think we give them a rich life. Certainly they have enriched ours. I use them to connect with students in class, as demonstrations in lab for structure, teeth, and behavior.

With deepest sorrow and grief, several of them have died in my arms at home after bouts with cancer or advanced arthritis, surrounded by the other dogs, my wife, and the attending veterinarian. We chose to purchase our home because it offered ample play space for the dogs and an adjacent state park to hike in. We choose our cars based on their ability to carry crash-resistant kennels, and readily cleanable surfaces that don't hold dog hair. Not that we actually clean our cars much, but we could, you know. The rhythm of our week revolves around the dog classes my wife teaches and the ones she takes; our days by feeding dogs and walks with them. Our social network is pretty much limited to others who are owned by their dogs. You could no sooner disentangle my dogs from me than you could pull out the tomatoes from tomato soup. It is similar to the way horse people feel about their companions, except you don't stick a dog between your legs and ride it, and the horse doesn't typically crawl into bed with you. How does such intimacy between species happen?

Dogs and humans get together

Dogs and humans have been dating quite a long time. Clearly domestication was well under way 10,000 years ago, and maybe started as early as 40,000 years ago. The photographic evidence is thin, there being no cameras at the time. Dogs left us few notes, there being no typewriters and no opposable dog-thumbs. We look for evidence such as artwork showing dogs, and graves with dogs deliberately placed in them. Our species is only a shade less than 200,000 years old. So let's consider.... Wait a minute. I am guessing right here and now you just glazed over those numbers because, well, they are numbers, and we will be seeing more of them, with lots of zeros, in the upcoming pages. These numbers really are unimaginably big. We need to get that time perspective, a deep-time perspective, or we can't really appreciate this unique relationship humans as a species, and domesticated dogs as a subspecies of wolves, have. Yep, they really are wolves.

Time out for a perspective on time

Time is a pretty odd experience. We know it goes back billions of years. If you look to the sky on a dark night, and you know where to see the Andromeda Galaxy, you can look back in time 2.6 million years. That is how old the light from Andromeda is, starting toward us about the time humanoid primates were poking around the African Rift Valley. To us, time is relative and not absolute. A fun day with friends and dogs can fly by in the blink of an eye, and for students the last minutes before class ends can drag into what feels like an hour. To my dogs, the time between placing the food dish on the floor and the release command to eat seems like eternity. The time for the food to disappear, a nanosecond. Physicists like Stephen Hawking argue that time is reversible, and maybe not even real, but a biological product of our experience. Interesting, but not helpful here. We can learn a lot about past time through geology, molecular clocks, old bones, and buried treasures, like dogs. History stretches back billions of years in easily observable ways. Yet we cannot see into the future at all. We imagine it, we forecast it, we plan for it. We do not see the future. In fact, we will learn later that we cannot even see the present. Looking back, what do we see, and how can we imagine something so variable as time?

Think of a pleasant walk with your dog, or a favorite walk with a friend, or a nice drive of about an hour. Or a Netflix episode of an hour. Maybe baking a lasagna for an hour. It doesn't much matter so long as you can picture and relate to an hour. I am picturing a walk into the state park by my house along a path that takes me to a beautiful ridge, then down a hill, and into a pine grove to an area we call Snowshoe Hill because we discovered it out on a winter hike. I can picture every step of the way because we hike it so often, summer and winter. Going there and the path back takes an hour.

An hour is easy to imagine; we experience a couple dozen of them every day of our lives. So if that hour-long walk represented the age of the universe (13,600,000,000 years), our lovely planet (4,540,000,000 years) is around for just the last 20 minutes of the walk. New comparison: If the hour walk is the age of Earth, mammals have only been around for the last three minutes and humans as a species for about two-tenths of a second. You read that correctly, we are literally the blink of an eye in the age of the Earth. My walk to Snowshoe Hill is the age of the Earth, and mammals have only been around about the time I leave the State Park coming back, cross into my woods, and see my house across the pond. Humans aren't a species until my foot is about to cross the threshold of the open door into my mudroom. A blink of an eye. Technically barely half of a blink of an eye, because those take three- to four-tenths of a second. But don't feel bad about it, because this is our only blink of the eye, so it is pretty darned important to us.

Domestication and selective breeding begin

Now let's make that hour-long walk be the time humans have been a species, again just shy of 200,000 years. Let's pick a middle ground for when domestication occurred, 20,000 years ago. That's a full 10% of the time, so the last six minutes of our hour-long walk.

Now let's turn the reference point around. The hour-long walk is the 20,000 years of dog domestication. How long have we been actively manipulating breeds? The American Kennel Club only started in the late 1800s. Modern genetics only dates to the mid-1800s. There is good debate about what constitutes a breed but that is not important here yet. We know humans were actively and selectively breeding dogs by working types for a few thousand years, selecting for herding, guarding, and pulling kinds of jobs probably without giving it too much direct thought. Let's use 3,000 years. If 20,000 years is our hour-long walk, then we have been selecting dogs by types for nine minutes, with formal breeding associations for 27 seconds. Look what you can do in under a minute! The point is, this is all happening pretty fast in biological terms and astronomically fast in geological scales.

Breeds, races, subspecies, species. It is hard to get good definitions here. Evolutionary ecologists think in terms of gene pools. Not much help there. We will return to this in a brief while. Let's think of genes as a family secret, passed from parents to kids, and from those kids to their kids. And let's ignore reality and pretend that they can keep a secret in the family. Let's say that the secret is an idea about how to do something, maybe a way to grow more nutritious and calorie-rich food. Some families had good ideas, some not so good. If the idea helps the kids survive and prosper, then the family lines with the good ideas would do better, and have more kids, leading to more kids and more descendants and pretty soon most of the lousy ideas are gone as their families did not have what it takes. If ideas worked like genes, we would all be pretty wise!

Why would the bad ideas get weeded out? Well, resources like time and food and adequate housing are limited. That would lead to some competition, right? If there is no competition, then all the ideas, both good and bad, and the families with them prosper until enough time goes by, their world gets pretty full, and then competition occurs. Sooner or later, they start wanting and needing the same limited stuff. In this metaphor, the good idea has to do with growing better food. If farmland is not limited, there will be farms growing good food, with lots of healthy kids, and farms with smaller, less healthy families because they had less nutritious food, and not as much to eat. Over time, the better-fed families have more descendants than the less well-fed families. If they don't share the secret of better food, over time, when property becomes scarce, guess who ends up with it.

Remember, a lot of time has gone by. If the ideas varied, and some ideas were useful in helping the families survive, and some of the useful ideas were passed down from parent to child to grandchild, more of the good ideas would be passed on to the next generations. Over time the good ideas prosper and the bad ideas get weeded out. Any modifications to good ideas, those that make them work better, will do even better in the ongoing competition. Bad modifications to good ideas don't prosper, so they disappear, too. Richard Dawkins (1976) called these ideas "memes" in his book *The Selfish Gene,* but that word now is used for fun internet images. At its core, still memes. Good ones get replicated, bad ones disappear.

In a nutshell, by the way, that is the mechanism of evolution called natural selection, except that the traits need to be inheritable, not taught. Traits like big teeth and camouflage hair are like ideas. There is competition for resources making the relative value of different versions matter. Those traits like the size of teeth and the quality of the hair vary by individual. Some of that variation aids in survival and reproduction. Some of that variation is inheritable, while some, like a broken tooth, are not inheritable. Over time, you gather more of the positive inheritable traits, and the not so good ones get weeded out and disappear. In nature, that happens by the unfortunate act of dying with fewer offspring than another. This understanding of the mechanism of evolution dates to Charles Darwin, who did not invent the idea of evolution, but he saw how it worked. He only supplied the first working mechanism for it. We now know of five mechanisms, but the other four are not very useful to us yet. Darwin is historically important, so I took a selfie just last week with his statue in the Natural History Museum in London. Geek, remember? For what it is worth, another came up with the idea independently of Darwin based on different evidence, Alfred Russel Wallace. I took a selfie with his statue, too!

We humans like to invent. So what if we started picking the good traits irrespective of their ability to help an animal survive, but more to help us? We could select for dogs who liked to be around people, or were good at herding, or were great defenders of the home. We could pick outrageous things, like polka dots in a dog coat. I'm looking at you, Dalmatians. In fact, in the biological blink of an eye we have done just that, picking lines of traits that meet our wants and needs, be it color or size (or breeding the dog to look like a wrinkled prune, a genetic defect in a skin protein that people decided to keep around), and we get it. Natural selection takes lots of time. Human selection is pretty darned fast. Starting with skittish wild foxes, in 20 generations researchers selecting for an ever more sociable version got a fox that looks a lot like a Border Collie. A friendly fox at that.

It is easy to see how we could domesticate a line of dogs to herd our sheep, guard our buildings, and curl up with us, once we realized what we had available to work with. But how did it start? Who knows? Written recorded history is only about 10,000 years old, and that misses the start of this marvelous relationship. But we can make some pretty good guesses.

I find that people like to have one good mechanism or explanation for something. Two if it is the weekend or a holiday. Life is usually not that simple. In the debate about how we domesticated dogs, there are several very plausible mechanisms, and each likely played a role somewhere since dogs were apparently independently domesticated in several places. The internet was quite limited 15,000 years ago, and postal delivery was pretty much nonexistent. Isolated groups of people could not readily share ideas like "Hey, this dog relationship is a pretty good deal. Look, we got us a dog that can haul all of our stuff around." Humans were as good then as now at inventing things and using tools, and the fact that this tool was alive unlikely presented any moral problems at all. Complex animal rights are a much more modern invention that required alternatives to using living things to help us survive. Morals and ethics are really great, and they keep society together, but back when we were first domesticating dogs, any groups that developed morals against using dogs would likely have been out-competed by groups using dogs as tools. Similarly, wolves are smart and social animals with pack communication, so you had a species particularly receptive to reading another social animal, humans. Domestication happens pretty fast when both species involved benefit.

My preferred theory of how and why domestication began

The explanation for domestication I like best is called "reduction of flight distance." It is similar to the fox study I mentioned earlier, where rapid selection for the less skittish in each generation led to a docile group in just 20 generations. For wolves, that process could happen in a single human lifetime. Humans had food and garbage, so settlements would produce useful attractions to wild dogs. Any wolves who were less afraid of humans than the others in the pack could move closer and stay longer in the presence of this extra food source, gaining some protection as well. Over time, there would be selection for shorter and shorter flight distances, meaning they could approach humans more closely before running. There would also be selection for dogs who were particularly good at reading humans. Selection here requires that these behaviors are genetically controlled. I believe the fox domestication study shows pretty clearly that they are. Being able to read humans would be selected for in those wild dogs. Distinguishing the helpful human throwing a scrap from the hurtful one throwing a rock would be pretty valuable. So would reading other human intentions. That human is mad and wants to kill me; the one over there is friendly and wants to feed me. Which should I move closer to? Focus on humans, read their basic intentions, and over time you get a dog who can hang out in human space and read people at least as well as people read people. This path is also called "self domestication" because the dogs could do all this without any intentional help from humans.

Dogs were pretty useful tools to these early humans. It is not hard to imagine that once you had dogs with lower flight distances, and a focus on humans, you could start testing how smart dogs are. Can they learn that if they do this task, I will feed them? Turns out, yes. Now we can train dogs. It doesn't take long to see how humans could leash them together into teams to pull sleds and drag logs. It probably involved a learning process like breaking a wild horse. Get the dogs used to a collar or rope. Then a harness of sorts. Note that flight distance is an inheritable trait, as shown by the fox study. Reading humans well, orienting to them, has also been shown to be inheritable. Wearing a collar and pulling things is a learned trait, and would need to be retaught to every new dog.

Other domestication paths

There are other reasons for domesticating dogs. Wild wolf packs guard resources. Get a dog with a human orientation and it will come to think of that human and its things as pack resources. That makes guarding livestock an inheritable trait, easily shown in the very specific inheritable herding instincts in dogs of the herding lines. Humans would keep picking the best dogs at guarding for those chores. Even simple alarm barking would have been a useful trait for decreasing the likelihood that someone else could successfully steal your hard-earned possessions. I sure wish someone had bred that out for our later cohabitation!

Wolf packs hunt, and many of their behaviors appear to be inherited rather than taught. The best evidence of that comes from our herding breeds of dogs who instinctively show behaviors found in wolves. Packs of wolves will send out younger, faster dogs to turn fleeing prey like deer back toward them. That is just the "Send" we use in herding sheep when we tell our dog to go circle around the sheep or cattle and bring them to us. Holding the herd of prey in place allows the larger, older wolves to approach stealthily and pick out their prey. Domestic herders use dogs to hold sheep and cattle in place. For wolves, selecting and isolating the individual prey to attack uses the same base behaviors we use to sort a flock, sending some sheep to a pen area and the others back to the field. Driving the herd back to the attacking wolves is the driving we do moving cattle into a truck. Selecting for a controlled hunt minus the actual attack leads to the ability to use dogs to manage domesticated goats, sheep, and cattle. Dogs who cannot learn to refrain from attacking are rapidly weeded out.

Still another domestication process leads more directly to companions. Wolves are pack animals and trainable. An orphaned puppy picked up by a human who sought a cute novelty would rapidly train their own puppies to be tolerant of humans. From there, the humans would keep selecting the best pup offspring. A few would wander off and interbreed with the local wolves, but many would stay near, and pretty soon you have a line of domestic dogs to sell or trade with your clubs and spears.

So far, these are all relationships that leave the dogs alive, with meaningful work and obvious precursors to many of our modern activities with dogs. But dog fur is very warm. Just ask any wolf in a Canadian winter. Keeping dogs around so you have a source of warm winter apparel makes a lot of sense before you learned how to weave wool. If you kept picking the best fur-bearing examples to breed, and using many of their offspring for coats, you would do quite well. Patagonia was not shipping fiberfill alternatives at that time, so staying warm pretty much meant using some unlucky animal's coat. Likewise, dog meat would be a ready source of nutrition, and would be pretty efficient at turning scraps of human garbage into edible protein.

Why wolves, and not coyotes or foxes? Good question. I am listening to coyotes calling outside right now, and they sound far more manageable than the eerie wolf howls I have heard in the northern wilderness. By comparison to wolves, foxes look cute, toy-like, controllable. Apparently humans could have selected for any of these and over time gotten a domestic version of what biologists call the "wild type." Maybe they did, but we haven't found the evidence for them yet. My best guess, and it is only that, is size. A wolf can protect a flock or village from coyotes, but not the other way around. A wolf can pull more weight than a coyote. A wolf skin is larger and warmer than a coyote's. Also, it is worth noting, but not central to our thinking here, that modern dogs derive from what wolves were tens of thousands of years ago, not from modern wolves. The wolf line in nature kept evolving after we pulled out a subset for our partnership. Then we killed off most wolves around the world so they would not eat our domesticated livestock or our kids on the way to chores. The common ancestor for modern dogs is not modern wolves, it is wolves as they existed 40 millennia ago. Modern wolves are mostly the larger, arctic variety rather than the prairie wolf or temperate forest wolf of pre-modern civilization.

It almost seems inevitable that humans would coevolve a relationship with another social animal that could help protect, guard, and defend them. But maybe that all came later. Maybe the low-flight-distance dogs were just pleasant to have along on the hunt, or in the village, or around the fire. Maybe the dogs just wouldn't leave. That is how we got our first dog. We don't really know how long ago speech and language was invented in humans; best guess is north of 100,000 years for limited language. The fact that something warm and furry can't talk much might not have set it that far apart from your other human companions back then, and maybe still doesn't. Even today, with humans having complex language, many of us find our dogs communicate just fine, thank you.

Companions, pets, or property

Legally our millennia of domestication created tools, of the property sort. While my father-in-law viewed dogs in that light from his Depression-era farm upbringing, many (most?) of us put the relationship more in the "friends" category. Through this book, I generally refer to our relationship with dogs that way, using "companion" most frequently. "Guardian" might be more correct, and the term reminds us that we carry unequal responsibilities in the relationship. Not once has any of my dogs driven me to the doctor or offered to fix my dinner. See how I used "my dog" there? Possessive. Doesn't sound fully equal. I don't like to use "owner" referring to us and our relationship with dogs. It reminds me of how possessive the relationship can be without true dog consent, and my expectation that "my" dogs will follow "commands" not "suggestions." As a biologist, I won't refer to our canine buddies as our "kids," or us as "parents." Biologically that would be inaccurate as dogs are a distinctly different species. I know, I am such a party pooper. I doubt any of the early domesticators of dogs thought about where this relationship was headed.

Selective breeding impacts

With domestic dogs, we no doubt also selected for cute. Been in a room and had someone show a picture of a baby human, and everyone instinctively says "Awwww"? The juvenile form of humans elicits a feeling of paternalistic care in adults. In fact, baby humans who were good at eliciting that help got extra care over those who didn't, and survived better. Yep, cute babies would do better than non-cute. And here, cute is anything that works to elicit paternalistic protection or aid. Looking submissive helps, while big ears appear aggressive, as does baring teeth and snarling. Human babies who avoid snarling would do better. So would dog puppies. The genetic traits that work for being a puppy are not the same as those that work for being an adult wolf. The genetic traits that work for being a baby human are not the same as those that work for being an adult human. Juvenile traits in a social animal draw out the parent and get the parent to take care of the juvenile. Adult traits have to refocus on securing food, finding mates, and defending these things and oneself.

Domestication often involves selecting for the combination of traits that makes animals successful wild juveniles rather than the traits that make for successful wild adults. In wolves, we would select for adults that showed those juvenile behaviors of turning toward us as pack leaders for guidance and sustenance rather than those where the adult helps themselves to whatever they want, including me, right? In fact, domestic dogs seem to be pretty good examples as adults of carrying that helpful bundle of juvenile characteristics that work for human babies. We selected for more submissive dogs who drew out the "aww" in us, and who relied on us to direct them. We tossed out (an admitted euphemism) ones who challenged us too much or ate our livestock or our kids. Over time, we got ever-more-juvenile-looking adults who resembled the traits in canine and human babies. Larger heads relative to ears, big eyes, smiling, and a focus on the parent. The condition of retaining inheritable juvenile characteristics as adults is called neoteny. Adult domestic dogs show many characteristics of juvenile wolves, including play and submissive postures, higher-pitched barks, and a whole lot less aggressive displaying. They also show traits eerily similar to baby humans.

Science as a way of knowing

I have been writing about evolution for a while, and it will appear throughout this book. I have people tell me "I don't believe in evolution." OK. Does it matter to gravity if you believe in it? Nope, set that glass down too close to the edge of a table and it starts falling to the floor. Disbelieve gravity all you want, the glass still falls, the glass stills shatters, you still live with the consequences. All, and I do mean all, available evidence in the physical world shows the earth to be billions of years old (4.54

billion give or take a few tens of millions of years) in a universe 13.79 billion years old, give or take few tens of millions of years. That number has changed a bit over time. Why? Because that is how science works: "Based on the best evidence today using this technique, I find…" Other scientists try to replicate the method while still others try a different technique and get a different answer. The accumulation of evidence, challenged and retested, leads to basic understandings. Geologist and astrophysicists may quibble about a few million years based on what method of aging is used. For example, how old is your dog? I could use cataract development and make a guess. Or I could look at teeth eruption or wear and estimate. I could X-ray the skeleton looking for arthritis and make a guess. I could look at changes in DNA in rapidly dividing cells versus slowly changing cells. Each would give a different answer, but the accumulation of evidence would allow us a reasonable guess. That information, the estimated age of your dog, would lead to different diagnoses and treatments based on results. One treats a puppy differently than a geriatric dog, right?

Science is empirical, in that we get hard data from experiments, such as tooth wear in your dog as we try to determine age. But science also requires interpretation of data. The tooth wear data indicated a younger dog, maybe 4 years old. Arthritis and cataracts made me think 10. So is this a prematurely aging young dog, or an old dog with a better diet than most? Now I apply my own interpretations based on the best evidence and my understanding, and I treat your dog. Likewise, this entire book uses my decades of training and study to interpret what we know about dogs, and make some reasonable conclusions. I guarantee you that if you put another biologist in the room writing this book based on exactly the same data, you would get some different results. We might quibble about when dogs were domesticated, but not if they were domesticated. We might argue about how many cells are in a dog's body, because no one counts them one by one. But we would not argue about the order of magnitude (tens of trillions). Make sense?

Science also is, or tries to be, logical. Studies rarely prove something does not exist or cannot happen. It is easy to show if something does exist, simply by finding it. Look around you. Do you see a pink elephant? If you do, you know it exists, assuming you test that it is not just in your mind. Don't see one? That does not mean it is not there. Maybe it is smaller than you think and you looked in the wrong place, or it is hiding behind you. Logically you cannot prove it does not exist, only that you did not find it. Remember this every time you read "This study found no difference between canine medicine X and drug Y, or diet X compared to diet Y." It does not mean the difference does not exist, only that the measures they used were perhaps inadequate to find a difference. But if they found a difference, that is interesting. Now look at their methods and how confident they are in the difference to see if you accept the information. Be critical. Think.

Beware of bias. Our brains have some built in biases, and we learn more along the way. On one hand, biases are great filters for too much data coming in. Instinct and experience train us to look for what we know to be more important. A red car cuts me off in traffic. Then later, a second one. From that, I learn to steer clear of red cars, and that works. No red cars have hit me. That confirms that I was right, I feel rewarded, and I move on. Except that I drive a red car and I don't keep score. This particular bias is called confirmation bias. After some initial experience, I expected to see red cars as a problem, so every time I see one that is, I remember it, forgetting all the close calls with blue and gray and black and white cars and trucks. We need to make careful, objective evaluations, especially about things we care deeply about, like dogs or our pet ideas about why they do what we think they do.

Don't despair when you hear "New study proves…." That is usually not correct. A new study adds evidence to the piles of existing evidence, and might cause us to reevaluate the evidence. It does not simply delete the old evidence. Rarely does one study prove anything. Please, please, and please again do not say to me, as you read this book, "But I saw a news story that said…which proves this…" That is not how studies work. They are individual pieces of evidence in a big court case where the body of scientists including practitioners like veterinarians are the jurors. The author of the study is one of the legal teams arguing a point. They, like you, are human. They have biases, assumptions, and professional backgrounds that influence their argument. I am describing the court cases in this book, with my own biases.

All that is to say that, if you live in the United States, you are far less likely to believe in evolution than in the rest of the world. The percentages cited vary based on the way the questions are asked. Either way you want to think about it, domestic dogs come from wolves, and wolves come from more ancestral mammals, and the evidence is overwhelming and informative.

TOUR 2

The Reproductive System from DNA to Intercourse via Taxonomy

Awhile back, in the last chapter, I started down a path of discussing gene pools. In my description of domestication, I repeated the term "inheritable." Neither a coincidence nor an accident. Describing what a dog is, and what isn't a dog but is some other kind of species, all depends on inheritable traits. And dogs don't pass on inheritable traits without a functional reproductive system. We really don't need to know too much about the mechanisms of inheritance at the sub-organismal level, but I am not letting that fact stop me from telling you. You might find it useful later when you are pondering a new dog and you hear about CRISPR, which has nothing to do with firm vegetables and everything to do with designer dogs and your future.

DNA

We do not need too much of a description of DNA itself for all this. You probably ought to know that DNA is a long molecule that looks like a ladder with rungs, twisted into a spiral. DNA stores information, including instructions on how to make an organism, in strings of molecules, much like the letters on this page string together to make words and then sentences. When DNA is being read to get the instructions, the DNA molecule splits down the middle of the rungs. Otherwise, it is all coiled up tightly most of the time except for the exact parts that need to be read by the particular cell at the needed time. Liver cells need different working instructions than nerve cells. The molecular tools in the cell can find the right part, uncoil it enough and split it open in the rungs of the ladder to read it, and even make minor repairs to it, all without tangling it up like a fishing line or pile of yarn.

Every cell in your dog's body, except sperm or eggs, has two complete sets of DNA instructions for making the whole dog, lock, stock, and barrel. That DNA in one cell, if you lined it up, would be about 6 feet (2m) long. Time for a reality check again. Cells are tiny spaces that are hard to imagine. A common cell size in a human is about 0.001 inches (0.025 mm) across. I just told you that a little tiny cell, maybe one-tenth the diameter of a human hair, has 6 feet (72 inches, 2 meters) of DNA coiled up in it. That surely deserves at least a passing "huh," maybe even a "WTF, are you sure?" I am. Use that at your next party.

In humans, that 2 yards of DNA in each cell is all stored in 46 pieces, each called a chromosome. Your dog stores it in 78 pieces, also called chromosomes, as do wolves and coyotes. Think about it for just a moment, and not much longer or it will make you dizzy. Each one of your 40,000,000,000,000 (FYI that is 40 trillion) microscopic cells has not inches, but 6 feet (2 m) of DNA crammed in it. While I cannot find a good estimate of how many cells a dog has, if an average dog is a fourth the size of a human, there would be about 10 trillion cells. Each cell has 78 pieces of DNA. That is enough DNA in one dog to stretch a really thin string of DNA to the sun and back to Earth about eight times. Or enough to reach from the Sun to out beyond Saturn. How thin is that DNA string? A nanometer. A dog hair is about 50,000 times thicker than that. Try not tangling or breaking that in every cell, every minute, every day, as you uncoil the DNA, read it, and close it back up. You should not ever wonder "What went wrong?" You should wonder that it ever goes right. But it does, day in and day out, year in and year out.

Stop, reread that paragraph. If that does not blow your mind, I am hard pressed to think of what will. But I promise to keep trying.

There are parts of the DNA that code for proteins, which do the work of the cell. Parts code for RNA, which manages the DNA. Parts of the code are stray or invasive remnants from viruses. Parts code for, well, we aren't sure what a lot of it does. Give us time, we will. Functional units, stretches of DNA that do something, are called genes. Your dog has genes for eye color, coat color, ear shape, fighting bacteria, sociability, and literally thousands of other qualities.

Chromosomes

Now let's think of each chromosome as a book. Remember, dogs have 78 of these in each cell. All mammals basically have about the same amount of DNA, just broken into different numbers of pieces, those chromosomes I mentioned. I am generalizing here, so those of you who understand molecular biology and biochemistry can roll your eyes because I am skipping polyploidy, rapidly repeated segments, etc. Back to chromosomes as books. As it is now considered an archaic and seldom used item, a "book" is an old, plant-based analog storage device. It is what you are holding. Since you have one here, let's stick with a book.

Imagine a stack of 78 books representing my dog at her genetic level in one single solitary cell of her body. We call this dog "Wish," but she is actually formally named MACH2 Brighteye Fairy Tail, with a long string of titles that follow. Way too much to say when you want to call her off a squirrel. Like fighter pilots and for similar reasons, she has a call name: Wish. We think of Wish as a dog, but for now let's think of her as a pile of 10 trillion cells. Wish has 78 books of DNA in each cell of her body. Half the books came from Wish's mom, Brighteye Amazing Grace, half from her dad, Offon Remington's Blue Steel. Even though chromosomes are all the same color, let's say for illustration that the Remington-supplied books are blue and the Grace-made books are pink. My dog Wish has 39 blue books from her dad and 39 pink books from her mom. The volumes (books) are numbered 1 to 39. Volume 1 from either her mom or dad has chapters or genes that code for a mix of things. These are not organized into the 39 books by function; nature does not tend to be that neat, and that organization would be disastrous in the long run of evolution. The first book might have coat spot shape, eye color, and fungal fighting instructions, and hundreds of others. Volume 2 might have instructions for adjusting body temperature and hair length and the number of toes on a paw. Volume 1 from Grace has the same instructional chapters as volume 1 from Remington. Thus, the pink and blue copies of volume 1 give the same kinds of instructions for the same kinds of things for every dog.

But volume 1 in dogs is different from volume 1 in people. Throughout the whole collection of books, all of the same basic traits are present, just the instruction set is broken up in different places. Same ideas, different instructions. Mostly the same order of material, but not at all identical. The blue set is identical to the pink set for most of its pages, but some chapters are different. And those differences are what made my dog Wish different from her mom, Grace, and her dad, Remington. One book, volume 39, is very different. Wish got the same version from Grace and Remington, so she is chromosomally a girl. Had they been different, she would be a boy. Probably still named Wish, but that hardly matters at all.

Females in mammals, chromosomally speaking, all get the X volume from their mom, and another X volume from their dad. Males, chromosomally speaking, get the X volume from their mom, and the Y volume from their dad. Grace, the mom, was XX. Remington, the dad, was XY. Wish, my dog, has an X from Mother Grace and an X from Papa Remington. Moms can only pass on X copies because that is all they have. Half of the sperm dads make have a Y, half an X.

All this is pretty detailed. You can skip it and return to it later if the next heading is irresistible to you. Otherwise I advise you reread the last two paragraphs, slowly.

Mitochondria

Mitochondria in each of your cells add another element to your unique DNA package. Unlike our chromosomes in strings, they have their own DNA type in a circular structure, and do their own DNA copying independent of the host cell's normal DNA. There are between 100,000 and half a million mitochondria in each of your cells with their own (common, shared) DNA. They are clones of each other. You got all of them from the egg your mom used to make you. In essence, your mom's egg was infected with mitochondria, and each of your cells carries up to half a million of those buggers. If DNA and your own metabolism make you alive, then mitochondria are alive and used to be independent of your own cells' DNA, accumulating their own mutations, evolving away. So they could outvote your own cells. By cell numbers, you are so much more them than you. Damn parasites. Except that they also give the host cell most of the usable energy it gets. Without them, the dog dies. In fact, it never even gets born.

Realize how messy this all really is. Like you, your dog got a set of DNA from its dad, full and complete. It got a set of DNA from its mom, full and complete. Together they code for some 20,000 different proteins with 3 billion base pairs. The base pairs are essentially the letters in an alphabet plus punctuation, but the code requires three bases for each letter. You could translate that roughly as 20,000 sentences coded by 1 billion letters. Since there are two sets of DNA (one from mom, the other from dad), we can cut that in half for this, and half again since only one side of the DNA double strand is read. Call it 20,000 sentences coded by 250 million letters. By comparison this book uses about 10,000 sentences coded by half a million letters and punctuation. Those sentences in the DNA are often 15 thousand letters long, and each cell has an awful lot of information in it! Your dog has a full set of mitochondrial DNA, too. Much smaller, only about 17,000 base pairs coding for 13 proteins. Most of the coding for mitochondria has moved, over time, from their own genes to the host dog, so some of your dog's 20,000 proteins are to make the mitochondria. Your dog, my dog, they are all just a mess of DNA from multiple sources. Sure, your dog got all of its mitochondria from its mom, but those mitochondria were an almost exact clone of her mom's, which were almost an exact clone of her mom's, etc. The regular DNA your dog got from its mom was a mashup of its dam's and sire's DNA. The DNA from the dad was a mashup of his parents. This all makes each dog unique, and it makes it easy to tell if someone is a direct sibling (same mitochondrial DNA if from same mom), and helps to figure out how closely related we are, à la every episode of CSI.

The DNA code determines what your dog is like, how it functions, and how good of a companion it can be from the heredity side. Remember, the home environment you set up and the training and nurturing you provide influence all of that. I just think it is worth remembering that so much is determined by 6 feet of DNA coiled up in every cell. DNA determines what a dog is, how well the species interacts with humans, and in many respects, why we do so well together. Copying and sharing genes is pretty messy, but thank goodness it works so well so often.

The act of mating

The only area of DNA sharing and sorting we have not yet covered is the actual act of mating. I am guessing you know what goes where and why, so I really don't need to cover that, right? But I will, anyway, because it is pretty interesting.

The male of most mammals has a permanently erect penis, accomplished with a real bone called a baculum. When called for, and too often when not called for, the male can simply extend his penis. Primates are among the few mammals that use a hydroskeleton for the penis instead of a bone. The baculum is highly reduced in most primates, absent in humans. There's lots of speculation about how that evolved, not likely just to keep Viagra in business. Horses also lack a baculum. In a raccoon, they have a wicked sharp bend in them. Why have a penis in the first place? It is a tool common throughout the animal kingdom, but far from universal, for placing semen as far into a female as you can, to get it past other male's semen. The more male competition in a species, the larger the penis. Humans, compared to most mammals, have a pretty small penis. Yep, you can blame that on your heritage, too. Now the walrus, that is the master of penis size in both absolute and relative terms for a land mammal; they are up to 2 feet long (or two-thirds of a meter for you metric types). The penis on a canid has blood engorged parts at the distal, or business, end of the penis such that a male can get physically locked to the female while mounted. This keeps other males away while his sperm settle in for the long haul. It also risks breaking the baculum. They can stay locked anywhere from a couple of minutes to half an hour, more typically around 15 minutes.

Worth noting is that semen is just a high-energy liquid that serves to provide a nutrient-rich environment for the sperm and to provide a plug to help prevent a competitor's sperm from reaching the holy grail of an egg. Individual sperm actually cooperate in many species. A cluster of sperm that lock heads swims faster than the sperm going solo. It is not first come, first served, as it were. It is also not the least bit challenging to see how a female dog, popping out a dozen eggs at a time, could comingle sperm from multiple fathers and have a mixed litter.

The parts involved in dogs are otherwise similar to what you have yourself, or had before surgery. In males, sertole cells in the testicles produce sperm. Sertole cells operate best at a bit below normal body temperature, so they hang out, as it were, in a sack called the scrotum. Once ready, they gather with materials produced by the prostate gland and get ejected from the urethra at the end of the penis. If all is going as "nature planned," that penis is in a muscular receptacle called a vagina. Through peristaltic action, the blob is moved up into the uterus and then into an oviduct. There are two of these. Functionally a dog has two uteruses, but since we are being technical, we count uteruses by the number of endings called the cervix. Dogs have one cervix at the end of the vagina, but that splits almost right away into two distinct horns or bodies of the uterus, each of which leads to an oviduct where fertilization usually happens;

these each connect to an ovary, home of the sacred eggs. When the bitch is in heat, she is shedding eggs, up to a dozen or so. Any eggs that meet up with sperm, if the DNA sorts without problems, becomes a fertilized egg with a set of Mom's genes and a set of Dad's genes. If they successfully implant in the uterine wall, they make a placenta that is ring-shaped, encircling the developing embryo. These develop for two months, get expelled by the mom, and the puppy begins: blind, confused, and no doubt hungry.

Sex

We need to talk about sex. We are all adults here, right? This is that talk where I sit you down, I look you right in the eye, and I tell you the least romantic thing I can. Let's be clear about sex. Biologically, all sex does is serve as a way to swap the same set of pages between the books from Mom and Dad so that the kids are different from the parents. Sex functions to take, for example, pages 29 to pages 153 from volume 4 from the blue book made by Dad, and swap those into the pink volume for the same pages in volume 4 from Mom. Not swapping whole chapters necessarily, just big chunks of pages. This only happens in sperm or egg cells. The entire rest of the cells leave Dad's and Mom's pink and blue books intact. Sex is swapping segments of DNA between the instruction set from Mom and Dad to make an altogether new book from the one making the sperm or egg. Aren't you glad we had this little sex talk?

Two questions should have popped into your head. Why bother? With the page shuffling, not with the sex stuff. And if the sperm has 78 chromosomes, and the egg has 78 chromosomes, won't the kid just have 156? The cell is pretty crowded as it is, so what gives?

These sexy little dog sex cells, the sperm and the eggs, each start with 78 volumes like any other cell, half from Mom and half from Dad. Remember, the blue books in total have all the pages needed to make a dog. So do the pink ones. After swapping, each volume has whole sections from the other parent's set of books. Then we pile all 78 books up into 39 piles, by volume number. Pile 1 has the blue volume 1 and the pink volume 1, each now with swapped pages. We go to each pile, flip a coin, and toss one volume into a box. There are two boxes in this analogy, where one starter cell with 78 books sorts chromosomes into two sex cells, each with half as many books. Each starter sperm or egg gets split into two final sperm or two final eggs. This is happening to the sperm in a testicle, to the eggs in an ovary, all before conception. For the sperm, it happens just a few days before they, uh, start their journey outside the body. More interesting, I think, is the fact that it is happening in the egg even before that ovary holding the egg is born. The egg that my mommy used to make little ol' me was already through this process before she herself was born. The process is called meiosis. If this were a cat book, I'd have to say "meowsis" but I won't.

Now that they have half the chromosomes, when a sperm and egg meet up later in a dark alley and combine, the new cell will be back up to the required 78 books. This is the process that keeps the amount of DNA from doubling every time conception occurs. We take the two volumes in pile 2 (chromosome 2), and randomly toss one into each box (cell). And so on 78 times. Each box (cell) has one full set of instructions, but only one set of volumes numbered 1-39, and each box (cell) has a mix of pink and blue books (chromosomes), and each book (chromosome) has a few pages (stretches of DNA) from each parent. Pretty good scrambling, and since we cut in half the number of chromosomes from 78 to 39, the sperm or egg will end up with the right number after all once they join together. Now recolor the cover of each volume (chromosome) in the box (cell) to the color of the individual doing the sorting (mom or dad) so each volume (chromosome) is now pink if it is being sorted in a female parent's body, blue in a male parent's body. We bubble wrap the box (yep, in this case the bubble wrap goes outside the box—the box is a sperm or an egg, the bubble wrap is all that gooey fluid that washes over the sperm or eggs) and we ship that box off via FedEx to join up with a box from whomever we are sharing our precious boxes of DNA-based instructions. When those boxes meet up, if you are lucky (or unlucky, I suppose, who am I to judge?), you get a new dog unique in all the world with a full set of volumes from their mom and a full set from their dad.

Again, why bother? That is a lot of work risking tangling or mis-sorting all that DNA, and it requires expense in time, energy, and frankly getting really close and distracted to another being who might rather kill you for a meal than share genes with you.

The lame answer is this: If it weren't so important to shuffle genes, there would be no sex, and critters would just clone themselves. Fast, safe, simple, efficient. What happens when you inbreed, crossing two closely related individuals, like my dog Wish mating with her brother, Sonic? Two major problems. You have no way to get rid of bad, unhelpful genes or mistakes that crop up, and they accumulate, and you more often get diseased or deformed or weak or otherwise less fit individuals than those that result from random mating with nonrelatives. We call it a "blood line" but it is really a gene pool. The successful mixing of genes is measured by diversity. The more diversity, the more the species can adapt to changing environments. In a changing environment, genetic diversity wins out in the long run. In the wild, the environment is almost always changing. In rare places where it does not, we do find species that clone themselves and skip all the brouhaha of sex. Why make it feel so good? You have to reward overcoming the risk of disease and dismemberment or no one shares genes, no reshuffling occurs, and the clone wars go to the asexual.

The impact of mutations

As if all that were not enough! Two more interesting details. First of all, all that gene copying, something like 3 billion functional units (think letters in words, or if you took chemistry, base pairs of nucleic acids) in each cell each time it replicates, there are going to be a few errors. A one-in-a-million error happens 3,000 times in 3 billion base copies, now multiplied by the 10 trillion cells in the dog's body. Lots of errors! Most errors are minor or unimportant. If the genes for making a good liver get messed up in the rapidly copying and dividing cells on my dog's skin, who cares? It is not getting used there anyway. Any bad mistakes that affect body cells (non-sperm, non-egg cells) might kill, but they can't get passed on to the offspring. Only copy mistakes in sperm or eggs matter in the long haul of evolutionary time. Only these can be inherited. Most mistakes in sperm and eggs result in offspring that are worse off than those without the error, and they either fail to replicate, kill the embryo or, if they are born, they get outcompeted and the error is lost to the lineage. But rarely, very rarely, a mistake makes for a slightly better version than the original. Over lots and lots of time—remember how long that time really is—those little changes add up. Indeed, everything that separates dogs from horses, and before that separates mammals from dinosaurs, and before that animals from bacteria, every single difference comes from the very few random positive errors adding up over a very long time. Most of the DNA we carry is what is working in all living animals, so it is common throughout. All living things share about 50% of the same DNA. Dogs and houseplants share half of the blueprint material. Humans share about 90% of their DNA with dogs, 99.8 % of their DNA with chimpanzees, our closest relatives, and 99.9 percent of their DNA with every other human on earth. Likewise, all dogs share 99.9 percent of the same DNA with each other, from Chihuahua to Mastiff.

From that, you can see that only a relatively small number of genes code for what makes us different from fish and earthworms. Dogs would be bacteria if it were not for these chance copy errors, known as mutations. Only mutations that affect the DNA in sperm or eggs count, and only those that give some advantage to the offspring remain in the gene pool. So the next time you stare lovingly at your dog, cat, or gerbil, compare them to a microscopic bacterium. Count your fortune in all those literally billions of years of accumulated differences that make our loved ones different from bacteria.

Inbreeding – the good and the bad

Inbreeding does bring a clear advantage, however. If a chance mutation leads to something we like, such as a new coat color or a particular texture to the coat, we can rapidly propagate it. Decreasing genetic diversity makes it easier to predict what offspring will be like because you get rid of a lot of extraneous options that you did not want anyway. Like many things, inbreeding is a double-edged sword. It is only messing with the 0.1% of the total DNA, the small part where one dog differs genetically from another.

In dog breeds, we see loss of diversity leading to trouble happening in highly inbred subgroups or breeds. A recent data-filled study (Dreger et al., 2016) provides a good overview, but for a better graphic presentation, see Beuchat's 2016 blog at https://www.instituteofcaninebiology.org/blog/inbreeding-of-purebred-dogs-determined-from-dna which found that Norwegian Lundehunds had the highest inbreeding (over 80%) of AKC recognized breeds. Bull Terriers were up there with 60%. Pugs, Irish Wolfhounds, and Bloodhounds were at 50%. Golden Retrievers were at 30%. Border Collies were at 25%. The least inbred? Jack Russel Terriers and Chihuahuas at 10%. For comparison, in the wild, it takes crossing two full siblings of the same two parents to get as high as 25% inbreeding. How much inbreeding is too much? In the wild, any inbreeding generally leads to depressed success in the long run, but in a domestic breed, it really depends on your tolerance of the negative effects of inbreeding balanced against the positive effects of more certain physical and inherited behavioral traits. It is worth noting that many of these mutations show up in wild dogs, and are quickly removed by selection as not useful. Something lethal in the wild type, such as really short legs from one wolf gene reinserted into the domestic stock sometime in the past, can be quite useful in a domestic, protected type like a Corgi. Aside from what many consider as cute, the short stance of the Corgi gave them a unique herding ability around livestock by putting their bodies down below the animals to be moved. But a wild wolf with Corgi legs? Dead.

Sex is just a way to scramble the pages so no puppy is exactly like their sire or dam. But think about it. All that sorting happens with 78 pieces of DNA, each set of 78 totaling six feet long (2m) in each cell (DNA) without getting tangled and without losing or misplacing any volumes. If mistakes are made, and they are made, the shipped box of books is incomplete or otherwise messed up, things die. If the basics in the DNA are wrong, the sperm or egg dies. If the chromosomes are mis-sorted, the newly fertilized cell dies. Errors often mean the developing embryo won't survive, or the puppy dies at birth once independent of the mom.

Selective breeding and artificial selection

Domestic dogs, the stars of our lives, are a set of wolf boxes of volumes with the parts we didn't like thrown out. We threw them out. Over the past 20,000 years we kept tossing out traits we did not like while keeping the traits we liked via slow, tedious editing. Liked or not, we also had to keep the traits that allowed dogs to live, because if the dog died, that whole set of books (genes) was lost. Put differently, you can't select for a dog that needs zero food and therefore never poops. Too bad, because that would be a popular breed! But domestic dogs and wolves can share boxes. Not a Chihuahua and a wolf. One of them is going to eat the other. Sure, in a laboratory their sperm and eggs can pair up. CRISPR lets us directly cut and paste the DNA, instead of needing dogs and generations of their mixing DNA, to get the same result. Now I ask, just because CRISPR is quick and new, is it really any different than what we have been doing for 20 millennia?

Traits that lead to more successful copies of oneself are selected for. That is easy to see with coat color, for example. If you have the wrong coat color, you become a target because you cannot hide. Or you don't get recognized as a potential mate. Other traits are also under evolutionary pressure. Consider lifespan. If being weak and dying young meant you could spend more energy on reproduction that made of copies of yourself that could later reproduce, then being fit or evolutionarily successful would mean "die young, you weakling." Conversely, if it means having big teeth and snarling a lot, so it shall be in the long run. At its most basic, you only get so much energy, and you can devote it to a finite number of uses including reproduction, growth, eating to get more energy, and using some energy for repair. Invest too much in repair, and the participants of the gene pool programmed to put less into that and more into reproduction out-copy you. Not enough into repair, and you die too young and don't make enough copies. Nature finds the balance through lots of time and experiments. By experiments, I mean unsuccessful individuals whose genetic lines did not pan out. They died.

In the wild, organisms have two types of lifespans. One is called the ecological lifespan. The other is the physiological one, or what the organism could achieve if the environment lacked threats like predators and diseases and occasional famine. The latter really does not exist in nature; it only exists in your home, because it is really dangerous out there. Your dog cannot live forever because they eventually wear out. But why wear out at 10 to 15 years, and not 80 or 90 like humans? For that matter, why do humans die at 3 score and 10 years, to get biblical or liberal artsy, when bowhead whales can live to be 200 years? The poor Sunda rat lives only a year.

Clearly there are biologically viable mechanisms that organisms can use to repair and replace worn parts for centuries. However, that kind of repair is very expensive in terms of energy. If your environment is full of danger, disease, and predators, it would be an utter waste to spend the energy to be able to live to be 200 years old when odds are other things will kill you way before that. The ecological lifespan a species lives in the wild is really the average lifespan of the population based on the threats it faces with some reserve to keep the average up. If your average wolf lives, say, five years in the wild, and less than 1% live twice that, there would be no selection for genes to help that species live to be 100. Individuals with genes to live that long would invest too much in repair, and not enough in reproduction. Kind of like investing in your retirement 401K to provide enough money to live to be 1,000 years old. It isn't going to happen no matter what, so most of that stockpiled cash would be wasted. Wasted energy is selected against.

The ecological lifespan for a species, in the wild where it existed, is the right balance of repair relative to other uses of energy that led to the most successful copies, with an extra margin for error. In a safe, stable environment with no predators, take your time. Grow old, reproduce a little along the way. In an environment where you are going to get eaten in a year on average anyway, like a rat, you might as well not invest in too much in repair, as you are a bit of a disposable species. Domesticating a species can add years to its life with good medical care, pain and arthritis drugs, etc. For dogs, the wild genetic source (wolves) doesn't generally live much longer than a bit over half a dozen years, so being programmed to repair much beyond that just did not pay off. That is why your dog gets arthritis and cataracts at a decade, and you were just getting warmed up at that age. Few wild dogs would live that long, and those that did would become easy prey. Could CRISPR find the genes for aging and change the game, making dogs who live 200 years? Probably, although it is unlikely that is where the best money can be found, so not where researchers would start. Aging is controlled by many genes, too, so it is also not a simple place to start.

Species, breeds, and hybrids

How did we get here when I wanted to talk about gene pools? Time to circle that back home and close out this chapter. Species are most commonly thought of as groups of organisms that can and do share genes. In our analogy, ones that can successfully swap boxes of books. No wolf is sharing boxes with elephants. Parts won't fit and the books are arranged differently. The elephant has 56 chromosomes, so they won't match up with the 78 dog ones. The groups live on separate continents. We call them genetically isolated. They have separate gene pools. Genetic isolation and enough time lead to separate species. These two are easily shown to be separate species by about any conceivable definition.

Wolves and coyotes share boxes on occasion, and they have the same number of chromosomes. Separate species? Yes, but not because of the same type of genetic isolation. Learning this next part will make clearer what a breed is and is not. Cross a wolf with a wolf, you get a wolf. Cross a coyote with a coyote you get a coyote. Cross a wolf and a coyote you get something we call a red wolf. Apologies to the biologists who insist that this is a separate species. Biologists argue about how much separation is enough. If you cross red wolves with red wolves, do you get a wolf, a coyote, or a red wolf? If you get a true breeding line, you have a new species. Cross a Labrador and a Standard Poodle, you get a Labradoodle. Cross two Labradoodles, what do you get? People are arguing now if the cross is a true breed. Skipping the politics behind it, biologically if you have to keep going back to separate original source groups (the Labrador and the Poodle) to get your Labradoodle, it is a cross-breed and not a true breed. If you cross Labradoodles with Labradoodles and get predictable consistent Labradoodles, you have a new breed, made the same way many of the old established breeds were founded. That red wolf is its own species if you get red wolves from red wolves. If you frequently have to go back and cross wolves and coyotes to get a red wolf, it is just a cross breed. Is it special? That is not a biological question.

When is a breed a new breed? This is not a biology question, but it's closer. There is a lot of subjectivity in what separates breeds. You say, "No there isn't, there are breed standards." Nature did not set up those standards, people did. They sorted and codified and voted and argued, listing what they valued and did not. Human capriciousness, not biology. Is it worth all the money? Cost is based on supply and demand, and this is not even close to a biological question. Is a breed a species? If one kept breeds true for long enough, sure, they could become genetically isolated enough to become separate species, but none so far rise to the level of separate species from the rest of domestic dogs. Despite being taught the contrary in my undergraduate biology classes, nature does not care about our definitions like "species" or breeds. They are what we say they are. Nothing more, nothing less. In nature, genes get swapped where and how they can without a worry about our feelings or our definitions.

Dogs are the same species as wolves by most definitions of species. Domestic dogs are but a subset of books (chromosomes) shared only amongst their own kind. That is all a breed is, too. Someone decides this is a good look and a good combination of traits and sets standards they like, and encourages only sharing books between like-minded members. And heaven help the soul who takes an individual from a line that can trace itself back to some sire like Multiple Best in Show–Winning Champion Floats Like a Butterfly and dam Multiple Best in Show–Winning Champion Stings Like a Bee and shares precious volumes of hard selected DNA with Never Won Anything Question-able Daddies Unknown Breeds Like a Rabbit, producing a mixed breed called Bubba. Still clearly a domestic dog but no longer in the carefully selected breed line. That line is a breed. It is a functional term, refers to a subset of a gene pool, and is a term used for human-selected packages of DNA instead of ones Mother Nature selected for in the kill-or-be-killed world.

Heritability versus the environment

Now you know a lot about genetics. But there is the inevitable curve ball that is worth making a cautionary note about here. It will return again, most notably when we look at behaviors toward the end of the tour. If there were flashing fonts in books, I would be using them here. Very few observed traits, if any, are purely genetic. Two identical twins fed different diets will grow to different heights, even though height is mostly controlled by a few genes. Sex (the biological distinction, not gender, which is the social one) is genetically controlled, unless something else genetic or environmental like a disease or a tumor of cells that produce sex hormones interferes. Bitter taste is genetic to protect you from plant toxins that can poison you, but if you like coffee or beer, you learned to ignore those genes. We calculate the heritability of a gene as the ratio of the variation in how that gene presents in the organism that is inherited versus that which the environment causes. We study that best by comparing identical twins (monozygotic, or from one egg) to nonidentical (dizygotic, or from two separate eggs) twins. So far, we mostly do that in humans.

Reproduction again

Evolutionarily speaking, the whole organism is optimized to get copies of itself into the next generation. Despite all of the focus so far, that is not the same as having offspring. Sit tight, hang on, because I am about to toss out having puppies as the only way to reproduce a dog! I got half my genes, the pink volumes, from my mom. And as we saw, I only got half of her genes, the other half went into another less fortunate egg called a polar body that was reabsorbed by my mom's ovary. Likewise with dad's genes, except that the other half ended up in a sperm that lost the one great race of its life. So, to my mom, my brother and I are each half a copy of her. Add in my sister, and there are one-and-a-half copies of my mom there. If my sister got half of mom's genes, and I got half of mom's genes, and the halves were split by chance, then half of my mom's genes that I got from mom are in my sister. Half of a half is a fourth, if you are keeping score. You best be keeping score, since that is the only point of this entire paragraph. My sister has a quarter of the same genes from our mom as I have, and a quarter of the same genes I got from my dad. My sister is genetically half of me. My brother is half of me. For a gene pool count, they equal me. As far as evolution works, getting copies of me into the next generation works the same if I help my siblings' kids survive, each a quarter of me, as if I helped half as many of my own kids survive. Two of their kids equal one of my kids, genetically. Remember, things that make copies of themselves tend to make more copies of themselves than things that don't. Mother Nature does not care if the copies are in my kids or in my relative's kids. Your evolutionary success is measured in copies of yourself scattered amongst other humans, not direct descendants.

Your exact genome exists as a package only once in all of history. Yeah you! Unfortunately, like the earlier chicken egg, you are just your genes' way of making more genes. If this is the only time the package (you) exists in all of history, it can't be very important (of course, it is everything to you). Once that unique set of genes gets polluted (mixed, you know, from mating with others), those offspring really aren't any more or less "copies of you" whether you actually help them survive or not. Getting copies of you into the next generation is the whole definition of what life is all about, biologically speaking. Non-blood relatives do not count in all of this. Remember, my wife's niece and nephew from her sister don't count for me because they have none of my genetic line, but they do for my wife, as they share the same common source, my wife's mom, who is their grandmother.

Now let's count up copies of Tim Lewis. My brother has three kids. My brother is half a copy of me and each of the three kids is a quarter copy of me. My brother's side is one-and-three-quarters copies of Tim Lewis. My sister has two kids, so they make a total of one copy of me (each niece adding one quarter, my sister a half). I am a full copy of me. I have no parents left, each would have added half a copy of me if they were alive. They are not alive, so they do not count here. Grandparents are a quarter copy, and I have none of those living, either. If I had any children, they would each be half of me. Their kids, my nonexistent grandkids, would each be a quarter of me. So I have three-and-three-quarters copies of me, but they are spread out in eight human beings. From an evolutionary point of view, I would have less success (copies of Tim Lewis out there) if I had zero siblings, no nieces or nephews, but had five of my own children. Or, to state that again, because this is non-intuitive: Having kids is not always the best way to get copies of yourself into the next generation from an evolutionary point of view. If I have five kids, that is a lot of food to procure. If copies of me are spread out in my siblings' kids, it costs me a few Christmas presents, but I do not have to feed them every day. Evolutionarily, I am a parasite, having my family raise copies of me so I do not have to. You would think I had to have my own kids to be successful in this evolutionary competition, but I don't.

In wild wolves, having five puppies seems like a good strategy to get copies of oneself out there, and indeed it works. But a wolf that could work collaboratively to build systems that helped assure closely related puppies survived better than their own pups would not need to make their own. Doing that requires a bigger brain, and a society or a pack, and you see where this is going? Anyway, most of my students average seven to ten copies of themselves when they count parents, cousins, siblings, and the occasional child. So biologically they are all more successful, more evolutionarily fit, better at making copies of themselves, than I am.

When I say my brother is half of me, I really mean that of the 0.1% of DNA we could potentially not share, we share half. For the other 99.9% he is all me, or I am all him, as we humans all share that 99.9%.

Recall that you are genetically unique, found only once in history, and really can't be what evolution is all about. Genes are quite durable. We even carry Neanderthal genes in us, and we have parasitic genes inserted by viruses. I kind of lied to you about the importance of making copies of you. In fact, the chicken is not the egg's way of making another egg. The gene is the primary unit. The egg is a gene's way of making a copy of itself, and genes that make copies of themselves endure and proliferate. Genes that packaged themselves in chromosomes did better than those that did not, making more copies. The egg is the gene's way of making more copies of the gene. The chicken is the egg's ways of making more eggs, which are really the gene's way of making more genes. We are amalgamations of successful genes on their way through history, currently packaged in you, or your dog, or any other living thing, enduring. For how long? Well, any one gene lasts no longer than you, except the one set in the successful egg or sperm you or your close relatives produced. I highly recommend Richard Dawkins' *A Selfish Gene*.

Before you start to wonder that if it is all about the genes, what about my dog? That package of genes—unique and together once in history in your dog—still created the being you so love and want to know more about. It really does not matter that the gene cannot think, and your dog is an incidental byproduct of self-replicating strips of DNA. They make for wonderful organisms, driven by emotion and thoughts. Knowing how that package works is what the tour in this book is all about, so the unique set of DNA housed in the bag of enzymes that is your dog can have a rich and rewarding time with the unique set of DNA housed in the bag of enzymes that is you, together on your trip forward through time.

All that is a very long way to say that inheritable traits we find in dogs were successful at helping make copies of themselves so they got into the next generation, but they do not always help the individual dog in question. A trait or gene that made the dog likely to save a human life at the cost of the dog's life works, if by saving the human the dog assured more copies of itself in other close relatives living with the human saved by the dog's sacrifice. Remember, there is no need for intention here. Dogs with a gene to do this in conditions where other siblings were around, like in early domesticated dogs, would just be successful despite the adverse impact on the individual. More accurately stated, a gene housed in any organism that caused the loss of itself, but with the result that other copies of the gene survived, would be just as successful. We will return to this when we look at dog behaviors near the end of our tours.

Evolution is not always intuitive, but it works and it set the stage for our dogs. I just tossed at you one of the most profound concepts humans have ever come up with. I really don't expect you to get that in just one read. Someday go back and reread this chapter. Slowly. Give yourself time to absorb it. The ideas, if they sink in, will rock your world. In the interim, go and take a minute to rock your dog, because that is what is most important. The rest of our tours are far more concrete, all built on this somewhat abstract idea that we inherit traits and why the variety exists.

Checking your dogs' evolutionary success is the same, really. I have heard plenty of people who breed their dogs argue about how successful their line of dogs is. I cannot disagree with them because I do not know how they measure success. Maybe money. Maybe geographic distribution or fame of their dogs. To Mother Nature, the only measure is copies of the dog in the next generation, not because copies are good in and of themselves, just that copies are copies. For us with our neutered dogs, however, evolutionary success still matters. Successful copies, those that make copies well, are exquisitely adapted to their environment. If there are lots of copies of my dog out there, odds are pretty good that the gene package is quite good. Wish, our 11-year-old Border Collie, was in a litter of six, five still alive. There were two other breedings of the same parents, and each of those counts as a full-blood sibling, or half a copy of Wish. She is the aunt of our youngest dog, Cricket. Cricket's dad's sperm has been frozen for years, so who knows how many of her siblings, half siblings, etc. are around. Gromit, our eldest, was adopted. For all we know, he may be alone in the universe. Or, by now, you may have figured out that if my kid is half of me, a blood-related cousin is an eighth of me, and you, the random person reading this paragraph, still share 99.9% of your DNA with me, and because we are all genetically related, a very tiny fraction of your genes are my genes. Over the 7.5 billion humans out there, there are plenty of copies of me, and a bit of me in everyone alive. And a lot of my dog's ancestors' genes are in me, and my distant ancestors' genes are in her. We really are all one family.

Oh, and did I mention we now know we have Neanderthal genes still in us? In fact, we seem to vary only slightly from their gene pool. Besides us and them, there were four other species of humans (our genus, different species from us, but like coyotes and wolves, likely able to interbreed with us). Three of these other species were all alive at the same time as we were working on this dog relationship, 20,000 to 30,000 years ago. At least one book claims dogs are why we outcompeted the other three species of humans, the Neanderthals in Europe and western Asia, the Denisovans in Asia, and the Flores humans (unfortunately popularly nicknamed the "hobbits"). In case you missed it, only ours is still around. Was that because of dogs and our unique partnership? We may owe a lot more to dogs than we like to admit.

A paws, I mean pause. Too often, people say that they do not want to believe that the world is billions of years old, or that there are trillions of stars, or that there are over 7 billion people, and that they are alone in their unique set of genes. It makes some people feel meaningless. It has the extreme opposite effect on me. There are tens of millions of dogs, and mine is the most precious on the planet. Time is seemingly endless, but my time is short, so every minute matters and every moment is priceless. So much so that I need to take my dog down to the river for a swim right now, just Cricket and me. If moments matter, in this sea of DNA and ocean of people in an infinite amount of time, I can do no better than giving joy to my dog who worries about none of these things, and so fills my moments with hope and love and happiness. See you after the swim.

What is life?

Biology is the study of life. (Can you believe I waited this long to define it?) Life is defined, or recognized by biologists, as having these seven characteristics:

- Living things are *organized*, typically into cells, to do some function.
- They maintain some level of *homeostasis*, regulating their internal environment as needed.
- Living things all have a *metabolism*, a process of converting energy into other forms and using it to build or repair things.
- Living things *grow*, either by volume or by number of cells.
- They *respond* to their outside environment, usually through their metabolism and often to maintain homeostasis.
- Living things can *adapt* to some degree to their environment.
- Perhaps most importantly, all living things can *reproduce*, making copies of themselves.

Note that if living things reproduce, they have to have some form of inheritance, not necessarily DNA. COVID-19 uses RNA instead of DNA. That will lead to evolution over time. The definition is not universal, nor always clear. Are viruses alive? What about prions, smallish proteins that reproduce all by themselves with none of the cellular machinery? Is an individual cheek cell alive? Turns out that last one is easy: Yes, if it is fresh. Defining when it dies is not biologically easy since you can freeze it and bring it back decades later. I can do that to whole organisms, too. Tardigrades, or water bears, are extremely common segmented and legged microscopic animals and can be frozen to minus 328 degrees Fahrenheit (-200 C), cooked to 300 degrees Fahrenheit (150 C), exposed to the vacuum of space for 10 days, and still come back from their survival inert state. We are finding bacteria, frozen, inert, but definitely alive in melting arctic ice, that have been there for up to a million years. Life is pretty durable, it would appear.

Sperm and eggs are alive. Each contains a full set of DNA, metabolizes energy, and shows all the characteristics of any other living cell in the animal body except that they have only one set of DNA volumes (23 in humans, 39 in dogs) not two sets (46 in humans or 78 in dogs). Sets of DNA do not define life. There are organisms with one set of DNA (such as a species of mites), two (like dogs), and up to four sets in one species of mammal (a rat)— four sets are also common in plants and some fish. The egg that made me was fully formed with the boxes of books packed and ready to go when my mom was born, 35 years before she and my dad ... can we not discuss that part? Male mammals, we pack those boxes just a few days at most before we ship them out. No sense hurrying that along. So how old am I? At birth, was I brand new, as we count birthdays? Was I nine months old, counting from when the sperm and the egg started to cohabitate and combine DNA? Or was I already 35 years old plus nine months because that living egg with half my instructions was primed and ready for kickoff that long ago?

So what? Why should you care? First of all, as I like to note, it is interesting and forces you to think about what it means to be alive. All that DNA in every cell, the sex cells getting only half the instructions, and problems galore if there are mistakes. It also means that we can arrange a sharing of boxes of DNA, say a few million sperm and an egg or two, hoping to get the great sociability of the mom and the beautiful coat of the dad, and maybe we get it right, like our dog Wish did. Or maybe we get the coat of the mom and the sociability of the dad, or both from Mom's side, or both from Dad's side. And since neither trait is covered by only one gene, most likely we get something that was a mix of sociability genes from dam and sire, and coat instructions from each, and all we can do later is say that we think this looks a lot like both parents, maybe. If only we could identify the particular traits we wanted and snip those pages out and assemble our own custom-made books or chromosomes.

Until a few years ago we called that science fiction. Then it was called wishful thinking (but not Wish-full thinking). With a hot, new molecular technique, we now call that CRISPR (known by essentially no one as its full name of clustered regularly interspersed short palindromic repeats). Genetic engineering has come of age. In my lifetime we went from Watson and Crick showing us how DNA made up the instructions of life, to the whole genome being read, even if we did not know what the words meant, to the ability to identify specific parts we want and the ability to make designer offspring. That is what CRISPR will do. Identify a desired part of the DNA, cut it out, and put it into the DNA of another living creature. In theory, but not yet in practice, I could grab the genes controlling running speed from one dog and slip those in with the personality of a second dog, and…your imagination is the only limit. Laws in many countries prevent doing this for humans, but we are going down that path with other animals. Truly designer dogs are probably just around the corner. I will just say watch out. People ask me if we should be doing this, and I tell them "should" and "should not" do not seem to be relevant when there is money to be made. There is gold in them thar genes. Remember the Golden Rule: Thems that has the gold makes the rules.

Finally, what a dog is

So, what is a dog? To get technical, and you knew I would, a domestic dog, *Canis lupus domesticus*, is a subset of a gene pool making up the species *Canis lupus*, in the group of dogs in the genus *Canis* of the family Canidae of the order Carnivora in the class Mammalia in the phylum Chordata of the kingdom Animalia, using the common but somewhat outdated five-kingdom model of taxonomy. Each group listed shares common evolutionary descent from a common ancestor with all others in that same group. So all animals come from a common source, and all mammals are a subgroup of common origin within the larger group of chordates and animals.

To work our way back down from large groups of living things to species, we start with kingdom (ignoring domains, but don't you think I don't know about them). All animals are multicellular with advanced, non-bacterial cell structures that, at least originally, got their energy by consuming others. Chordates are animals that have four common traits: a dorsal tubular nerve cord (your spinal cord), a tail (shows in your five coccyx bones or tailbone), a notochord (a stiff rod, in you and your dog the discs between your vertebrae), and gill slits (which you and your dog had as an embryo, but they got repurposed into your nose and mouth cavity and other parts). Mammals are chordates that all have seven diagnostic characteristics, most of which I won't bore you with here, but they include milk from sebaceous glands and hair, and do not exclude laying eggs (cue the duck billed platypus, echidna, and spiny anteater). Carnivores are mammals that eat primarily meat and have a very characteristic pair of teeth called the carnassial pair, which your typical dog uses to gnaw on bones and chew toys. Carnivores also have claws and larger canine teeth than most other mammals. Weasels, bears, raccoons, cats, seals, walruses, and wolves are all in the order Carnivora. Canids are carnivores with nonretractable claws, adapted for speed and pursuit. There are over 30 species of canids, including our beloved domestic dogs, dingoes, jackals, foxes, dholes, and wild dogs. The genus *Canis* includes foxes, jackals, and wolves. *Canis lupus* is an isolated genetic group of common evolutionary descent including wolves and domestic dogs. There you go, no extra charge. Next time someone dares to ask you what a dog is, let them have it.

Science as a way of thinking - Part 2

I want to close this discussion on reproduction and the basic genetic lineage of dogs with a framing paradigm that shapes my thoughts about dogs and helps me deal with the split personality brought on by both studying and living with dogs. My love of my dogs in particular, and dogs in general, colors almost every aspect of every day. My day starts with Cricket climbing on my chest, back, or side, depending what part of me is facing the ceiling while I am asleep, whereupon she noses my face until I get up. She then curls up on my pillow to go back to sleep, the first task of her to-do list for the day complete: Get Tim up, he has to go to work. But she does not seem to grasp weekends and holidays. See what I did there? I assigned meaning and motivation to her actions. The observation is that at 5 a.m. every day Cricket noses me until I get out of her way. Is it a to-do? Do I start the process by stirring, and this is her way of booting out the one disturbing her sleep? Is she trying to help me get to work on time? Does this really happen every day, or do I only remember when it does, and not take note of the days she does not do this: a form of observational bias?

We can test that. That is the other half of my split personality. I am a scientist, which means I subscribe to a philosophy based on two assumptions. Those assumptions put the limits on what science is good for. That philosophy, that way of knowing, assumes that the world exists in such a way that there are rational repeatable non-miraculous forces that explain all actions, some argue including decision-making and free will. Secondly, the philosophy assumes that our senses are valid ways of learning about the world. Science is a perspective based on careful observation and rigorous testing of ideas through actual experimentation. Apologies to the theoretical physicists amongst you. If you can't test it experimentally, it is not science. It is likely worth thinking about, but it is still not science. As our ability to test things expands, so does what is in the realm of science. For example, I used to teach that love and beauty were areas outside science. Modern experiments prove that I was wrong. Each of these has a strong basis in evolution and some genetically influenced aspects. Many dog behaviors we train are testable scientifically. Mostly science gets directed to where the money is, so most interesting questions you will have about your dog probably have not been tested. Testing is slow and can only answer one question at a time.

We scientists love to be proven wrong. That is how we move knowledge forward. Science is based on testable facts. That means that I have no more added perspective on morals and ethics than the next person. Are dogs moral beings with rights? My being a scientist gives me no more gravitas to that opinion than you have. I will try to keep my focus on biology, and my opinions clearly marked as such. I will provide a lot of contextualizing, which is necessary for informed interpretation, because science is not only facts and experiments.

Science is also a body of knowledge; the many observations, facts, and experiments are assembled into models, our interpretations based on the best explanations for the facts. It wasn't called science then, but early observations of the Earth's shadow on the moon showed people that the Earth was round, and that the sun and moon both orbited the Earth. The orbiting part was interpretation, a model that best explained the sun and moon's increasing separation from the Earth's eastern horizon every morning throughout the day, and at the same time decreasing the separation to the western horizon. More observations, now of other bodies in the sky, the wandering stars known as planets, led to the better explanation that the Earth orbits the sun and the moon orbits the Earth. Over time, these ideas could be tested experimentally, from measuring gravity to experiments with orbits, which is pretty much where we are today, with apologies to all professional and amateur astronomers for the quick, sweeping generalizations there.

The body of knowledge is great, and like any field of knowledge, it is easy for an outsider to get lost in the jargon and details. Scientists are trained to be exact and precise. When someone from the general public asks a scientist a simple question, we tend to gum it all up with details, rare exceptions, and conditional statements. The body of knowledge needs to be accessible, because you really deserve to know how utterly astounding that dog is. By the time we are done with our journey together, you will know enough basic biology to talk meaningfully with your veterinarian, to have better information about diet and herbal remedies and to know why your dog does much of what they do. You can also become the life of the party. You will be able to answer such crowd pleasers as: Why do dogs vomit so easily? Why do dogs only live a decade or maybe two? Can my dog be depressed? Are dogs colorblind? Which came first, the chicken or the egg?

You know that last one already. What your answer is tells us much about the rest of our journey together. If your response is: The egg, by a few hundred million years, since eggs are found in all of the animals preceding chickens on the Earth, you have the perspective of a logician. If you read into the question the word "chicken" as in "which came first, the chicken egg or the chicken adult," this can go two ways. If you thought, "Whatever a chicken is, it was blueprinted by the DNA in an egg. So the chicken egg had to precede the chicken." Factually correct and implies that the DNA is the defining factor of being a chicken. This is also an evolutionary perspective, with emphasis on the perspective of molecular biologist. If you thought, "No matter what a chicken is, it is the adult form eating and being able to make more chicken eggs that counts" then you are more of an evolutionary ecologist, and probably adhere to the mindset of "gotta make successful copies that can reproduce to count you" school. If your answer was, "Chickens are so cute, we should have one as a pet," you are a helpless aesthetic, and you bring a bit of joy wherever you go. If you thought, "Who cares, wings sound good for dinner," you are an optimal forager, and will continue to be invited to nonvegetarian parties, and actively excluded by vegetarians. If you thought, "Oh my gosh, what nut job thinks of all these things?" then you know why I am not invited to those parties!

TOUR 3

A FLOAT TRIP DOWN THE DIGESTIVE SYSTEM

As I start on this chapter, it is Thanksgiving morning. The irony is inescapable, but it also provides a good focus on what a wild dog spends much of the day doing, and what is central to my Border Collies as they watch me write: food. I could have started with sleep, too, but that is for a small part in another chapter. Holiday or not, my dogs start waking us up at five, because they learned that is when I normally get up, typically to go to work. Try as I might, I have been unable to explain to them that humans have weekends and holidays, and many of us like the idea of sleeping in. To my dogs, whatever else we are, we are the means to food, and their morning meal comes right after the day's first trip outside. Check those two boxes, and it is naptime for them. Their meal with preparation time lasts minutes. Eating takes a few seconds. The phrase "wolfing down your meal" had to come from somewhere. Like the Thanksgiving feast we will attend later today, food preparation takes way more time than eating the meal. I will return later in the next chapter to everything it took to get their food to the storage bin, so I can address some issues about the food itself.

Much of what fills a wild dog's day consists of locating and consuming food, something you do for your not-so-wild dog at home so they can sleep more. Refined through evolution over millions of years, much of what any dog is stems from the need to effectively and efficiently find, secure, process, ingest, digest, and dispose of food. None of this happens with tools or weapons. There are no grocery stores for wild wolf packs, no butcher shops they can stop at for a side of moose, no distribution network of dog-driven trucks, and no chef dogs in white puffy hats. Until domestication. Now you do those jobs for the dogs. We took over all of those roles in some form or another, and we fill the day with other activities that take advantage of that wolf heritage. Who domesticated whom?

You might as well learn to do those jobs better. I find that if you know how your dog works, how it processes and digests food, and what can go wrong with all of this, you will be a better domesticated-by-my-dogs kind of person.

Feeding the cells

It was my first day of college as an 18-year-old, at my first class, which was the general survey of biology offered at most colleges in the country. I sat in a big lecture hall at a small college in central Illinois, surrounded by a hundred other students, eagerly awaiting wisdom and, of course, checking out my classmates. After a brief and insincere welcome to college, the instructor described his wife as simply a big bag of enzymes. He asked us why that really wouldn't work, just one big bag instead of the trillions of little bags we actually have. He was driving to the point of specialization. If she were an unorganized bag, what would distribute the food and oxygen throughout the bag? How would the bag move about, getting food? How would the bag defend itself? Is size the only constraint?

Could a single cell function as simply a bag? Turns out, no. My youngest dog, Cricket, is by necessity far more than just a bag of enzymes. Even the simple cells she is made of, all 10 trillion of them, are highly organized. Each has organelles, really parts of a cell with specialized tasks, analogous to the organs in your body. I will briefly describe a few because I cannot resist doing so, two others because they are necessary to our tour through the dog's body, and overall as homage to the fact that cells are what your dog's eating habits are all about, and therefore why they have legs, and teeth, and a tail. Besides, learn this part and a trip to the veterinarian or pet food store will make a lot more sense to you.

Cells are tiny, right? It takes 10 trillion to build one 30-pound (14 kg) dog. Picturing 10 trillion is difficult. OK, it is darn near impossible without making analogies. It is more than the current estimate of galaxies in the universe, but that is not going to help. If each of your dog's cells were as large as an average grain of sand, they would fill a box 35 feet (10.6 m) on each side. That is a three-story house with 1200 ft2 (111 m2) on its first floor, a midsized but tall home.

I am writing this text in my office at home, necessitated by the current global lock-down caused by a virus. I sit in a room that is 10 feet by 10 feet (3 m by 3 m), with an 8-foot-tall (2.5 m) ceiling. I am going to use my office, which you cannot even see, to give you a picture of what one cell in your dog looks like, a typical cell. Please note that there really is no typical cell; each specializes, and they vary quite a bit in size. Skin cells are different from intestinal cells, which differ from muscle cells, which differ from nerve cells, which are way different from sperm (tiny cells) and eggs (largest of cells), to drag sex back into this, because dogs and food alone might not hold your attention. You need to know that cells differ. You don't need to know how they differ, at least not yet.

If the room I am in were a living cell in a dog, the room would be filled all the way to the top with a thick, gooey liquid called cytoplasm. Floating in that goop is a 3-foot-wide (1 m) ball, like one of those big yoga balls, holding the DNA in its 78 fragments that we covered in Tour 2. Now you know this is a dog cell, because I used 78. And I got to remind you about the previous chapter. That ball is the nucleus, holder of the crown jewels, the instructions for life, the very molecules that make your dog what it is and keep it from being an elephant or a tomato. Like a museum, most of the stuff inside the ball is simply sitting, gathering dust as it were. Depending on what kind of cell we are in, different parts of the DNA are actively being read, and molecules of instructions written on RNA are coming out of the nucleus through the many openings in the ball. RNA is a lot like DNA, except it is only half of the twisted ladder that makes DNA, and with a different sugar as its building block.

The cell has other organelles floating in the sea of goo, structures that do specific tasks. One critical structure your cells have a bunch of (and by bunch I mean somewhere between 70,000 and 10 million, so a sizable bunch at that) looks like an acorn (look it up if you don't have oak trees in your area). They are called ribosomes. They read those RNA instructions to make proteins that do things for the cell. One of my favorite structures is called the Golgi apparatus (how can you not like that name?). These layered organelles look like a short stack of pancakes that modify proteins made by those ribosomes so they can be exported from the cell and shipped around the body via the blood stream for later use. There is a whole complex set of filaments that make up an endoskeleton. Picture the steel girders that make up a big building or the trusses overhead in a barn or arena. This is a framework running through the cell, and bags of proteins made by ribosomes and packaged by the Golgi apparatus can be moved along it. In addition, if the cell needs to change shape or sort chromosomes, these filaments do the moving.

Converting food to energy

The organelle I really want you to remember is called the mitochondrion (that is singular, "mitochondria" is plural, and you rarely catch one alone). We talked about them in Chapter 2, in terms of their DNA. Now it's time to talk about what they do. This one is an imposter, a parasite, not really part of you at all but found in every cell. Think of the mitochondria as the charging station recharging lots of little batteries, and everything else in the cell is run on those rechargeable batteries. Busy place, the cell. For what it is worth, and it is worth a lot to me but not to my editor, those mitochondria were once free-living bacteria that successfully invaded animal cells. They parasitize us for their food, and in exchange they give us their leftover energy so we don't boot them out. They have their own kind of DNA, but over time, most of their DNA moved into our DNA in the cell nucleus. Thankfully antibiotics we use don't kill them, or we would be goners. Without it, you are dead. Intrigued?

In our office example, these bugs are about half a foot (15 cm) across and look like a pill, one of the old-time capsules that were two-colored and felt like they were made of plastic. If my room is a cell, there are likely hundreds of these mitochondria in the room. What are they doing in there? They take two ingredients the cell gets from the blood, carbon and oxygen, and release a molecule that stores energy. The mitochondria chemically burn carbon found in simple sugars from food you fed your dog using oxygen that your dog breathed in. Like a campfire, only chemically controlled to burn cooler. From that, they make a molecule called ATP from a precursor, ADP. A pause. You are going to hear a lot about ATP. In fact, you will have 35 more encounters with the acronym, and without ATP you are dead. Gone. ATP stands for adenosine triphosphate. Go ahead and forget that, but not the letters so when they pop up again in a few chapters you don't go "huh?" for too long. The T in there is for tri, the D in the other is for di, three versus two. The phosphate to phosphate bond stores a lot of useful energy. Break the bond, you release energy you can use. These organelles are taking loose phosphate (phosphorus combined with a few oxygen molecules) in the cell and sticking it on ADP to make ATP. Other parts of the cell take the ATP, pop off a phosphate that releases energy, and they use that energy to do things.

This paragraph implies one of those really cool, fun facts that I want to make explicit, so you can drop it into conversations with your erstwhile friends. When you give your dog some food, that food gets broken down into molecules made of carbon. Your dog breathes in oxygen in the air around them. The mitochondria strip out a carbon atom ingested as food and combine it with oxygen your dog got from breathing in air, leaving carbon dioxide to breathe out and free energy to use. Overfeed and your dog stores the extra carbon and energy as fat. Underfeed and that fat is burned with oxygen, releasing more carbon dioxide. When your dog goes on to lose weight, that lost weight exited as carbon dioxide. One loses body weight by breathing carbon out, not the temporary and easily fixed losses from pooping, peeing, or sweating water out.

All of what follows in this chapter is basically this: how to take a complex mix of food, like a piece of kibble or the leg of a moose, and break it apart into little enough parts to process down into simple sugars, so mitochondria can burn them to make ATP. Dogs burn ATP so that in the long run, testicles can locate some ovaries, and make copies of themselves. Dogs who do this show up in the next generation. Dogs who do not, not so much. In the short run, dogs convert food to ATP so they can leap over a set of bars, cruise through a tunnel, push some sheep around, or just stay alive while we watch a movie.

ATP is ATP, whether it derived from kibble or the bloody flesh of a recently killed rabbit. Food is the raw material. The digestive system breaks it down to useful chemical parts such that once inside, it matters little what it came from on the outside. If this is the case, then why does food source matter at all? Food is a lot more than energy. It carries vitamins, minerals, and a few toxins. Different starter foods, meat versus grains, for example, get processed differently once we get them into the digestive system. In the end, most of what we eat goes to make glucose, a simple sugar, used to make ATP in each and every cell.

The digestive system - a tube within a tube

My introductory biology professor finished the first day of class stating that the body plan of most animals is simply this, a tube within a tube. Most properly, the tube or path from your dog's mouth through the stomach, intestines, and out the anus is like the inside of shirt sleeve. That inside space is not inside the fibers of the cloth, it is just a space for your arm to pass through. Your arm never becomes part of the sleeve, except in science fiction. Your arm goes through the space, but not into the fabric. Likewise in the intestines. It is not really inside you. Swallow a rock (please don't), and it will emerge from the other side pretty much intact, unless it was limestone. Stomach acid digests that one. Whether the path is inside you or not is a matter of perspective. To a physiologist, no. To an ecologist, yes. I am an ecologist, so let's go inside the tube known as the alimentary canal. Consider this, now, as a journey through the canine digestive system. Our journey starts at the saliva-dripping tooth-filled mouth, and ends up in a pile, hopefully outside the house.

Teeth

Dogs are I 3/3, C 1/1, P 4/4, M 2/3 (explanations to follow below). That pretty much says it all, right? I just listed the tool substitutes in the primary toolbox dogs carry with them all the time. Sit and watch a dog for almost any length of time, and sooner or later they will pick up or pick at something with their mouth. We reach and grab with hands. Canines, well, use their canines. In mammals, there are four kinds of teeth by function. These get modified through evolutionary pressure, and feeding puts a lot of pressure on an organism. If you are not good at feeding, you die. If you die, you tend to make fewer copies of yourself than if you were alive. A good look in the mouth can tell you a lot about what feeds the beast in your kitchen. A word of caution. While your dog may be tolerant of you prying open their jaws against their will and probing around with your fingers and a flashlight to check on what I am going to describe, be alert to your dog's responses. My dogs, no worries. I could probably reach down their throat and pull out a missing sock from their stomach. Some dogs will simply add your fingers to their stomach. Know your dog, and proceed gingerly, maybe first by parting the lips and looking at the clenched teeth. I can't be responsible for you and your dog. If you are unsure, just trust my descriptions or look at the photo. I am hoping, however, that you are about to embark on a slime-covered journey into the cavernous abyss of the dog's buccal region.

Imagine you are really hungry. You go to the store for some food. You pick up manageable sized pieces, be they parts of a cow or portions of a corn or rice field. You take them home, maybe cook them so they are easier to chew and digest, and head off for some dessert. In the wilds of your kitchen, mudroom, or wherever you feed your dogs, you give them bite-sized portions of kibble or raw food. Almost certainly you don't toss out a whole goat for them to eat at once. Seriously, if you are doing that, you have issues. If you do, I presume you, uh, processed that enough to keep the neighbors from calling the police. You, the butcher, and the food factory system use a boatload of tools to process the food for easy handling. Knives. Scissors. Scales. Bowls. You carry larger portions in bags or boxes, Tupperware, Ziploc bags, and nylon treat bags. In the wild, dogs don't even have hands for this. Their mouths serve as their toolboxes, their scissors and knives, their hands for carrying things around, and their bowls and bags.

Incisors (I) are chisel-shaped teeth at the front of the mouth. They are used for biting off a piece of something, like you might with an apple. They are useful for grasping things, like a pair of tongs. They are set into the jaw with only one root. If you really want to pull hard, you don't use your incisors, because that one root is not the strongest connection between tooth and jaw. They are also good for a nip at something. Being way out on the jaw, the leverage for them is not so good, so you don't get your strongest bite there. Dogs with the full, normal wolf set of teeth have six incisors in the front of the mouth on the upper jaw, and six on the lower jaw. A caveat rests in that last sentence: normal. Domestic dogs are a fairly inbred group, as are all domesticated animals. Defects, which are any deviation from the wild type, are more common in inbred groups. If your dog has extras, no worries. My eldest dog is missing his lower incisors. Too much tugging, or maybe chewing on rocks, or maybe a bar fight, but one day I noticed he was walking around with a gaping hole where four of those lower front teeth used to sit. Another note. If the center of your dog's face were a line, the six upper incisors would be set three left of the line, and three right. The left side would be symmetrical to the right. All I really needed to say was that your dog had three upper incisors because we refer to quadrants or quarters of the mouth. Upper left, upper right, lower left, lower right. Left mirrors right. Upper does not always mirror lower. In the formula I started this section with, I 3/3 translates to three upper incisors and three lower incisors per quadrant. Left and right are always a duplicate of each other in the wild types, but upper and lower tooth numbers vary. A white-tailed deer or a bovine or a sheep is I 0/3. No upper incisors. This tells you nothing about tooth shape but a lot about what the animal eats. The tusk of an elephant is a long, continuously growing incisor and looks nothing like your dog's incisors. Placental mammals, the non-egg-laying, non-marsupial or pouched group, have at most 3/3 incisors. Marsupials can go as high as 5/4 incisors. Monotremes, the egg-laying group of mammals including the duck-billed platypus, lack teeth as adults.

Next in line along the jaw are **canines (C)**. These are easy to find in dogs. Yours are barely bigger than your incisors, unless you are a vampire. Generally, canines are shaped like daggers and pretty much function as them. In mammals there are never more than 1/1 canines. Some, like the walrus, get ridiculously large. But no fast-running mammal can have huge canines; they would get in the way. I mean none like a walrus has. The saber-toothed tiger had some pretty respectable canines. In dogs, canines are for piercing prey, digging deep, and holding on. Wild dogs that grab large prey use their canines to sink in and hold on. These teeth have deep roots, well anchored in the jaw. For something small, like a rabbit, wolves tend to use the incisors to hold the prey and shake their head vigorously to kill their victim. Every time my dog, Cricket, catches a Frisbee, she shakes her head and spins around. I tell her "kill it," which does get me strange looks from my friends, but that is all she is doing, an instinctive killing of smaller prey. For large prey, grab the jugular or hamstrings with your canines, and hang on. Not all dog bites are the same. A dog that is really trying to hurt you, since you are large prey, uses their canines to grab for the kill. A bite with only the incisors on larger beasts, like humans, is usually a warning or an attempt to move you away, or to intimidate, not to kill or eat.

Now we enter the realm of **molars (M)**. Molars are for processing food. Your dog started with a "milk set" or baby teeth. It is a set of smaller, sharp and pointy teeth for a smaller mouth. It has all of the same number of incisors and canines as the later adult set. However, only some of the adult molars are found in this first milk set. Technically, a molar with a milk-set precursor is called a premolar (P). A true molar, no "pre" in the name, is found only in the adults. Thus (I have been waiting to use that word, it is so snobby) we differentiate them in the dental formula. Dogs are 4/4 premolars and 2/3 molars.

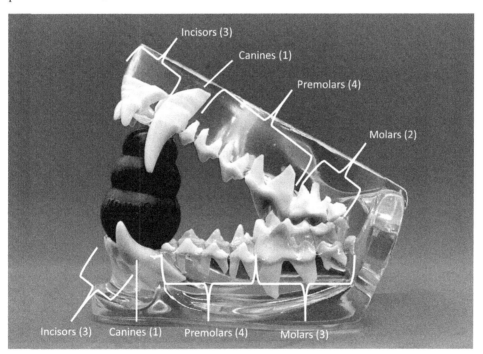

If you are a horse or a cow, your molars are big, broad, and flat with grinding surfaces to tear open plant fibers. Dogs in the wild eat meat. Not much to process. Cut it up and swallow the pieces. You should run your tongue along your own molars. Broad and flat, not so big as a horse's, but not like your dog's molars. Look inside at your dog's back teeth. They look pointed, sharp, and not at all made for grinding. In fact, your dog can't grind its jaw, moving the lower jaw back and forth to the side. You can a little. Watch a cow or a horse eat and you will see that lower jaw moves very far side to side. Molars in dogs do the cutting. That shape is called secodont, not that you asked. Watch a dog chew on a bone or some leather chew toy. They will be using the largest molars they have: a pair of teeth in the side of the jaw halfway back that sets up like a guillotine, with a huge upper premolar opposing a large lower molar. That pair is strong enough in wolves to crack a moose femur. Get your fingers in there and you will feel the joy of some serious damage if your dog is so inclined. Now we get to what is distinctively carnivore. Any of the molars are shaped to process meat, but that largest pair is called the carnassial pair, and it is diagnostic of this order of mammals. Even the grass-eating panda shows it.

Now we finish out with two upper molars and three lower molars, all shaped to cut meat. The last upper molar is pretty small and offset from the others. All of these molars help hold on to prey. Set into the back of the jaw, they have incredible leverage. While bite force is hard to measure, the force of a wolf's jaw can reach to upward of 600 pounds (270 kg), similar to a lion. Your dog is likely half that, which is still three times what a human can do. Great for holding on to squirming prey. The carnassial pair of a wolf can generate 1,200 pounds of force per square inch (psi) (8274 kpa), twice what the jaw overall can do. Compare that with most domestic dogs at 200 psi (1380 kpa). Rottweilers have the strongest average bite force for domestic dogs, followed by German Shepherds and American Pit Bull Terriers. A word of caution: If you peruse the internet, you will find bite force values for dogs as high as over 2,000 pounds (900 kg) (note, without the area so no psi or kpa available). Other sites use the 200 psi (1380 kpa). Some websites claim that the higher value is just myth. You need to watch units. A 200 psi bite is not spread over a full square inch. In the bite-force studies, they typically give the jaw clamping strength. Think toothless jaw. In reality, that force gets concentrated at the tooth tips, giving them enormous piercing pressure. Skin tears at well below the bite force of most dogs, because sharp, pointy things like knives and teeth cut into the skin, not just push against it with crushing force. Every dog has the musculature and teeth to bite, and bite hard.

How do they do that? Run your finger down the center of your dog's skull in back. You will feel a couple of ridges that the jaw muscle, or masseter, connects to. The one that lines up with the spine is the sagittal crest. In many dogs you can also feel the occipital crest, which goes left to right across the skull in the back. Another part of the jaw muscle originates at the zygomatic arch, the wide part of the skull above the upper jaw, below and slightly behind the eyes. The masseter ends or attaches to the lower jaw. Overall, this is a pretty big muscle. In cows and horses, this muscle pulls the lower jaw left and right in a grinding motion. In dogs, the jaw is tightly hinged with no lateral motion, so all of the force goes into pulling the lower jaw into the upper jaw.

And you feed kibble that barely needs to be chewed, or raw meat that is not really fighting back. No wonder our dogs like chew toys.

Digestion

Digestion is all about taking long chains of repeating molecules and breaking them into small units that can be absorbed. Proteins get broken apart from long polypeptides to amino acid building blocks by the stomach enzyme of pepsin, and the pancreas' trypsin and chymotrypsin. Stomach hydrochloric acid also helps. Fats are long strings of glycerides. Bile from the liver breaks the fat globules into smaller and smaller drops. Then enzymes like lipase from the liver and pancreas break these chains down into smaller, one- or two-part pieces called mono- or diglycerides. Digestible carbohydrates enter as long strings of sugars, and get broken into single or double sugar units. Starches are broken apart by amylase into glucose, or into maltose, which is just two glucose sugars bonded together. Milk sugars are broken apart by lactase, which breaks the two-part sugar of lactose into glucose and galactose, a close molecular relative. Much of our diets now include sucrose, a two-part sugar broken down by sucrase into fructose and glucose.

Since this is such a sweet topic, let me try building these sugars from the ground up so you can remember them. Sugars are single units or doublets that when strung together make carbohydrates. The sugars come in different families. Common ones we consume all have six-carbon rings. They are glucose, fructose, and galactose. Glucose is mainly what plants make from sunshine and carbon dioxide in the air: you know, photosynthesis. Fructose is a plant storage form, now commercially derived from corn syrup and from sugar beets. Sugar cane makes for the best cocktails, in my opinion, but is really the same sugar. Galactose is not usually found by itself, and is not very sweet, but I think it has the most awesome name.

These simple sugars are often found in nature combined in pairs. Put a glucose with a galactose, and you have lactose, that stuff many are intolerant of in milk. Sucrose, or table sugar, is a glucose and a fructose. Two glucoses make maltose, the malt in beer and malted milkshakes. Honey, or bee vomit, is fructose and glucose, or table sugar with some extras. Maple syrup is sucrose, also with some extra flavors. The agave nectar I add to my margaritas instead of sucrose, because it is so much better, is a fructose and a glucose. Yep, table sugar again. Long strings of sugars called carbohydrates just get broken down into simple sugars so they can be absorbed. Leave a starch in your mouth, like a piece of bread, and it begins to taste sweeter as the amylases in your mouth break out the sugars.

Moving down to the tube toward the stomach

Several organs in the abdomen of the dog contribute to digestion, this chemical breakdown of large molecules of sugar or protein or fat into smaller pieces. In a way, digestion is just microscopic chewing and swallowing, breaking big chunks of food into manageable pieces. The enzymes that break down food are really just chemical teeth without cusps and roots, and you know, real teeth stuff. The pancreas and the liver secrete material to aid digestion, but let's start in the mouth. While the teeth cut the meat into, hmm, I guess bite-sized pieces, the saliva glands in the mouth are squirting away with a slimy liquid to lubricate the food, and the tongue pushes it to the back of the mouth. There we encounter one of the worst designs in nature. Just thinking about it gets me all choked up. The trachea, grabbing air for the lungs, moves from behind the esophagus, the muscular tube that connects the mouth to the stomach, and passes in front of it. That would be fine if they took some bypass route. Instead, the trachea and esophagus cross paths in the same space. There is a one-way valve, the epiglottis, that is supposed to keep food doing the mouth-to-stomach trip from taking a detour down the nose-to-lungs path that is meant for air. But if you have ever inhaled a little food or water, you know it is not a perfect system. Evolution works with the parts it has, and design is not always optimal, and here we see a good example. Once I inhaled a piece of chicken while dining with the world-famous marine biologist Sylvia Earle. I left the table, too embarrassed to admit I was going to die in her presence, and somehow had the wherewithal to self-Heimlich when I reached the hallway. Immediately after forcing the chunk of chicken out of my mouth, I thought, "What a stupid arrangement this is." Like I said, I am a geek, even near death. And no, "stupid" was not exactly the adjective I used, but I hope you will forgive that indiscretion, there being death on the line and all.

The stomach

The bolus of food now is actively pushed down the muscular esophagus with waves constricting it much like you squeeze toothpaste out of a tube. These are called peristaltic waves, and they continue to move food all along the digestive system. The food is dumped into the stomach for storage and for processing. In the wild, a wolf will gorge on an enormous quantity of meat and keep it in the esophagus and stomach. If it is an adult with no pups, it will lie around and digest for a day or two. If there are pups, the adult will return to the den and when stimulated by the puppies licking their face, the adult will regurgitate food to the puppy. So yes, before your puppy gets trained to lick your face by your giggles and cooing, they did that instinctively to get you to vomit up a little dinner. Maybe not as cute as you once thought.

In the stomach, the food is sloshed and churned with stomach acid and enzymes like pepsin, which helps break down the food. The stomach is a very muscular sac, so it closes off valves on the incoming and outgoing sides and constricts the bag like you might mix dough in a Ziploc bag. When it is a good slurry, it is moved into the small intestine. In humans and in dogs, this takes about 15 minutes for liquid foods, and up to three hours for a solid meal. Little nutrient absorption takes place in the stomach; it is really about breaking down food into basic chemical components and liquefying into a paste-like consistency for better absorption. There is some evidence for taste buds in the stomach, and you will learn later a bit about the enteric nervous system, known as the "second brain" or the digestive nervous system. Certainly the stomach detects toxins and expels detected toxins back the way they came in. That is why dogs vomit so easily. They evolved to scavenge questionable foods, and they have to be able to launch those back out on a moment's notice. The food-holding mechanism was also important in wild canids so that they could carry meat back to the den for pups to consume, partially digested along the way.

All along the digestive tract, there are special cells called goblet cells that secrete mucus that helps protect the lining of the digestive tract from being digested. Think about it. A wild dog gobbles up the intestine of the deer. It has to digest that deer intestine while not digesting its own. Mucus lines the intestines and helps protect them. The small intestines have little projections called villi that increase surface area 10-fold, and each cell in the villi has microvilli adding another 20-fold increase in surface area, and protrusions to increase the surface area even more. The small intestines, stretched out and flattened, would cover a large area. Sources vary, and they are all estimates because you cannot flatten out cell surface protrusions, but 200 m2 is a pretty good guess for dogs. That would be a square a little over 40 feet on a side. Picture the surface area of a single story 1,800-square-foot house, or a tennis court, or a little less than half a basketball court. That is a lot of area wrapped into an average-sized (think 30- to 40-pound) dog. The small intestines are the primary place of fat and nutrient absorption, and the only place for amino acid and single-sugar absorption.

The intestines, large and small

The first segment of the small intestine, called the duodenum, receives the acidic mess from the stomach. It has a duct or tube from the gallbladder for bile, and another from the pancreas with its digestive enzymes and acid buffers. There are also some lymph nodes, important to the immune system and protecting the dog from what bacteria and viruses might be coming down the food disassembly line. By now the food is pretty liquid, and no longer recognizable as to its source material. The next part of the small intestine is the jejunum. This is the longest part of the small intestine and where most food and nutrients are absorbed. Because the warm, moist environment used for digestion is ideal bacterial breeding ground, the small intestine also has immune systems in place to help fight the spread of infections. The final area of the canine small intestine is called the ileum. It is rather indistinct from the preceding section, but it does specialize in breaking down and reabsorbing the enzymes used in digestion. Recycling is important in the body.

All that should give you something to think about when you encounter an indiscrete, indistinct pile on your freshly shampooed carpet. If the pile on the floor has recognizable parts, even unchewed kibble, it is most likely from the stomach. If it is a brown watery-liquid mess, smelly and, to me, has a bit of a chemical bouquet, it is from the intestines but came out the front of the dog. Same look, maybe a bit thicker in consistency but with a more, well, shit-smell, or fecal bouquet, if you prefer? Rejected from the intestines out the back end. Semi-formed feces? The rectum was where the eviction notice was received. Ponder that in your next cleanup.

The smaller units of sugars, proteins, and fats are absorbed across the intestines into the bloodstream that bathes the small intestine's walls, and are transported up to the liver for more processing and some detoxification. That sentence covered a lot of complex biological ground because there are different ways to get the now molecular-sized pieces from the lumen of the small intestines into the cells lining the intestinal walls. The liver processing includes building new molecules of cholesterol and some proteins for fat transport out of the amino acids absorbed in the small intestine. The digestive products are then distributed throughout the body via the circulatory system.

Again, the small intestine is where most of this digestion occurs. In your average dog, this section of the canal is around 12 feet (4 m) long (it's 20 feet [6 m] in you, and 70 feet [21 m] in a horse). It is all about food quality and digestibility. If you are eating meat, you only really need to break down proteins and fat, and then absorb the rest. It is a chemically easy task, so you don't need much length. If you eat grass, which is hard to digest and requires cohabitating fungi and bacteria to break apart cellulose, you need a lot more storage, processing space, and retention time. The small intestines of a horse are long. A horse is large because it has to lug around a huge digestive system for processing grass. A dog is small, as the digestive needs are far simpler. In dogs, body size is also driven by prey size. Wolves eat deer and moose, so they need to be pretty big. Coyotes eat rabbits, so smaller body size. Foxes eat mice. Smaller body size. In each case, eating meat means a shorter small intestine. The human small intestine is intermediate in length as we evolved eating both plants and animals.

An adequate description of digestion requires pages and pages, but I haven't the stomach for it. However, we cannot ignore what is happing to this now liquefied food, called chyme. It is in this brew that we need to start thinking about what food is, what it is made of, and what it gets processed into so you can decipher the labels on your dog's food bag, or meaningfully argue if feeding raw is better, or knowing if it really matters what you feed your dog.

The intestines, being warm and wet, are prime breeding grounds for bacteria. As nutrients are pulled out of meat, bacteria are reproducing and accumulating. The now smelly mess moves downstream into the large intestines. The purpose of this larger tube, 2 feet (0.6 m) long in a typical dog, 5 feet (1.5 m) in a human, and up to 25 feet (8 m) in a horse, is to wrap up digestion, and actively absorb all the water dumped into the stomach as acid and in the intestines to emulsify and liquefy the food. Can't be losing all that. Ever seen a dog with diarrhea? Of course you have. By the way, I am writing this paragraph while eating lunch, and it occurred to me how indifferent I am to thoughts of liquid stools and my Greek salad, but I apologize if you are reading this over lunch. Back to the question: Ever seen a dog with diarrhea? That is how liquid the material in the small intestines is. The large intestines dry out the food coming through, and absorb a few minerals.

The end of the tube and what comes out of it

The final stop for the material is the rectum, a muscular organ that stores and eventually expels the now solid waste. The final exit is controlled by a muscular sphincter, the anus. Once opened, we get those lovable little gems we bag and tag.

In a wolf, the feces is full of hair and bits of bone. Our dogs are dropping mostly bacteria and indigestible leftovers. Total time from ingestion to excretion? In you, about a day, give or take half a day. In a dog, 8 hours, give or take a couple of hours. It takes less time to process proteins and fats than hard-to-digest plant fibers.

A good dog partner becomes a connoisseur of poop. You really have to know your shit. Changes in feces are good indicators of changes in your dog. More liquid means lower retention time in the large intestine. The occasional soft stool is rarely cause for alarm. A hard, dry stool indicates constipation, too much retention time in the large intestines. But changes in texture or color when the diet did not change mean something is different inside the digestive tract. It could be as simple as exercise or stress promoting motility in the food. Canid feces is typically brown from the bile secreted to aid digestion. Changes in the digestive enzymes from the pancreas or liver can indicate problems there. Some intestinal parasites like tapeworms can be visible from a standing position over your dog; they can look like white flecks or even grains of rice in the feces. Dark or red color can mean blood in the feces or an ulcer (hole or sore in the digestive system). Tarry black can be from an ulcer, as well. If the feces looks like raspberry jam, it could be hemorrhagic gastroenteritis, severe bleeding in the digestive system with often uncertain causes. Greasy looking or overly gray feces can indicate poor digestion of fats that can be from pancreatic disorders. Green feces is usually grass or plant material, but it can indicate a parasite or poisoning. Orange or really light brown color in feces is common in material that traveled too quickly through the intestines to pick up the bile needed to aid digestion and give it that reassuring brown color. Yellow color is typically mucus. It often comes from a rapidly changed diet. Understanding that the biology inside your dog affects feces color and texture, it can be the first indicator of a problem or some reassurance that all is fine. Knowing what is normal for your dog will help you see what might need a veterinarian's attention. Not every change is panic-worthy! Blood in the feces or obvious parasites, though, probably need rapid attention.

Before you read on, as if the preceding paragraph did not suffice, let me remind you of my warning in the Introduction of the book. You did read that, didn't you? I think it is the best part of the whole book. Anyway, I am a biologist. Poop is a veritable treasure trove of information. When studying deer, I collected coyote scat to determine what they were eating, particularly looking for deer hair in the scat. With our dogs, I check out most defecations, both from a standing distance and as I pick it up, to see if there are changes in texture and color. My wife and I daily report to each other what we observed, a bit like high priests reading the stools of a prince or king. So it may come as no surprise to you that I periodically sniff what I pick up. You need to know what normal smells like. On cheap dog food, my dogs' feces stinks of gross putrid smells that seem a cross between decaying road kill and petroleum products. On a good diet, on a normal day, they actually smell slightly sweet and pleasant to me. For what it is worth, I sniff my dogs' ears, too, but mostly because their ears smell unique and are a way to remember them. Scent is a powerful evoker of memory.

Bacteria in the stool are one of the causes of foul smell. Bacteria broadly writ come in two kinds: aerobic, which thrive in oxygenated environments, and anaerobic, those that thrive in places without oxygen. For example, aerobic bacteria often break glucose, a common sugar, into carbon dioxide and water. No smell. In the anaerobic environment of the intestines without oxygen, that metabolic path does not work. Instead of two odorless byproducts, the anaerobic pathway can lead to carbon dioxide or methane and lactic acid, which smells like vinegar. They also release ketones, sulfur, and hydrogen, which humans find, shall we say, unpleasant. Fiber is more poorly digested in dogs, as they are not equipped with the intestines to break down cellulose found in plants. Fiber absorbs many of the smells, but also slows down the time it takes food to flow through the intestines, so waste is retained longer and picks up the smells. A high-quality diet, raw or kibble, will have smaller feces that smell less bad or have no adverse smell.

What to do with millions of tons of dog feces? Biologically, it will biodegrade outside. If people walk there, they will likely step on it before the several months it takes for the sun and bacteria to break it down has passed. Biologically, that works. But as it is breaking down, the bacteria are washing downstream in the rain and snow. What options do you have? If you live in the wilderness outside of a national forest or park, or the North Woods off the beaten path, and you are confident no one is going to pass that way or drink from water within say 30 feet (10 m) of the deposit, you can likely leave it. But short of those rare, rare (did I say rare?) situations, your choice is to pick it up or pick it up. If you don't, your community will pass ordinances prohibiting dogs from all of the interesting places, because dog shit is full of bacteria that can make people sick, and a surprisingly high number of people are intolerant of stepping onto a warm, moist pile. I go nowhere but the shower without a dog poop bag on me. Pick it up.

But now what? Generally speaking, it really should go into a toilet with your feces for sanitary processing at your city sewer treatment plant or your septic system. That is pretty messy, frankly unreasonable, and in many places illegal. Tie the bag off and put it into the garbage. That puts tons of biologically active waste into the landfill. How much? I thought you'd never ask. In the United States alone, domestic dogs produce about 11 million tons (10 million metric tons) of feces per year. That is more waste than all the humans on the planet produced the year I was born. Granted, that was a while ago. But even then, we had huge sanitation systems to deal with human waste. Eleven million tons is something like 10 cubes each 100 yards by 100 yards by 100 yards (100 m per side) (an American football field without the end zones wide, deep, and tall, or a bit less than a soccer field length). We don't treat most of it, and we do bury much of it. One interesting option is biodegradable poop bags. Seems like a great idea. I offer some cautions. Modern landfills are anaerobic, meaning no oxygen in them. Not much decomposes in a landfill, that which does decompose releases methane gas because of the oxygen-free metabolism of the bacteria. Your biodegradable waste in a biodegradable bag in a landfill takes something like months to a year to decompose, but it will decompose. In a plastic bag, the bag has to decompose first. That takes between 10 and 1,000 years depending on how close the plastic is to other actively decomposing items, moisture of those other items, and a host of other variables. Someday it will decompose, but not soon. There are good, cellulose-based plastic-like poop bags out there, and some cheap imitations. Make sure you read the labels and claims carefully. Their decomposition rate in nature with modest moisture and warm temperatures is measured in months.

TOUR 4

A SIDE QUEST TO LOOK AT DIET AND FEEDING YOUR DOG

This seems like a good point to step out of the digestive system and apply what you have learned to how and what you feed your dog, how to select the right diet, and how to analyze food ingredients.

Let's look back 36,000 years to the wolf ancestor of our household dogs. If their diet was similar to that of modern wolves, they ate a lot of meat. I refer you to a 2006 scientific article from the *Journal of Nutrition* on the feeding ecology of North American wolves, written by Stahler, Smith, and Guernsey. (Stahler et al., 2006) Winter diets are mostly large ungulates, like moose. But in the summer, prey source is more varied and includes invertebrates like insects, and also plenty of grass. Plant material shows up in 74% of 530 scats (poop piles). Even winter kills are not just meat in the common way of thinking of it: muscles from steaks. They eat the fatty livers, chew on bones, kidneys, lungs, the works. Wolves do not eat the digesting plant material found in the prey's stomach, so no haggis for them. The raw plants consumed add vitamins to the diet, and important roughage that is poorly digested but may help reduce intestinal parasites.

Domestic dogs, while genetically a subset of wolves, differ in a few ways induced by human selection. In 2016, Arendt and others published an interesting article in the journal *Heredity* looking at domestication and dog diets. (Arendt et al., 2016) Unlike their wolf ancestors, domestic dogs have genes for amylase, which allows for digestion of starch. This would certainly be an advantage when your food source is leftovers from early agricultural humans, who were starting to fill up on starches. There were also changes in fatty acid digestion in dogs. These two digestion-related adaptations are some of the key changes in domestic dogs from wolves. It is right here, in the small intestines, where that first huge modification shows up. In particular, it involves duplication of genes to make amylase. Each copy adds a tad over 5% more amylase; wolves and coyotes have two of these genes, domestic dogs up to 22. This gene expansion is not uniform in domestic dogs. Some domestic dogs have only the ancestral two, mostly those breeds derived from indigenous arctic dogs or from Australian dingoes. Most others have on average nine. This affects the conversion of starches into glucose, the sugar those hungry mitochondria use. Starch breakdown — and a whole metabolic pathway to make it into glucose — evolved, was selected for, and utterly changed what domestic dogs can effectively eat. Cooking food also helps break down difficult starches, so you really can get calories from cooked celery but not so much from raw. But even fully trained and domesticated dogs don't cook their own food. Domestic dogs got a new banquet of food when humans started growing starches; those dogs who had the new ability to digest starches proliferated. Humans learned to cook, and their scraps became even more valuable. Dogs in close association with agricultural humans diverged from those associated with nomadic hunter-gatherers.

What different dogs eat varies a lot. Given adequate variety, the canine body is well adapted to pulling out what it needs and passing on the rest. Needs vary over time and are health dependent, so a commercial diet meant to be all things for all times has to include quite a bit of variety. I will take just one kibble recipe list from one manufacturer's product, popular with a lot of my friends. Surprised to hear I have friends? If you feed kibble, go get a copy of the required ingredients label and let's run down what a single mouthful contains. This is what Fromm Gold Adult dog food has in it: Chicken, Chicken Meal, Chicken Broth, Oat Groats, Pearled Barley, Brown Rice,

Chicken Fat, Menhaden Fish Meal, Dried Tomato Pomace, Dried Egg Product, Whole Oats, White Rice, Chicken Liver, Whole Barley, Potatoes, Cheese, Flaxseed, Salmon Oil, Brewers Dried Yeast, Duck, Lamb, Carrots, Sweet Potatoes, Celery, Alfalfa Meal, Salt, Monocalcium Phosphate, Potassium Chloride, Chicory Root Extract, Vitamins, Minerals, Yucca Schidigera Extract, Sorbic Acid (Preservative), L-Tryptophan, Taurine, DL-Methionine, Sodium Selenite, Probiotics. Note that these are in descending order by weight, so there is duck in there, but it is the 21st ingredient.

Like the duck, some of the ingredients are obvious meat protein sources, but in such low quantities as to make me think they are there mostly to sell the food to you. In even less mass than duck we find lamb. The primary protein source in this mix is chicken in three forms as meat, pulverized dried tissue, and broth from cooking the chicken. I do not know Fromm's methods, but for most dog food you are getting not just meat, but all of the organs listed as byproduct. That might sound gross to you, but to a dog that is a rich and varied diet similar to what they had in the wild. Later down the list we see chicken fat and chicken livers. There is menhaden fish meal, which gives the dog the whole fish and its varied nutrients, and salmon oil. Eggs and cheese. We see four grains: oats, barley, rice, and flaxseed. There are some vegetables like tomatoes, carrots, celery, and potatoes. So far, it sounds a lot like my Thanksgiving dinner. Then there are smaller amounts of ingredients to balance the nutrition, and even chicory root extract to make sure the symbiotic gut bacteria get what they need. Likely, the gut bacteria would get what they need from all of the other food coming down the alimentary canal. However, I like the thought of being deliberate about nourishing the gut bacteria themselves, giving them a little consideration for all they do. I don't think there is much science behind chicory root, but I like it anyway, because I want to feed the microbes. Your ingredient list will vary, of course. The proportions on this meal are at least 25% protein, 16% fat, and no more than 5.5 % fiber, leaving 54% for carbohydrates. What is ideal? Talk about a hotbed of controversy. Most veterinarians say 18-25% protein, 30-70% carbohydrates, which includes the indigestible but necessary fiber, and 10-15% fats. The Association of American Feed Control Officials (hereafter AAFCO) is the group that sets standards for pet food. They list 18% protein as a minimum for maintenance (22.5% for growth formulas), 5.5% fat (8.5% for growth formulas), all as a percentage by weight. Protein source matters, too, depending on food allergies. If your dog develops issues with beef protein, switching to salmon can help. And so it goes with each ingredient on the list.

Cooked versus raw diets

So let's start poking the bear (a figure of speech, not some wolf-bear slap down) by asking what I am so very often asked: Is it better to feed my dog raw meat or a fully raw diet rather than processed kibble? The first thing I ask back is, "What is your measure of better? Whom do you trust? How complex is your decision matrix going to be?" Most often, when you get a simple answer, you are not getting the full story. Which is better, kibble or raw? I have given talks on this, and people show up ready for a fight. This is not a topic human companions of dogs tend to discuss civilly, likely because the scientific data do not provide a clear answer. When the facts do not support your case, talk louder. Lawyers say, "If you cannot pound on the law or the evidence, pound on the table." I guess that is the strategy.

If you feed raw, and you are careful about contamination and you are including more than just muscle meat, great. Your dogs will do well. If you feed a high-quality processed food, your dogs will do well. If you feed cheap food built to meet minimum AAFCO standards, your dog will still thrive. Thrive, by the way, for AAFCO means they do not die and do not exhibit signs of malnutrition. I see (and smell, and feel) a significant difference in feces between those on a high-quality food, including raw, and a poor quality kibble. Frankly, the better food leaves less obnoxious fecal pellets, and a shinier coat. People tell me their dogs live longer on raw. Very little quality scientific data exists to address this question. So please put your weapons away. I will only say that I see value in any high-quality food, and since not dying is the main measure for food out there, it is hard to quantify the value of better foods. I eat better foods. I am guessing my dog will do better with better foods. What are better foods? How many grains and carbohydrates are optimal depends on how many amylase genes your dog has. It also depends on the gut microbiome. Once you start feeding a diet, the kinds of microbes in the intestines change to those adapted to the food composition you are feeding. Switching foods requires switching out the flora and fauna inside your dog, and that takes time. So the best diet will vary by criteria used to define "best," by the genetics and cohabitants in your dog, by your pocket book, by the time you have to feed. But you aren't going to be able to prove your version of best in ways that convince many dog partners unless they agree on your definitions and measures.

Evaluating dog food is as complex as evaluating human food for many of the same reasons. Tour 1 showed how diverse and unique we each are. So let's admit up front that because of individual variation in genetic makeup, digestive physiology, variations in metabolic rates and physical activity, and microbes in the intestines, no two dogs will have exactly the same response to the same food. In addition, what we want from that food varies. There are several results of that. What works for your dogs might not work well for mine, and it will not be a matter of simply researching online or in a book to find the best diet for my dog. Furthermore, what works for my puppy is not what my middle-aged dog will need, and when that dog ages, their needs will change again. I never promised you an easy answer related to diet, and anyone who does is selling something.

Food analysis, testing, and regulation

Let's start with an easy question. Note that my students would be warning you that when I say something is simple or easy, it is anything but that, and if I ask, "Which is better?" they learn to respond with, "That depends on..." In order to assess best diet, we have to determine what outcome we want. Federal law (the Federal Food, Drug, and Cosmetic Act enforced by the Food and Drug Administration) requires any commercial pet food be "pure and wholesome, safe to eat, produced under sanitary conditions, contain no harmful substances, and be truthfully labeled." Perhaps your measure is simply the FDA "safe to eat" criterion. If my dog does not become ill after successive meals, all is OK. On the other hand, maybe you want more.

Most commercial dog food manufacturers try to meet AAFCO standards. Keep in mind (as if you knew this before!) that AAFCO is a private organization made up largely of state government officials and leaders in the pet food industry who want some standards for the pet food industry and who stand to profit from some of the standards. AAFCO does not test or certify pet food themselves. Their labeling instructions and food ingredient definitions are often incorporated into state laws. According to pet industry data for 2018 — the most recent currently published because, as of this writing 2019 just ended a month ago — the U.S. market was $91 billion, and globally $125 billion. Human food in the U.S. is $6 trillion per year, by comparison, but the $100 billion in pet food is hardly chicken feed. With AAFCO setting the guidelines, and industry sitting at the table setting those guidelines, one might wonder about the proper checks and balances. On the other hand, it is in the pet food industry's best interests to set guidelines that work. It is just that their definition of "work" and mine are far apart. I put that in for full disclosure, because the science behind all this is not the driving force, and the science is mostly funded by industry and proprietary to the funding industry, so not widely available. Complicate all that with the fact that legally, my dogs are not family members, they are property and protected more as if they were a lawn mower than a person. It pisses me off beyond belief that so much good data that we could use to make wise feeding decisions is now privately funded so the results are unavailable to the public. The government stepped out as the once-neutral source of such things. In research, privatization results in marketable but controlled information instead of commodity knowledge free to all. I am an academic, and pretty angry about this. I will step off my high horse now, but I want you to know why this is so difficult to answer. If I am a bit vague on the food wars, know that I come by it honestly.

To meet AAFCO standards, the dog food product needs clear labeling with product name, the intended target for the food, how much food is in the container (net weight), guaranteed analysis, ingredients in descending order by weight, a statement on nutritional adequacy (with treats and snacks exempted), feeding instructions, and the address of the manufacturer. For fascinating bedtime reading, look up AAFCO Appendix B, "AAFCO Pet Food and Specialty Pet Food Model Regulations Label Review Checklist," to learn the incredible nuances in those food labels. Foods that meet the "complete and balanced" standards to serve as a dog's sole food have to pass a feeding trial and meet a long list of nutritional requirements that AAFCO produces, others test, and AAFCO monitors, studies, debates, and amends. Note that AAFCO establishes standards, they "do not regulate, test, approve, or certify pet foods in any way." Dog food manufacturers are responsible for formulating their foods, while state and federal agencies are tasked to ensure that the labels are accurate and truthful.

The nutritional standard has profiles based on whether the dog is on a maintenance diet or if it is growing, pregnant, or nursing. By AAFCO feeding trial rules, the feeding trial that must be passed has to have a minimum of eight test subjects, and six of the eight must complete 26 weeks. It is worth pausing here. One of my editors wrote in the margins at this point "Are you fucking kidding me?" Another penned in "This has to be wrong." Still a third said "You mean six to eight of each sex for each breed, right?" A fourth called me and said "What a joke. Is that really all AAFCO certification means?" Remember, AAFCO does not certify food. Instead brands claim to meet the AAFCO criteria. For the record, let me repeat that the minimum acceptable, and therefore a widely used testing standard, is to have a minimum of eight test subjects and six of the eight must complete 26 weeks on just the food being tested. Since these trials are private and proprietary, I cannot guess what percent use more test subjects than the minimum. I can tell you that more test subjects cost more money, so I am skeptical that there are good, well-designed, large-scale studies going on out there. My hope in humanity is that there must be some really diligent high-caliber food manufacturers out there using good science to derive better quality food.

For these food trials, a veterinarian checks the dogs before and after for general health, body, and hair condition. Four blood values are measured: hemoglobin, packed blood cell volume, serum alkaline phosphatase, and serum albumin. A dog can lose up to 15% of its body weight over the trial. So if "maintaining most of your dog's weight over half a year without significant loss in four blood measures in three-quarters of your very small sample size of dogs covering nowhere near all of the breed and sex variations out there" is your measure of success, any AAFCO-based diet will do. As a scientist, I find the "experiment" of only 26 weeks measuring minimal traits necessary, but not close to sufficient. We are way better off having some trialing data, but alone it cannot be the measure of success. So I sincerely applaud the incredible effort, research, and monitoring of AAFCO. It is an important first step, but like any set of standards, it sets a bar to be cleared, not the end all be all. Federal Environmental Protection Agency minimum levels of "ingredients" in my drinking water set a base for safety, and we need that. However, all of my water goes through a reverse osmosis filter before I cook or drink it to move me well beyond the minimum. So it is with food; I want to do a whole lot better than the minimum.

Most of us cannot afford monthly blood panel work-ups on our dogs, and few veterinarians would prescribe that, but it might be the best way to measure how my dog is doing and to look for problems. Annual blood checks are good, and some nutritional failings can be detected that way. Most people should use at least the following signs of nutritional healthiness. I would monitor body weight, some measure of activity and playfulness, comments on coat color and texture, breath, and fecal conditions. I recommend that you actually keep notes as you try different foods, because your memory is not a perfect recorder, and it will change to match expectations. You will see what you hope to see (this is called confirmation bias). Regularly, monthly even, record these parameters. Or just go ahead and wing it. But then don't preach to me about how much better your dog's diet is than mine.

Dogs evolved as scavengers and predators with no AAFCO guidelines, no one watching their coat, and no one fretting over every nuanced behavior. People fed dogs for centuries without regulations and minimal nutritional analysis. Dogs thrived because, like most mammals, they do well with a varied diet with adequate calories. Their metabolism does the rest. Commercial dog foods are not a varied diet; they are a balanced diet that meets the best estimate of long-term needs. If you feed your dog, and supplement their diet with a variety of treats like carrots and apples, and avoid the bad human foods like grapes and chocolate, your dog will almost certainly do well. But is well good enough? Do you compete in a speed sport where a tenth of a second matters? If so, finding that slight edge is important. Show your dogs? That slightly better coat is game-changing. Maybe you just care so deeply about your dogs that you want to do the very best for them by giving them the best food you can? Well, the data are pretty sparse, and the measure there is hard to get. And what are your criteria for "best"? But the motivation is noble.

The great debate: what to feed

Back to raw versus kibble. Fists out, are you in your fighting stance? Let's do this. Raw food diets are, broadly defined, mostly raw meats, bone, fruits, and vegetables. You know, what all the dogs 30,000 years ago ate if they lived near a grocery store and only lived for up to three years. In the 1990s an Australian veterinarian started promoting a raw diet of biologically appropriate raw foods (the acronym seems so inappropriate but is actually used: BARF). The claim was based on the idea that dogs did not evolve to eat grains. But the genetic data shows that those dogs thriving near human agriculture did in fact evolve to have the needed genes to digest grains. Blows the basic premise out of the water. I know, maybe you don't like letting facts get in the way of a good argument. Those who feed raw contend that their dogs have shiner coats, healthier skin, better teeth, more energy, and less smelly and smaller feces. If one is careful about providing a balanced diet, especially to growing, pregnant, or lactating dogs, and if one is scrupulous about sanitation and bacterial infection from salmonella and E. coli, and if one is careful about excluding bones that can cause choking or crack teeth, the evidence is that this is a quite adequate diet. Note, I am not arguing better. Definitely not worse, either. Just different, dependent on your own outcome measures.

If you really want to compare a raw diet to a kibble diet scientifically and objectively, the kibble has to be exactly the same ingredients as the raw diet with the only difference being that they are cooked. Otherwise the differences found might be the food sources or the food types, not the rawness or cookedness. No, that is not a real word. And even if you did the proper experiment, what is your measure for being better? A friend of mine says, "Just look at the coat difference." I say fine, but does that really matter if health or longevity is my measure? Is there any evidence that a shinier coat is a clear indicator of anything other than a shiny coat? Is it the equivalent of a waxed car compared to a dirty but otherwise identical mechanically sound vehicle? A person at a dog conference over dinner said to me, "My first dog lived 10 years on kibble. Same breed, second dog lived 15 on raw. How much more proof do you need?" I cringe to admit I said that this was about as worthless as data can get. Maybe the second dog would have made 16 or 17 years on kibble. Individuals vary. What killed each dog? Was it diet related? Were you in the same house with the same life stress level with the same number of other dogs of the same health? How did you measure each of these factors? I am not saying it was not the raw diet; there is just no way with that story to know if diet played any role whatsoever in the longevity difference. Are there others with the opposite result? Needless to say, we did not share another meal to carry on this fascinating conversation.

Remember, dogs are not wolves, even if they are

Domestic dogs have up to 30 times as much genetically coded amylase as wolves. Amylase aids in digesting starches found in human food. So one genetic change domestication brought to dogs was the ability to digest starches in ways wolves cannot. You can argue kibble versus raw diets, but if your argument rests on what wolves ate, it ignores the selective evolution that occurred in domestic dogs. Raw diets provide variety that increases assurances that dogs will get all the nutrients they need. In evaluating diet, you probably should also ask how many copies of the amylase genes does your dog have? Bet you don't know. I sure don't. But Border Collies have been hanging with agricultural humans quite a while, and their ancestral stock is not recently arctic, which lack most or all of the amylase genes. My dogs seem to digest starches just fine. Yes, it is very unscientific of me to note that; it sounds like the raw-diet arguments I just shredded, except mine has a bit of science behind it with genes. Your experience may vary. The most vehement preacher of "feed raw" I know is a friend who has Siberian Huskies. For them, yeah, raw is a lot closer to their digestive system and they likely lack amylase genes. Is that better? Maybe. Maybe not. Best evidence so far indicates that the shinier coat really is like the car wax, in that it comes from higher fat contents in most raw diets, not the rawness itself. In fact, cooking aids digestion. But I do like a shinier coat.

If feeding raw makes you more attentive to what your dog eats, I am all for it. If it makes you give higher-quality ingredients, I am all for it. If it becomes a tool for shaming without the evidence to back it up, then it seems like bullying. Likewise on kibble. If reading ingredient labels makes you study nutrients and you move to a higher-quality food, great. If you learn that meat byproducts means brain, spleens, lungs, kidneys, stomachs, and intestines, all the better. But if your high-quality kibble is a just a tool to shame a person who cannot afford to or does not want to feed what you choose, it seems like bullying. Can you tell I get assaulted after my food talks by people who just want to convince me that they are right on a topic far too complex and unresearched to have a one-size-fits-all solution? Show me properly constructed, properly controlled studies with adequate sample sizes and detailed statistical analyses that meet the experimental design, and I am all in. Without that, we really are just pounding on the table for effect.

For the record, I do not feed raw. Or at least exclusively raw. Or even close to it. I have not the time nor cash resources for managing a raw diet. I see no evidence that it is superior to other high-quality diets with varied supplements. However, I am very attracted to the idea of feeding raw, and it removes my wonder at "what else" made it into the kibble. I see no evidence that kibble is superior to raw, either. Sanitation matters more with feeding raw, but it is manageable. Some examples of what we feed our dogs beyond their likely overpriced kibble: cheese, meat scraps, jerky, sausage, selected fruits and vegetables, dried cod, sprats, and high-quality commercial treats composed of god knows what. That is a lie, we read the labels. Sounds a bit like raw. Maybe we are trying to have it both ways?

We changed our dogs' kibble off of pea-based grains not because there was good enough data for me based on the scientific literature. To get that would take years to accumulate, but because there was no gain in using it and a lot of questions of late about it causing dilated cardiomyopathy (DCM). Even the FDA published a caution. Now we note a little less energy and their coat color is a bit duller. So we will try another good-quality kibble. Does any of this guarantee my dogs' perfect nutrition? Nope, but they live with us and are our family, so we can't help but try. We certainly can't wait a decade for science to sort it all out.

Guidelines and cautions

The AAFCO minimums are the best guide for the lowest bar. You will need to experiment by tweaking small changes in your dog's diet if you are so inclined. Dogs evolved as scavengers, so mostly you can't mess them up too far. But there are human foods from the cornucopia of our grocery stores you really should avoid. As in most things, the dosage determines the toxicity. A large dog eating one small listed food is not likely at any risk, and a small dog eating a lot of the listed foods likely is. You should right now get your area's 24-hour hotline for pet emergency care and poison control, put it in a prominent place, and watch what your dogs eat. The ASPCA Poison Control number is 888-426-4435. Stop reading. Right now, go put that on your refrigerator or have it tattooed on your phone dialing finger. I will wait. Did that? No? Go on, we are waiting. Post it somewhere. Don't later try to rifle through this book looking for it when you need it. Just in case you do, I will make that easier for you to find.

ASPCA Poison Control: 888-426-4435

The following is not an exhaustive list of dangerous foods for your dog because sources vary, as do dogs.

Knowledge of toxicity requires extensive lethal testing. Canine-specific toxicity information would require a lot of dogs dying for the cause. I am not a fan of that. Incidental anecdotes based on dog mortalities is less helpful than a controlled study, but a more ethical (if slow) way to collect information.

One calculates the LD50, literally the dose that will kill 50% of those getting that dose. Breeds, individual genetics, and sizes vary. The concentration of the toxin in question varies by food source. Extensive literature on the LD50 of these items in dogs is practically nonexistent. So it is best to avoid letting your dog eat foods on the following list. Built on material from WebMD for pets, one of the better objective sources on the web, we should avoid the following foods for our dogs:

- Alcohol is toxic to livers and harmful to brain function. See the word "toxic" in the word "intoxicated"? An ounce of alcohol is the amount found in half a bottle of a craft beer or a full 12 ounces (0.35 l) of mainstream beer, or a shot (or jigger or 1.5 oz or 44 ml) of hard liquor, or a glass of wine. In your large body, that is one thing, in a 30-pound (14 kg) dog, an altogether higher dose. My dogs love beer. But they get a lick off my finger or the very last backwash in the glass. Don't intoxicate your dogs!

- Onions and garlic evolved those strong-smelling chemicals to protect them from being eaten by the likes of us. You are large enough not to get a toxic dose in normal culinary settings. Your dog likely is not so large. Cooking seems to help with digesting these. Garlic shows up in a lot of dog food. Remember, dosage determine toxicity. For what it is worth, garlic appears to be more toxic to dogs than onions and leeks.

- Caffeine is a stimulant. Again, the dose OK for you is too high for your smaller dog. In addition, dogs don't metabolize caffeine well, so it builds up in their systems faster than yours even if they weigh as much as you do.

- Grapes and dried grapes (raisins) are a problem for your dog's physiology, which differs from yours. This fruit can cause kidney failure in canines. Scientific studies have not yet identified the culprit ingredient in grapes. Grapes are very toxic, so a small dose really matters.

- Milk and milk products. Like many humans, many dogs do not have the genetic ability to produce lactase, needed for digesting milk, so your dog may well be lactose intolerant. If yours tolerates cheese, they may tolerate milk. But many dogs do not.

- Chocolate is widely known to be toxic to dogs. It is theobromine in it that matters, so it's those with higher amounts like dark chocolate and baker's chocolate that are most toxic. Dogs don't metabolize this alkaloid well, so it builds up. Cocoa plants produce the alkaloid to protect them from predators. Like dogs.

- Any pit-filled fruit like plums and peaches present a choking hazard to dogs. Technically these should not be in a list of toxic foods, as it is a mechanical problem, but I want you to be aware, OK?

- Bones that fracture easily, like chicken and fish bones, can create slivers that lodge in the esophagus. Large bones can crack teeth.

- Macadamia nuts appear to be toxic to dogs. I can't find which ingredient is the culprit.

- Avocados have a huge central seed like a peach does, only bigger. They also have persin. This ingredient can be toxic, and the seed can block intestines.

- Raw eggs and raw meats including fish can have high bacterial counts: salmonella for chicken, E. coli for the beef products. And some contain parasites, although trichinosis is pretty much no longer an issue in western pork supplies. One reason we cook our foods is to reduce these bacterial risks.

- Raw dough such as bread dough can rise in the warm stomach environment of your dog. Even a small amount can be a blockage problem, worse if it ferments and produces alcohol as a byproduct of fermentation.

- Baking powder and baking soda are toxic to dogs in larger quantities. They combine with stomach acids to release gas that can damage or rupture the digestive system.

- Most spices evolved in plants to ward off predators. We use them sparingly to "spice up" our food. If your dog exceeds the trace dose we use relative to our large body mass, many spices can be toxic or even fatal.

- Xylitol is a food additive for humans that tastes sweet, so naturally it is found in a lot of products. It is found in such items as toothpaste and mouthwash, a lot of types of peanut butter (seriously, so check the label), fruit drinks, cereals, jams and jellies, many baked goods, chewing gum, some medicine pills, and many other processed foods. It causes a massive release of insulin in dogs, leading to dangerously low blood sugar.

Cleaning, sanitizing, and sterilizing

One of the challenges of feeding raw comes from bacteria. It is worth a slight detour to consider cleaning and cooking, and how good of a housekeeper you might be, not that I am judging. Raise your hand if you wash your dishes. Good. How about if you let your dog wash them first? While that cleans (removes food remnants), it certainly does not sanitize (kill foodborne diseases from bacteria and viruses). After handling raw chicken, do you wash your hands? Do you sanitize them? Do you disinfect them? Is that all the same thing? Do you really want to go where I am about to go, into the microscopic shop of horrors?

Consider the cutting board you used to cut up raw chicken, for your dog or for your dinner. Obviously if you are a vegetarian and do not feed your dog raw chicken, you will just have to use your imagination. Raw chicken, or any meat, unless it has an active infection, is pretty much sterile in the original whole organism or carcass. Processing and handling it exposes it to pathogenic bacteria aerosolized (in the air) from other chicken digestive systems, from handlers' gloves, and so on. If you could zoom in to look at the surface of the chicken meat and the cutting board, you would find each is very uneven, like a rugged landscape, with lots of hiding places for bacteria. You clean these surfaces by washing them. You might use water, a pretty good solvent. You might add a detergent, which helps carry away debris and break down fats, which do not otherwise dissolve in water. It does only a little to remove bacteria, but things look nice and shiny after a good washing with soap. That takes away sources of contamination, reduces surface area for bacteria, and washes away many bacteria, but does not really kill the bacteria hanging out in the nooks and crannies all over the cutting board or the meat. Cleaning, done well, removes up to 98% of bacteria and 93% of viruses. Good, but maybe not enough. If you are at home, and everyone already shares the same bacteria, clean is more than enough. Where diseases are present, maybe from a sick person or a salmonella-carrying chicken thigh, you need to sanitize. If you plan to surgically insert something somewhere — not what you ought to practice at home by the way — then you have to do better than sanitizing. You need to sterilize.

In order to kill more of the potentially offending bacteria than a good cleaning, you need something stronger. A sanitizer. For our example, you best be using a food-safe sanitizer that reduces bacteria and kills most harmful foodborne bacteria. At home, you clean the dishes. Some home dishwashing models use steam and actually sanitize dishes. Commercially, like at restaurants where one does not want the liability of passing diseases from one customer to the next, they sanitize the dishes and all of the eating surfaces. You need to clean the surface first for a sanitizer to work, as it needs to reach all areas of the surface. Common sanitizers include chlorine-based sanitizers like sodium hypochlorite, ozone, sodium hydroxide, and phosphoric acid. Those sanitizing wipes you use on the carts at the grocery store? Those are typically alcohol based and not considered food safe. You would have to rinse the surface off before you eat off it. Great for killing germs on counter tops, but not for the plates and silverware. It is OK to wipe the cart handle; you presumably do not eat off it, although I see lots of kids licking them. Once the alcohol evaporates, no worries anyway. These typically kill 99.9% of the bacteria and viruses if given at least 30 seconds of contact with them. Likewise a good hand-sanitizer. Just don't eat that stuff.

To sterilize or disinfect, to kill 100% (99.999), well, that is a lot harder than you think. Bacteria are tough little buggers. Actually disinfecting food and food preparation areas in one's home is not common, but it is a standard not really needed given how much bacteria are already inside you. Sanitizing kills bacteria and viruses at the level needed to fight the spread of pathogens, especially those carried by food. Sanitizing these surfaces in public gathering places is more important. Actual sterilizing requires high heat or pretty toxic chemicals with 10 minutes of contact time, and is generally reserved for the medical industry, baby changing stations, and other high-need areas.

Want to sanitize the chicken? Cook it. Heat is a great sanitizer. Were I feeding raw, I would cook my chicken. Oh, wait, that is not raw. I would learn about food-grade sanitation, and I would regularly sanitize my cutting surfaces and counters like commercial restaurants do. A hot dishwasher offers a grade of sanitizing that handwashing does not, but unless you go with a commercial-grade dishwasher with a steam setting, you are mainly cleaning really well. Is that enough or too much? It just depends on your risk tolerance. Mostly you wouldn't even need to clean your dishes, let alone sanitize. But that sounds pretty gross to those of us who do not live alone. The cost, however, is occasional food poisoning. Having spent a day of food poisoning laying on the floor of a hotel bathroom huddled around the toilet (talk about yuck, not likely clean and certainly not sanitized), wishing I were dead but too weak to pull it off, not worth it. Your dog pees on the carpet? You can clean and/or sanitize. Sanitize without cleaning and you just have bacteria-free pee on the floor. Clean without sanitizer for pee, likely just fine thank you. Plan on eating off that floor? Sanitize it.

Who to turn to?

Who are you going to believe in all of the diet controversies? Going to the internet is a lot like going to a crowded shopping mall and shouting your question. You will get crackpots. There will be well-intentioned but ill-informed responses. There will be well-informed but ill-intentioned people. There will be reams of data that are hard to digest. There will be purported experts. There will be real experts. There will be charlatans. How do you decide? Check credentials. Does this source have a bias, a reason to claim one thing over another? If I am selling you a product, I am more likely to think my product is better than it objectively is. Does the site come from an impartial source, assuming such sources exist? If I sell kibble, I am going to cite how inexpensive and convenient it is. If I am proselytizing about some food category, I will overemphasize the perceived benefits over risks. If I am a government agency, I am going to set minimum guidelines. Government scientists, and those at universities, usually offer unbiased advice. It does not hurt to check who funds their research, however.

You must be thinking that this is a lot of work. I am afraid so. It ain't easy being an expert, I should know. Why? Because with the exception of a very narrow set of fields where I do original research, I am not an expert. I have to get my information the hard way like everyone else. I have better-developed tools for evaluating information than most people because I have like two decades of formal education and three decades as a professional scientist and teacher. Still, I have to constantly check and recheck, challenge assumptions, and I get called out on errors. One does not teach 70 smart college freshmen, out to prove they are smarter than the next, without getting challenged every day! You obviously want those evaluative tools, too, or you would not have gotten this far with me. Kudos to you. Don't think this is the easy path, believe you me! But it will get you better results, healthier dogs, and that warm fuzzy feeling of really knowing when you are right.

So many words of caution are needed at this point, and for the rest of our time together. True objective data and results are rare as hens' teeth. Worse, we are biased to see what we expect to see. Again, it is called confirmation bias. If I think the new diet will make my dog healthier, I will note all of the signs of health and discount the facts that contradict it. We all do this. We have to so we can sort all of the conflicting information in our lives. Psychological studies show that the more time or money you invest in something, the more you will like it. This helps rationalize the expense you made. Purchase expensive kibble or prime cuts of meat, you will see more benefits simply from the price you paid, irrespective of reality. Labor for hours processing a raw diet for your dog? You will see more benefits than exist because of that time investment. The cure for this is time, really careful objective observations, time, well-thought-out experiments, and time. In the meantime, do your best and try not to hurt your friends and neighbors.

On dog health-related issues, I go to those who have devoted their lives to caring for my dogs' health: veterinarians. But I never trust just one source. I look at the reasoning for the arguments and the evidence, and I use what I know to see if what they say makes sense based on what else I know. One reason for this book is to give you enough basic biology so you can better evaluate the barrage of information you are inundated with. I read a lot from multiple sources. Shout outs to Pet.WebMD, the *Whole Dog Journal*, and Tufts University *Your Dog Journal*. I also praise Dogwise, publisher of great dog books who I relied on for years, but you should note now the potential conflict of interest here, since that is who is publishing this work.

Overfeeding your dog

Obesity and problems related to it are very common among the pet dog population. Surveys and research consistently find over half of all pet dogs are overweight or obese. That makes dog obesity a larger problem (by percent affected) than the human obesity problem. Human companions of dogs often pick a food and continue to feed even as a dog ages and requires fewer calories and less fat. It's why as you age and stop running marathons you don't need to eat four power bars a day, because you aren't burning off the amount of energy that you used to. Overweight dogs are less healthy. Do you really want your veterinarian and your food supplier to get more of your money than they need to? More importantly, do you really want your best friend to be less healthy?

Energy

Let's take a few pages and focus on energy. In nature, energy is like money. The more you have to spend, the more choices you have available to you. Much of the fussiness of digestion is about extracting energy from food so your dog can use it. At its most basic, and of course I won't leave us there, your dog eats food with carbon in it. Your dog breathes air that has oxygen in it. Oxygen is pretty reactive stuff. Toxic. It releases free radicals. It reacts with lots of material in your dog's body, causing it to age and creating problems with its DNA. In the end, it can kill. Of course, go a few minutes without it and you're dead, too. In a campfire, oxygen combines with the carbon in wood and releases energy as heat and light. Digestion puts the carbon into forms that a living body can slowly oxidize, using mitochondria in the cells. One adds the oxygen to the carbon, releasing energy one uses to stay alive, also releasing heat that keeps it warm, and the waste product called carbon dioxide. That exits via the lungs. Incidentally, and as noted earlier but repeated for effect, if you put your overweight dog on the needed diet, the weight they lose is not lost as feces or urine. It is lost as carbon dioxide, out the lungs.

The chemical reactions for digestion and metabolizing the food go faster and more efficiently at warmer body temperatures. The hotter the better, except that at higher than about 104 degrees F, or 40 degrees C, proteins start to denature. To cook. Brains are made of temperature-sensitive proteins. At high fever, they cook. Cooked brain might be tasty — I am not trying it — but it sure does not work well inside your dog for learning to freestyle dance. That protein-destroying temperature sets the upper limit for the warmth a body can generate for digestion. If a mammal can keep its body constantly warm, that has a lot of advantages, not the least of which is it won't freeze when outside in the winter. The higher operating temperature also means your dog runs faster, and for longer. Consider your dog versus some large reptile, like an alligator. The alligator has a lower metabolism and lower body temperature. It depends on the sun to warm it up, and has a slow idle speed. It can sprint a whopping 10 or 20 yards (same in m) total. Then it has to rest and let the metabolism catch up. It can hit 30 miles per hour (50 kph) for a few feet of distance. A dog with similar mass could run at 15 miles per hour (25 kph) all day, and hit over 40 miles per hour (60 kph) in a sprint. In the snow. The alligator could not run at all in the cold. One gains a lot of speed and flexibility with that high metabolism. But it is very costly in terms of energy. Energy, like money, is always in short supply.

A calorie is a measure of energy needed to raise a gram of water 1 degree Celsius. A Calorie, with a big C, is the energy to raise a kilogram of water (about 2 pounds, or about a quart of water) one degree Celsius. The big C calorie is the one we use for measuring food, so a candy bar with 300 Calories could raise 300 quarts (or liters) of water, or about 75 gallons, one degree. A human is about 16 gallons (60 l) of water, so 300 Calories in that candy bar can raise your body temperature about 5 degrees. Or, put another way, you use on average 2,000-2,500 Calories per day, and almost all of that is to manage your body temperature. At colder temperatures, the alligator burns fewer calories, while you burn more to stay warm. The alligator slows down at colder temperatures, you speed up. Below freezing temperatures, the alligator cannot stay alive. You make snow angels.

It is energy expensive to stay alive in cold temperatures, but it sure beats dying. The cold outside really does not significantly change how long your dog can live on a fixed amount of Calories. That is because most of the energy your dog consumes goes to just keeping your dog alive, the basic metabolism they have all the time, and most dogs are extremely well insulated from heat and cold.

A dog needs roughly 30 Calories of food per day per pound (or 66 kcal per kg). The formula is, for an average dog, 110 Calories times body weight in kilograms raised to the 0.75 power. A kilogram is roughly 2.2 pounds. More active dogs use 125 Calories times the body weight raised to the 0.75 power; 90 Calories is the starting number for more inactive and senior dogs. By the official calculations, my 26-pound Border Collie needs about 800 Calories a day. You get that from 125 times 26/2.2 to the 0.75 power. Order of operations matter. Do the 26/2.2 to get kilograms (Wish=11.82 kg.). Raise that to the 0.75 power ($11.82^{0.75}$=6.37). Then multiply that by 125 for an active dog.

This formula is not dog-specific. For humans, with refined data, the leading multiplier in Calories is varied by sex, age, and general activity level to refine the numbers. The formula shows an interesting biological trend, however. Energy needs do not increase linearly with mass (weight). If it did, a 200-pound (91 kg) organism would need twice as much energy as a 100-pounder (45 kg). It needs less than that. Per pound of weight (kg of mass), larger organisms are more energy efficient than smaller ones. Some, but not all of that, is due to surface to volume ratios. Smaller critters have a lot more surface relative to the body warming mass inside than larger critters. Volume increases cubically (to the third power) while surface area increases only to the square, or second power. Sorry, a lot more math than you probably wanted. It shows that per pound (kg) of dog, a St. Bernard needs less energy than a Beagle, for any given activity.

Back to Wish. She needs 6.37*125 or 797 Calories per day. Her kibble is a high-quality food with 400 Calories per cup (237 ml), so you would think she would get two cups (473 ml) per day, what most people would feed with those numbers. The "books" say she needs 800 Calories a day. However, she puts on weight at that amount, so the books are not the end all be all, or Wish is not reading those books. Wish gets 2 measured 1/2 cups (118 ml) of food a day (each half cup or 118 ml is 200 Calories), one at oh-dark-thirty after she has woken us up, and one in the evening around 5 p.m. That is only half of her reported daily caloric need. Every night she gets a dog biscuit at 60 Calories (currently salmon flavored, tastes like cardboard to me). She is active, and gets extra treats for training. We estimate that at most is another 200 Calories, most often only 100 Calories of treats. So Wish gets 560 to 660 Calories a day, even though the formula says 800. When she puts on weight, we cut back the kibble. If she is looking like a good breeze might push her over, we round up the cups of food. She would eat all day if we let her, but she would look like a sausage and her arthritis would be way worse. Cricket is a tad heavier than Wish, equally active, gets about the same food, and is equally maintaining a lean body form while being very active and healthy. The moral is do the math, but feed the dog, not the math formula. Likewise with me. I log my own foods. Geek, remember? I am "entitled" to 1950 Calories to maintain my weight. I do not log my activities, so that is the energy budget for a sedentary person, although mostly I fall into the active to normal range. I should be losing weight, especially since I hold myself to 1700 Calories per day. At 1900 Calories I slowly put on weight, at 1700 I maintain. Metabolism is quite variable and adjusts to a new normal, which is why Wish can maintain her activity and weight at fewer Calories than calculated by the formula.

Avoiding obesity

We have a serious obesity problem today. I am talking dogs here. Most of the dogs I see, and most my veterinarian friends see, are overweight. To repeat from earlier, research also shows most pet dogs are overweight. There are objective measures you can use, otherwise your confirmation bias will most certainly take over, and you will declare, "Looks good to me!" You will rationalize that being overweight makes your dog happy. Food certainly does. But being overweight does not. If your dog lives with you, you feed them. Most dogs don't saunter over to the refrigerator, pop open their own beer, grab some chips and kibble, and settle in for a good movie. You give them their food. You are responsible. Most overweight dogs have human companions who do not realize it. Ignorance is not bliss. If your dog is overweight, except for rare medical conditions, that is on you. And it is on me if I do not convince you here.

If you are unsure, tell your veterinarian to be honest with you. Most medical professionals don't want to lose you as a customer, but they also don't want your dog to get pancreatitis, joint problems, diabetes, unnecessary muscle or heart damage, breathing issues, or liver failure, and be at greater risk if surgery and associated anesthesia are ever needed. Does that get you listening? Now pay attention. Your dog may be fine, but knowing this may help you help another. No bullying. No shaming. Just give helpful guidance so dogs can be healthier.

Using PetMD as a guide, here are the criteria you should use:

Too Thin: Ribs, spine, and bony protrusions are easily seen. Much muscle mass is lost. In short, a bony and starved appearance.

Underweight: Ribs, spine, and other bones are easily felt. Dog has an obvious waist when viewed from above and abdominal tuck when viewed from the side.

Ideal: Ribs and spine are easily felt, but not necessarily visible. Dog has a waist when viewed from above and the abdomen is raised, not sagging, when viewed from the side.

Overweight: Ribs and spine are hard to feel underneath fat. Waist is distended or pear shaped when viewed from above, sagging abdomen from the side.

Obese: You can see and feel large fat deposits over the chest, back, and hindquarters. No waist from above. Sagging abdomen from the side.

Athletic dogs run lean, or underweight, as do athletic people. If your dog looks skinny as heck, but is active, it is great! I have worked with sled dogs whose ribs were showing, lean as any cross-country runner, bony but with clearly defined and robust muscle mass, able to pull a sled all day at a run. Overall, the risk associated with being a little underweight is much less than that of being overweight. One nationally known veterinarian friend of mine says that your dog is not too lean if they are active and playful. Remember, there is nothing magical here. Calories in must be no more than Calories out, or weight is gained as fat. Most Calories go to metabolism, idling speed as it were, so you cannot easily exercise your way out of overweight. Walking my dogs for an hour only burns about 60 extra calories, or one night-time treat. You need to both reduce Calories and increase exercise. If you don't exercise, metabolism slows to compensate for the reduced calories. Do me a favor. Take a break from this book and let your dog take you for a walk. I'll wait right here while you go. No, I don't care if it is raining. But if it is late or you might feel unsafe, go a little extra long tomorrow.

Mostly when we think about food for our dogs, it is a chore of pouring money out to a store to get the kibble or other food ingredients, drop it into a bowl, and clean it up when it eventually comes out the other side. Knowing the parts and steps in the process helps a lot when something goes wrong. Otherwise, like my Thanksgiving dinner, I try not to think too much about where the food comes from and where it will all end up. I know that feeding is such a strong evolutionary pressure that I can use it to reward my dogs and teach them to do crazy things, energize them to play in extremely cold or snowy conditions, or survive tropical heat. The digestive system weighs only about 2 pounds (empty) in a 30-pound dog (1 kg in 14 kg), so you get a lot of bang for your buck.

TOUR 5

THE MUSCULOSKELETAL SYSTEM

Except for Halloween, we don't tend to think too much about skeletons. We see them far more often than we realize, we just don't tend to recognize that what we see is a skeleton. While it is true that when I look at my dog, she would be unrecognizable without her skeleton, and it gives her a basic dog shape, that is not what I mean. First, we need to consider what skeletons are for. Fundamentally, skeletons give a place to attach muscles so an organism can move. The only animals without muscles that can still move depend either on ocean or air drift, or they are so small that their cell-based cytoskeleton with its microtubules can do the work of muscles and bones because they are made of only one or a few cells.

Interestingly, muscles can only contract, and once contracted, they need a muscle pulling the opposite way to stretch them back out so they can be used again. That kind of mechanics requires something sturdy to pull against, hence the skeleton. Skeletons serve a second, valuable purpose: They protect like armor. Actually, they are armor. They can (and do) have tertiary roles, like blood formation and mineral storage, as well.

Endoskeletons and exoskeletons (innies and outies)

Ever look closely at an insect, even a giant one in a sci-fi movie? How about eat oysters or mussels? That outer shell is their skeleton, called an exoskeleton. It adds protection to the list of roles, rather than just giving a scaffold for muscles to attach to. Football padding, police body armor, and even hardened kneepads help protect in the way an exoskeleton of an insect does. Like a snail's shell, or a turtle's shell, they add great protection but they limit growth and mobility, and they weigh a lot. There just are not a lot of large animals that have only an exoskeleton; there are some giant crabs and shrimp, but they live in water, which helps support the exoskeleton. Sea turtles can get quite large, and their shell is a functional exoskeleton, but they also have an internal or endoskeleton like we do. In fact, their shell is just their ribs modified through evolution. With an exoskeleton, muscles can attach to the external shell to function.

If mobility and speed are your thing, an exoskeleton just won't cut it. Watch your dog play for half a minute and you will see behaviors and positions impossible with an exoskeleton. If you are large, relative to an insect, you also get to skip the weight penalty of a large and heavy shell if your skeleton is inside. Instead, you can put that mass into muscles that actually do things. In your typical 30-pound (14 kg) dog, there are three pounds (1.4 kg) of bones and 10 pounds (4.5 kg) of muscles, so an endoskeleton is a pretty efficient way of structuring. Which is better, an endoskeleton or an exoskeleton? Obviously, that depends. For lobsters, the exoskeleton is ideal. For the mammalian way of life, an endoskeleton is ideal.

Briefly let me remind you that evolutionary history also plays into this since evolution works only by modifying existing structures. Mammals, depending on speed and mobility, evolved using the basic skeleton of their reptilian ancestors, which also lacked exoskeletons. If your parents don't have a trait, like an exoskeleton, you won't have one either. A short pause to remember some genetics. "If your parents don't have a trait" does not mean your parents have to show the trait. That depends on how many copies of the trait you get and how those traits are regulated by the environment or other genes. Evolution can only modify existing strips of DNA with little copying mistakes or other chance errors, including chunks of DNA accidentally moved from one location to another. There is no intentionality, no wholesale big leap, no "something from nothing." Those new traits come about only through tiny changes over very long geological periods of time. You might imagine a seagoing mammal, a whale perhaps, that could benefit from an exoskeleton. But like you, it has mammalian genes, and an exoskeleton requires a bunch of genes found in arthropods like spiders, insects, and crabs, but not us. Evolutionarily we parted ways 600,000,000 years ago. We cannot just grab their genes and get those traits. At least not yet. CRISPR again, cue the dramatic music.

Now back to our regularly scheduled programming.

Skeletal framework

Dogs are skeletons with muscles draped over the framework, and skin wrapped around all that. It is worth looking at that skeleton first as an engineering structure to get the basic parts down and to help understand what goes where and why. A dog, or most any mammal including humans before we started to walk upright, is a long supporting beam with four appendages, two at either end, that keep the beam off the ground. You would do well to think of it like a suspension bridge (actually a cable-stayed bridge, but give me a minute here) with the arms and legs being the pylons or pillars on which the road is built. The road is the spinal column. The chest and belly are suspended from the spinal roadbed. Bridges work by distributing load from across the span to the pillars that reach the ground. Stresses between the pillars pull downward on the roadbed. Suspension bridges, familiar to many as the Golden Gate, Mackinac, or Brooklyn Bridges, have a cable that runs above the road bed, strung from pillar to pillar. The cable distributes the load of the bed to the pillars that keep the bridge from falling down. This is pretty close to how a dog works, except there is no cable going from pillar (arms) to pillar (legs). In fact, if you are a bit of a bridge fan, you will see that the dog is a cable-stayed bridge like the…uh, hmm, well…that is why I started with familiar suspension bridges. Cable-stayed bridges look really neat, but are less common. We have one right over the St. Croix River where I drive every week. You likely have one near you, but they are more regionally known. Cable-stayed bridges have pillars that rise above the roadbed, and cables go directly from the pillars to various parts of the roadbed, holding up the load, rather than to a cable that runs the length of the bridge. That is pretty close to how a dog's skeleton functions.

The spine

Picture the spine as a flat rod held horizontally in front of you. Give it a bend, concave down (like this: ∩) so that it makes a small arch, which is structurally stronger than a flat rod in this setting. Set the rod down on two bricks, one at each end. The front brick is the pectoral girdle (front limbs and the structures that tie the limbs to the spine), and the back brick is the pelvic girdle, which ties the back legs to the spine. Place a hard ball on one end, the head, extending out beyond the front legs, and also extend the rod a bit beyond the back legs to counter-balance the head; now you have a tail. Call it Fido, and you have a dog. Any weight on the center of the rod will put it under stress. In your dog, that is most of its body weight. If your dog is overweight, the added body fat is mostly in the abdomen or the belly, certainly between the front and back legs, putting extra downward stress on the spine and joints. Keep this bridge structure in mind. The difference, of course, is that dogs move around, and bridges ought not to be wandering the town. You need those structural elements of bones to move and flex. A fixed solid spine won't allow any real jumping and sprinting and twisting and turning. That is accomplished by parsing the spine into smaller pieces and tying them together. The spine is not a long fixed rod of bone. It consists of many pieces called vertebrae, tied together with straps called ligaments, kind of like packing tape. Between each vertebra is a smooth padded disc, the remnants of that notochord all Chordates have. These, and the smooth articulation surfaces where bones meet, let the spine bend and flex so the head can pivot around and lick body parts, while the spine bends walking and turning, and the tail can flail and serve as a counterbalance.

Essentially, your dog has the same skeleton as you do, with a few interesting exceptions. Overall, humans generally are said to have 206 bones and dogs 320-ish. But the differences come in places that don't change our basic story, mostly accessory bones that do not count in the 206 we humans have but do count in the 320 dogs have. Veterinarians and human-medical doctors do not go to the same medical schools so they get to count things differently. You have 32 teeth, a dog has 42. Your tail is only five bones long (the coccyx), the dog's varies by breed, but 23 would be the most. You get 12 thoracic vertebrae and rib sets in the chest area, a dog has 13. We have collar bones, dogs do not. But I am getting ahead of myself. We don't need to know every bone in the body, but knowing the types will help you understand your dog far better.

The skull

Let's go head to tail, then down the limbs. The skull is made of two functional parts, the cranium that covers the brain like an exoskeleton, and the rostrum, which includes the nasal areas and the jaws and teeth. Bone shapes vary, such as the nasal bones that are longer in long-nosed dogs. Suffice here to say that the bones protecting the brain are strong, the bone that work the jaw and the jaw itself are strong, and because a heavy head is a tough load to carry, the facial bones are light and delicate. Some interesting differences: A dog's skull has a wide-open arch (the zygomatic arch) where you have closed cheekbones. That gives the dog a large surface for those big jaw muscles. The orbit around the eyes in humans is all bone, but in a dog the bone only covers three fourths of the eye circle. The last bit is covered in cartilage, leaving the eyes more vulnerable but making the skull lighter. Teeth were previously covered in detail in the chapter with digestion. The turbinate bones in the nose will get coverage in a later chapter about senses including smell.

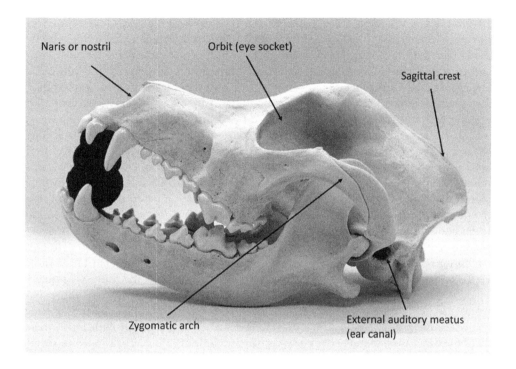

Naris or nostril

Orbit (eye socket)

Sagittal crest

Zygomatic arch

External auditory meatus (ear canal)

Vertebrae

Any look at a dog will show that supporting a large jaw and many sharp teeth changed the shape of the skull from that of a human. The skull rests on a specially shaped vertebra named the atlas because, like the fabled god, it holds up the world. The skull rests on it, and that bone pivots around the second cervical vertebra, called the axis, together giving the head a good range of motion. Vertebrae have spines or tabs sticking off of them for muscles to attach to via tendons, and for ligaments. Note that tendons are the duct tape or packing tape that attach muscles to bones, ligaments are similar and connect bones to bones. You can feel some pretty prominent bones over the shoulders sticking up if the dog is standing. Those have muscles attached that hold up the head. Think of holding a 5-pound (2.3 kg) weight extended straight out in your arm. Gets pretty tiring. A dog's head is always being held out beyond the front legs, and it takes some pretty good musculature to do that well. A dog also has some fixed ligaments that attach the back of the skull to the spine to help hold up the head. Processes or tabs extending off the sides protect nerves that come out between most vertebrae, and some big processes called ribs provide some protection to the vital lungs and heart. Arguably, however, the more important rib function is to allow a fixed space so lungs can be inflated and deflated easily.

Limbs

Coming off the spine are four limbs, two in the front and two in the back. There are four limbs for the same reasons a car has four wheels. It is a very stable layout. Six would be better for stability, but would slow the dog down and would inhibit turning. Two limbs work in some forms of locomotion, like humans, but that is a pretty recent adaptation in primates, 6 million years in the human line of descent. Limbs are basically all the same, front and back, as far as parts go. For each limb, closest to the body where strength is needed for really big muscles, you get a large single bone, the humerus or the femur. Heaven forbid we would use the same name for both front and back. We could call them all femurs or humeri, but we don't. What you call a knee gets called a stifle in a dog. Then you get two bones for the next set of the pillar. Two smaller rather than one larger bone allows a bit more mobility, twisting and turning with one rotating around the other, fused in the rear limbs. In all mammals, we call those the radius and the ulna in the front, the tibia and fibula in the back. The "backward knee" or hock in a dog or horse is really the ankle. Then, when we need lots of flexibility, we get lots of bones. In fact, about half the bones in the body are in the hands and feet or paws. We go from the pair of bones that make up the "shin" or "forearm" (radius/ulna in front limbs, tibia/fibula in rear limbs) to a mess of bones in the paws. Each foot starts with a row of three bones which articulate on four more, so seven bones in the wrist or ankle (8 in humans) called carpals in front, tarsals in back. We are ignoring the numerous and variable sesamoid bones, those accessory bones I mentioned earlier. Each digit (toe, finger, whatever) is named differently for front versus back feet (those anatomical naming devils). For example, the thumb is actually called the pollux and the big toe is the hallux, when they really are the same thing. No wonder so many students dread anatomy class, missing the amazing structures in a sea of names. Each digit (toe) starts with a long bone, bound together with four others from the other toes, to make the body of the hand or foot (metacarpals in front, metatarsals in back). Then each finger or toe is made of three small bones called phalanges, placed end to end. The thumb or the big toe is missing the middle phalange, so there are only two each for these shorter digits.

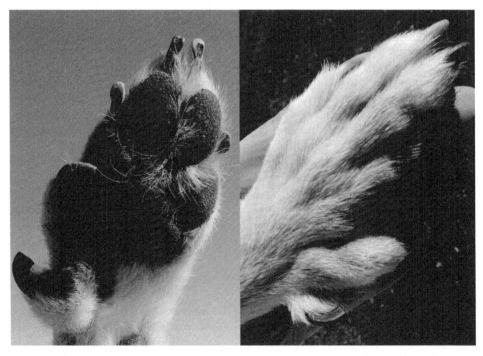

Go ahead and check. It is easier to do on yourself, but maybe your dog can use some attention right now. If you are a bone accountant, that is four bones per digit times five digits, minus one for the thumb for 19 for each foot. Add in the seven wrist carpals or tarsals (because heaven forbid we just say front or rear carpals), and you are at 26. Four feet have a total of 104 bones. That is a lot of pieces and explains why foot issues are so common in dogs. Sure, your dog's footprint only shows four toes. The fifth, if it was not removed surgically (and you are not a Norwegian Lundehund or other polydactyl mutation with a sixth toe) is farther back on the foot, the dew claw.

Shoulders and hips

Shoulders and hips are where the limbs join the body axis or spine. Dog hips are a secure ball and socket, where the large hind bone (femur) has a ball that sets nicely into the hip structure. This lets the hip transmit the tremendous force of running, which uses the whole torso in a dog, through the hip and out to the feet where the rubber meets the road, as it were. Dog shoulders do the same function, but they do it very differently from the hips. There are some 25 muscles that tie into the dog shoulder, giving a wide range of movement. The head of the long arm bone, the humerus, sits in a shallow socket in the shoulder blade. This allows a wide range of motion. Thank goodness for the 25 odd muscles that support the shoulder! Since the capsule holding the long bone is smaller than the corresponding hip, there is a wider range of motion, but the joint has to be held together with ligaments and muscles instead of bone. Less sturdy. These soft structures hold the shoulder blade to the spine and the breastbone (front of the ribs over the heart, also called the sternum). These allow the extra movement, which lets dogs turn on a dime (a U.S. coin) and make all those great sports moves.

Standing still, a dog puts about 60% of its weight on the front limbs, and 40% on the back. Dogs are a bit front-heavy for two reasons. The head naturally adds weight to the front. But that more forward center of gravity helps with cornering. Note that the center of gravity is the balance point for the dog. If you placed your dog on a stick at their balance point, they would be level, not tip forward or back like a teeter-totter. If the center of balance on the ground remains between the four feet, all is good. Get too front heavy, such as when a dog leans too far forward in a turn, and she (Wish, always Wish, tumbling and rolling) loses her balance and falls. I have seen a few French Bulldogs that I thought must be so front heavy as to topple forward on their noses, but to date I have not seen that happen. A friend back in Ohio said this was why she did not castrate her male Frenchies, testicles were the only counterweight they had! I digress, again.

Great skeletal anatomy to consider, lots of parts, especially in the feet. Let's not forget what the skeleton is made of. Living, calcium-rich cells hardened (ossified) in the familiar structures. Since bones are alive, they can heal if broken. Bones can change as stresses cause them to add tissue in some areas, reduce it in others. By exercising you strengthen and reshape bones. So go for a walk with your dog and enrich that skeleton. Bones can become diseased. Many minerals needed for use elsewhere in the body are stored in the skeleton. The bigger bones are hollow, to save weight at little loss of structural integrity, and that space is filled with stored fat and the cells that make blood, especially the parts of blood in the immune system. So much more than just a great Halloween decoration, right?

Muscles

Bones largely exist to give muscles something to work with, although my bone-scientist friend takes offense at that statement. Muscles only work by contracting. They are pullers, not pushers. You can pull a rope to drag a weight, but pushing on the rope is just not very effective. All skeletal muscles work by an elegantly simple mechanism, repeated over and over. Instead of pulling on the rope to move the weight, muscles are the rope, and the rope contracts. When my dog Blizzard lifts his right rear leg to pee, muscles on the outside of the upper rear leg that connected the femur (large single upper-rear-leg bone) to the pelvis (hip) contract, pulling the leg up. When he lowers the leg, gravity helps. But muscles opposite the first muscle contract, lengthening out the first one. We talk about the place where a muscle starts as its origin, and where it pulls against as the insertion. The muscle in his hip contracts, pulling on both ends, the hip (origin) and the lower leg (insertion). The hip is tied to the whole rest of the body, which is braced by three other legs. It is not moving, so the lower leg moves instead and rises. When he walks, different muscles pull the leg forward, with an opposite set to pull them back. To be graphic, one of the main ways a wolf disables large prey is to bite through the hamstrings. That cuts the muscles that pull the leg back. The injured animal can pull the affected leg forward, but not re-extend it. It can no longer walk or run, or kick at the wolf.

The muscular system is just a series of contracting ropes, anchored on both ends, with a hinge (joint) in between. In general, the muscles that move an area are located closer to the body than the part they move. Feet are flexed and extended by opposing muscles in the lower leg. The lower leg is flexed and extended by muscles in the upper leg.

The upper leg is flexed and extended by paired muscle groups found in the main body attaching to the pectoral or pelvic girdles and the spine. It all rests on the strength and integrity of the spine and abdomen, the core. Understanding that muscle groups are paired, and that they work only by contracting, will help you understand how your dog walks, sure, but more importantly it will help you to understand injuries, how paired muscles need to balance each other in strength, and the value of core (abdomen and back) strength.

Conversely, knowing which muscles get lots of use, like the large leg and arm muscles, versus the small one inside the spine that help curl it inward, will help you know your cuts of steaks and why prices of these vary. Heavily used muscles make for tough but cheap steaks or hamburger. Seldom-used muscles, like tenderloins, are less tough. They are all nutritionally pretty much the same. Butchers hate it when you ask for cuts by proper muscle name, and veterinarians hate it when you describe your dog's injury as "perhaps an injury to the round steak." But give it a try, it might be kind of fun. It might also remind you that if you eat meat, you are eating parts of a real animal that walked and ran. I am fine with that, no problems. My vegetarian friends and family often say that is part of why they won't eat meat. If you do, maybe the next paragraph will make you look more closely at your next steak.

Ropes are made of threads twisted together into cords, which are in turn twisted together to make ropes. Muscles are the same, without using twisting to hold them together. At their core, muscles are made of small segments of protein, actin and myosin, which ratchet along each other. Think of one of them as fixed, and the other sort of climbs the fixed piece using a lot of the ATP made by the mitochondria. You remember ATP, right? I asked you to not forget it. That really important molecule that stores energy in the cell? Kind of like the ropes we climbed in gym class as kids. Do they still do that in school? Each segment that climbs, or the climber, ratchets passed the fixed piece. These proteins are microscopic. The protein strands are grouped into little units. Each of these units, called a sarcomere, is 0.00007 of an inch or 0.002 of a millimeter across. These are stacked up in line in fibers with hundreds of thousands of these lined up like the boxcars on a really long train.

Muscle movement

Here is where nature gets really interesting. If the muscle were one really long sarcomere instead of a string of many of them, so just one long actin and one long myosin molecule, contracting at the pace the actin and myosin move past each other of about 0.001 inch (0.02 mm) per second, it would literally take your dog all day (about 16 hours) to reach out with their foot to take a single step. Actin and myosin are really slow. Moving that slowly will get you eaten in the great wilds of nature. Instead, the pieces of actin and myosin are really short. They are stacked like Legos or bricks. Each Lego piece or brick contracts slowly, but they are all doing it at once, stacked on top of each other. Picture that Lego wall or brick wall with each piece squeezing in just a little. Instead of taking 16 hours to contract something as long as a leg (making each actin and myosin rope and climber be 20 inches [half a meter] long in one long muscle), now it goes really fast. Each sarcomere (Lego or brick) contracting together makes the muscle fiber contract at 100 inches (2.5 m) per second. Now the leg could move forward in just 1/12 of a second. But it goes even faster than that because the muscle is pulling on the near end of the leg bone moving at 100 inches (2.5 m) per second, swinging the far end of the leg bone 10 times faster than that. Think about holding a baseball bat and swinging at a pitch. You twist the bat handle with your wrists moving the handle a few inches, and this makes the far end of the bat go very fast over an arc of several feet (a bit over a meter for this vague comparison). Stacked sarcomeres and the mechanical advantage of leverage accelerate the process of contracting muscles from hours to fractions of a second.

Leverage is a powerful force multiplier. Go to a playground and imagine a teeter-totter or seesaw. I think these are mostly removed now as they were deemed too dangerous in the United States thanks to mid-1980s federal safety rules resulting from so many cracked kid skulls, but if you can find one, try this. You can simulate a teeter-totter on a table with a pencil or a yard (meter) stick, some balance piece in the center, and somethings to stack on the ends like poker chips or Oreo cookies. Put two people (or weights) of equal weight on it, one on each end. They balance and can go up and down all day with little effort. Put a small child on one end and an adult on the other, and the child cannot move the heavier adult. Now move the adult toward the center. At some point close the center, the child can now move the adult as they balance. The child uses distance, employing a lot of up or down motion to move the adult a little distance in the opposite direction. That is leverage. The balance point is called the fulcrum. You can trade distance for force. A joint in the skeleton is a fulcrum with bones as the lever arms. Muscles can attach close to the joint or far away. A small muscle moving over a great distance can apply a very heavy force just past the joint. Or, going the other way, a very large muscle near the joint can really move the far end very fast. Locomotion, or any muscle movement, is a combination of microscopic movements caused by chemical reaction using materials from digestion to power it, amplified over distances because these tiny groups all contract in unison, amplified still again with mechanical advantages of levers, so that feet can move really fast at the far ends of legs, powered by large muscle groups closer to the core of the body. Parse out that last sentence, it has a lot of steps in it! Some muscles pairs are more balanced. The muscles that turn your dog's eyes to the left are pretty much exactly balanced by the ones turning the eyes right.

The skeleton and the muscle system work closely together. There are some 650 muscles in your dog, about the same as you have. There are something like two dozen muscles per shoulder, 17 per hip, so let's not go through all of them. If something moves in the body, there is a muscle attached somewhere to the motion. Move a toe, and there are muscles in the paw and forelimb involved. Move the forelimb, and the upper limb muscles get into the act. Move the whole limb, and the torso is involved. The nervous system coordinates it, the circulatory system feeds it, but it is the muscles doing the work. What moves the blood? The heart, a pump made of cardiac muscle that does not attach to any bones. Moving food through the intestines? That is smooth muscle contracting to make the tube-squeezing motion.

Movement is all really very complicated. If any of this activity gets out of sync, you get uncoordinated spasms. Imagine a seizure. I really don't mind if you gloss over the details of actin and myosin. I hope you understand how the body amplifies a slow chemical process into lightning-fast action. I will be sorely disappointed in you if you do not realize that any action in the leg affects the other limbs, and therefore the torso or core, and that almost every single movement requires coordination of hundreds of muscles controlling hundreds of bones all at once. Watch your dog jump, run, walk, or even stand up, and be amazed. Be truly amazed that it works at all. I just now watched Gromit run to the door to bark as my neighbor drove by in his truck. Gromit went from lying down next to me on his bed to standing up, on alert, and over to the door. His eyes shifted, ears oriented to the sound, head up. He had to stand up and initiate balance and start trotting to the door. This involved tail balance, steps, limb locomotion, and twisting around doorways. Take a slow-motion video of any activity your dog does and watch the elaborate, exquisite array of motions and counter motions literally from nose to tail tip. I'd say it leaves me speechless, but I am investing over 200 words expressing my awe, so I am anything but silent.

Muscles do some pretty interesting things besides flinging limbs all about and wagging tails. Your ribs make up a fixed chamber where your lungs take residence. We do not force air into our lungs like a frog does by "swallowing" air. We lower the air pressure in that chest chamber and air is sucked in by the virtues of a relative vacuum. Air is then actively propelled out by muscles, too. One big muscle, the diaphragm, separates the thoracic or chest cavity from the abdominal cavity. It is domed-shaped and curving around the liver and digestive system. When the muscles between the ribs contract and the diaphragm flattens from dome shaped to pretty flat, the area in which the lungs abide increases. They, being elastic in nature, stretch, and that increased volume sucks in air. Exhaling is the opposite: Relax the diaphragm and contract muscles inside the rib cage.

The heart
Another quite interesting muscle is the heart. Like skeletal muscle, it contracts with all of the usual means. But cardiac cells are particularly susceptible to an electrically propagated signal that makes them contract in a wave that squeezes blood into the heart, and then actively ejects it, setting up blood flow. This happens regularly, with a rhythm tied to the metabolic needs of the cells in the body, day in and day out. My oldest dog, Gromit, has a steady resting pulse of around 75 beats per minute for the last 7,626,000 minutes. That is over half a billion beats so far in his life. Not too many machines have that high of a mean time between failures. Thankfully, the beat goes on.

Did you see what I did there? I paid close attention to my dog. I counted his breaths. I checked his pulse. I stared at his face. I do this a lot. I do this because Gromit has a very poor ability to say sentences like, "Tim, old boy, I am feeling a bit under the weather today. Maybe a bit stressed about it. Maybe today is not our best training day." Since he can't say that directly, and he will hide pain normally, I have to look for other measures. I absolutely need to know what normal looks like so I can recognize abnormal. Watch your dog breathe at rest, after play, while sleeping. How do the breaths differ? Deep or shallow? Rapid? How rapid? Watch for short, timed, 15-second intervals. Multiply the result by four to get breaths per minute. Learn normal for your dog. Do the same for heartbeats. Use the same place to measure where you might check yours, usually along the wrist (and learn where your dog's wrist is!). Is the beat strong or weak? Rapid or slow? What does normal feel like in your dog? Write down the numbers in a notebook with the date, a count, and a comment like "resting" or "seemed anxious" or "just finished a walk." It is not hard to do, it gives you a physical connection to your dog, it leads to an odd Zen-like relaxing moment, and it will help when the proverbial fecal material hits the rotating blades of an electric air mover. By the way, that happened to a student of mine when she was younger. Her dog had diarrhea right into a fan and blew drops of shit all over her. She knew that wasn't normal! But it is one of my favorite dog-student interaction images in my brain.

Fully 10 to 15 pounds (5 to 7 kg) of a 30-pound (14 kg) dog are muscles. All of the speed, twisting, and turning: muscles. All the poop squeezed out the back end: muscles. Hair standing on end? Muscles. Heart beating? Muscles. Lungs inhaling? Muscles.

Muscles and bones are a team

It is worth tying this all together for two goals. One is to be aware of what can go wrong, and how this all fits together to get some work done. In general, the pattern is like this. A pair of muscles oppose each other. Think biceps to flex the lower forelimb, opposed by the triceps to extend the limb back; remember, muscles cannot push. Mammals all have this pair; their relative sizes and exact places of attachment to the bone vary, but the body parts and the genes for them are all pretty much the same. The muscles attach to the bones at either end through tough connective fibers called tendons. These do not stretch much, which is good, so they convey almost all of the power of the muscle. But when the force is too great, they tend to tear, not stretch. This is painful. The biceps (technically the biceps brachii: bi for two upper ends on the muscle and brachii meaning arm) originates, or attaches, on one end to the scapula or shoulder blade in two places (the "bi" in the biceps). The other end inserts or attaches beyond the elbow on the radius, one of the bones in the forelimb. The muscle helps turn the palm by making the radius rotate, and it helps flex the forearm relative to the upper arm. Pulling opposite it is the triceps (technically the triceps brachii: three attachment points for moving the arm). The triceps originates on the humerus, the long bone separating this pair of muscles, and on the scapula or shoulder blade. The other end inserts or attaches to the back of the ulna, the other bone of the forearm, at the elbow. You can easily trace your hand along these on your dog. Do it gently, no pinching. Contract the triceps, the arm straightens, the biceps stretches out. Contract the biceps, and the triceps stretches out while the arm bends.

All this pivots around two joints. The joints are held together by ligaments that attach the bones. For example, there are four main ligaments in the elbow, and three in the shoulder. There is cartilage in the joints, because cartilage is slipperier than bone, all lubricated by synovial fluid. The shoulder has six bursa in it, and there's one in the elbow. Bursa are liquid-filled sacs that help muscles and tendons slide past the bones to make movement work better. There are maybe 350 joints in a dog to go with the 320 bones and 600 muscles. Sound complicated? That is the point! Why do you think veterinarians have to go to school for so long? Just to learn the limbs, they have to know all the parts, how they go together, what can go wrong, and what it looks like when something is going wrong. Not for the first time, let me remind you that I am telling you all of this is so you can understand the basics and have meaningful conversation with a veterinarian. There is no way a book or the internet can substitute for the knowledge it takes to put all these parts together and to diagnose a problem with any degree of certainty. No way that a veterinarian can replace the watchful eye of a dog's human companion who keeps a good lookout for changes in their companion. Good veterinarians listen to the dog handlers. Good dog handlers listen to their vets or other care professionals. Together we can do a much better job with our dogs.

Oh, the second reason for tying all of this together? Because, as I said earlier in the book, wow factor.

A by-no-means exhaustive list of what can go wrong in just the shoulder area I described: You can have malnutrition or a metabolic disorder so the muscle proteins malfunction. You can have a problem in the nervous system so the muscle movement is uncoordinated. The digestive system might not be breaking down or absorbing the sugars and proteins needed for the muscles to work. The circulatory system might not be getting the raw materials such as sugar and oxygen to the muscles. The muscle fibers themselves might be bruised (damaged blood vessels leaking all over the place), stretched, or torn. The tendons might be damaged. The bursa could be inflamed (bursitis), the cartilage in the joint can be damaged and interfering with the joint. The bones themselves could be broken or damaged by arthritis. Any of the living tissue can be infected by bacteria or invaded by cancer.

How do you know what is wrong? Lots of tests, since you can't get too much out of an animal who cannot speak our language and evolved not to show pain on penalty of death. Some tests are simple, like listening to a joint or feeling a limb. We had a dog whose arthritis was so bad you could hear it when you flexed his foot. Some tests use very expensive equipment like an MRI, ultrasound, or X-ray. After the challenges of diagnosing the problem, your veterinarian has to know the treatment options, ranging from letting the body heal itself to physical therapy, drugs, and/or surgery. If you get the impression I admire veterinarians, it is true. Veterinarians have to be every bit as smart and educated as the human-medical students, learning biochemistry, physics, and biology, as well as human psychology and business management. Unlike human doctors who only treat one species, veterinarians learn to treat birds, turtles, cats, and dogs, and they have to know normal and abnormal for each. Toss in as an aside that they typically do that for far less pay. I love my veterinarians (or I immediately switch!). I spend a lot of my time marveling that anything works right at all, let alone works well most of the time, and admiring my students who go into veterinary medicine because, well, how many humans bite their doctors? I have to admit that my pediatrician and dental friends say I would be surprised!

Two activities described next can show how much more complicated this all is, or how wonderfully coordinated the body is.

Eating

The mandible is the lower jaw and holds just under half of the dog's teeth. It is opened primarily by one muscle (the lateral pterygoid) but also by some smaller ones that come off the hyoid bone under the tongue. The hyoid is one of the rare bones that does not directly articulate with another bone, and most people don't even know it exists. How sad. The mouth is closed by pulling up the lower jaw. This job is accomplished primarily by the masseter, the really large muscle that goes from the top of the skull to the bottom of the lower jaw, plus one or two other helper muscles. As your dog chews, this is coordinated with tongue movements to manipulate food in the mouth, smooth muscles in the esophagus to transport the food away, and coordinated with breathing so the dog won't inhale the food through that esophagus-trachea-crossover intersection. All of this can be done with no conscious control, but can be interrupted when needed. You can get your dog to stop chewing, for example, if you call their attention away while they are eating. While chewing, neck muscles are keeping the head in position over the food bowl, eye muscles moving the eyes about to watch for distractions, and the ears might rotate toward a sound. That is just eating.

Gait

Walking gets really complicated, what with four limbs thrashing about and uneven terrain to balance on. Can't be having those paws just move randomly, you won't get anywhere. Walking requires the coordination of hundreds of muscles moving over a hundred of the bones (mostly in the paws) in precise patterns depending on what speed the dog is going. Walking, two types, is different from trotting, which differs from two forms of running and bounding. Locomotion like this is most certainly not just the legs. The back and abdomen muscles are used in every step your dog takes.

Before you read the next few pages, if you can, take your dog for a walk. Watch the footfalls, the steps, the leg motions. Then read the next part. It has information you cannot see because your eyes and brain are not fast enough. These intricacies required slow motion film technology to discover, first with horses. Then, after reading about gaits, go for another walk. You will see more, and you will be frustrated at what you still cannot see. There are some really good YouTube videos out there. Search "dog locomotion and gait analysis." Or try slow motion on your own camera.

Four-legged animals are called quadrupeds, meaning literally "four feet." Humans are bipeds, walking on two. But we evolved for four so we have the same muscles and bones. Our posture and gaits differ. Let's start with foot position. Humans stand flatfooted with the heel on the ground, called plantigrade. When we run, we move up onto our toes, called digitigrade. It lengthens the limb, giving it a little more mechanical advantage and the ability to move faster. Dogs and cats are both digitigrade. If you could run on your toenails like a ballerina dances, you could go a bit faster still, at the expense of turning speed, since less would be hitting the ground. That is called unguligrade, and it is what deer and horses and cattle do. Their hooves are just toenails. Their many bones in their "paws" have fused over evolutionary time to make the foot strong enough to maintain toenail running.

Your dog's foot will leave four toe prints on the ground, each from the pad that supports the toe. In addition, depending on how closely you trim your dog's nails, you will see nail prints. The fifth toe is farther back on the foot, and since the dog is digitigrade, that lifts the thumb or big toe (pollux or hallux!) up off the ground, giving no traction except in extreme maneuvers. That fifth toe still strengthens the foot. It is not vestigial; it has a purpose or else evolution would have gotten rid of it long ago, so I do not recommend getting rid of it.

Dog prints look different from cat prints. First of all, cats, except for cheetahs, retract their claws to keep them sharp so they only show nail prints when cornering tightly. Cheetahs are normally found only in Africa, so unless you are there, if the print otherwise matches a dog and shows nails, it is a dog. Dogs almost always show nail prints, as they rotate weight forward on the foot when they step off. All those dog designs you have showing a main footpad and four toe pads, but no nails, are really cat prints. Dogs show the nails. Most people don't like how that print with nails looks on a jacket, jewelry, or tattoo. To some it is cluttered, to some almost sinister. There really is no accounting for art preferences. I am told time after time to let it go, but I just can't. In addition, most dog prints are longer than they are wide, while cat prints are wider than long. Don't feel bad about what you have. While I was in graduate school in wildlife ecology, the Nittany Lions of Penn State used a five-toed logo for their lion. We all knew from wildlife work that only weasels and bears (of the common sports mascots) show all five toes in a print. Eventually biology won out over copyright (the real reason, not ignorance, that the Nittany Lion had five toes). But we sure had fun mocking the wildlife biologists at Penn State at conferences. Geek fun, I know. They switched their logo back to four toes in 2006. My sister-in-law, having heard me whine one too many times about people mixing up dog and cat prints painted hundreds of toenails onto a really cool sweatshirt of mixed color "dog prints" she bought my wife, her sister. She matched the colors on the jacket perfectly, and my wife now gets to explain why she has the one-of-kind jacket. One of my regular Vermont dog campers had a tattooed track of, well, cat prints running up her back. After hearing me, she went back and had the artist tattoo on nail prints. The next summer she proudly showed off the improvement. Looked awesome. At last, I have permanently changed a student!

Types of gaits – walk, trot, canter, gallop

When you walk, you pivot your hips, left side forward when your left leg goes forward. It helps move the leg. Likewise, your dog flexes his pelvis left side toward their head when the back left leg goes forward. That imparts an s curve in the spine, which is offset by the opposite shoulder going forward at the same time. Left hip, right shoulder. Left rear foot forward as the right front goes forward. Plant those feet, pivot on the hips and shoulders, so the right rear leg goes forward while the left front foot goes forward. This is called diagonal walking, the most common walk in dogs. But you can move the left side front and rear and then the right front and rear in unison. This is lateral walking and is often used by puppies, and generally has to be retaught to an adult dog if you want to use it in something like freestyle dance moves. Overweight dogs will learn lateral walking to take stress off their joints. Losing excess weight is a better way to remove stress from joints. Lateral walking keeps the spine straight while one side and then the other moves forward. In both gaits for dogs, there are always at least two feet, and generally three, in solid contact with the ground. A trot is essentially a well-timed diagonal walk where two feet are off the ground at the same time.

Pick up the speed, and the dog will break into a **canter**. This is a three-beat pace where one hind foot hits the ground, say left hind (beat one), followed by the right hind foot and the left front foot together (beat two), followed by the remaining right front foot (beat three), called the leading foot. Some dogs lead right, some lead left. Canters and trots are not very fast. A **trot** is a speeded-up walk, a canter is essentially a slow run that can easily switch to a full run or gallop. I find it amusing to walk with one of my dogs, slowly increasing the speed, to find where my dog switches from walk to trot and trot to canter. If you do this on level ground with a smooth surface like a mowed lawn or level sidewalk, you should get pretty consistent results.

There are two types of gallop, or full runs. In one, the pattern can be one foot at a time, so four beats, or two beats with two feet on each beat. In a two-beat pattern, both front feet hit the ground followed by the back feet landing right where the front feet just were. So as the back feet come in for landing, the front feet spring up and out of the way, reaching forward again. Here the prints often look like only one left foot and one right foot since the back foot goes right where the front foot was. To really crank up the speed, the same two- or four-beat pattern can have the rear feet land in front of the front feet, outside them. The front feet land, and momentum and good abdominal muscles pull the spine into a curve. The front feet stay planted, close to each other, and the rear feet land outside and in front of the now-planted front feet, landing together so that the prints of the rear feet are just in front of and outside the prints of the front feet. The curved spine with stretched muscles acts like a spring straightening out and propelling the front feet forward for the next steps. If the feet hit a bit out of time, you can have one front foot land just before the other, and then one back foot on the same side as the lead front foot land just before the other rear foot, again with rear feet landing outside of and in front of the front feet. The first kind of gallop can be sustained for long periods of time, the second gallop is very fast, but only for short sprints.

What I really want to put here is a really cool table with dog breeds aligned down the left side and average speeds for different gaits across the top. Sadly, there is so much variation out there. There is a complex peer-reviewed article published in the *Journal of Applied Animal Research* in 2016 with a title you are just going to love: "Biomechanical characteristics of gait of four breeds of dogs with different conformations at walk on a treadmill." (Vilar et al., 2016) It convinces me that there is just too much to consider to make the table I want. For example, one has to factor in body mass and dog age and neck length and leg size and kinetics. Lots more searching just resulted in incredible detail, but not the generalizations I wanted. So I am going unscientific here, and I am giving you some anecdotes, mixing and matching breeds because I think this still accurately drives home my point: wow. At a walk, my BCs don't switch to a trot until about 4 mph (6 kph). Wolves can cover 100 miles (160 km) in a day, most of that at a trot. Sled dogs average 7 to 12 mph (11 to 19 kph) at a trot all day, with rest breaks, speed depending on snow conditions, for over 10 days at a stretch. In shorter one- to two-day races, that trot can be faster at 15 mph (24 kph). Greyhounds (the dogs…the buses can average highway speed limits but their feet are wheels, so no fair) race at 40 to 45 mph (64 to 72 kph) for 500 yards (460 m). So I am going out on a limb here (pun intended) and say that a dog walks at…remember this varies by dog breed, age, fitness, geometry of legs, and a gazillion other factors, so your Dachshund and my Border Collie will change gaits at radically different speeds. But generically, with asterisks and hemming and hawing, and a sincere need for someone to show me a chart like I want, here goes. Dogs walk at less than 4 mph (6 kph), trot from 4 to 12-ish mph (6 to 19-ish kph), and run from maybe 15 mph (24 kph) to their top speed, in Greyhounds an astonishing 45 mph (72 kph) over a 500 yard or meter course. Now think about this. The Greyhound can accelerate to that 45 mph (72 kph) from a standstill in six strides, or 32 yards (30 m) in 1.5 seconds experiencing a 1.4g acceleration, if I did all of my calculations correctly. That is second only to the cheetah in acceleration. The cheetah can hit 70 mph (110 kph) and maintain it for 200 to 300 yards or meters, a horse a bit over 45 mph (72 kph) for up to half a mile (0.8 km). The Greyhound can run at 35 mph (56 kph) for 7 miles (11 km)! The Greyhound heart rate in a sprint is over 300 beats per minute, or 5 beats per second, or one beat every 0.2 seconds. Nice transition into the next section on circulation, if I do say so myself.

Watch your dog next time you go for a walk. You can pick up some of this looking at prints in sand or snow, or wet feet on dry pavement. Use your smartphone to record your dog walking and running and slow down the replay. People really did not understand gaits until photography came along and gave us time-lapse to let the slow human brain see the too-fast run. While you are at it, remember why I provide all of those metric conversion. Most dogs do not live in the U.S., and we need to remember that our experience is not theirs. For example, dogs in the United Kingdom have to walk on the opposite side of the road, for heaven's sake.

TOUR 6

The Circulatory System: Blood, Lungs, Air, and the Heart

Every cell in the body needs a constant supply of oxygen and sugar to make ATP (yes, that molecule again), the energy currency of living things. Getting oxygen and sugar into every cell where it is needed to make ATP is the job of the circulatory system. Need the actin and myosin to slide past each other and contract a muscle? Convert ATP to ADP. Need to produce digestive enzymes? ATP provides the energy. Need to actively move a protein across a cell membrane? That will cost you ATP. Cold, but need to be warm, or warm and want to cool off? ATP. Want to ponder that fun family gathering, the latest new movies, this book you are reading? ATP. In fact, in a day, your body uses and reuses about its own weight in ATP, constantly converting it back from ADP to ATP at the expense of energy from food, so you can accumulate energy for all those activities by turning ATP into ADP. Earlier I said energy was like money so ATP is the dollar bill (or euro, pound, peso, dinar, or rupee, you get the idea). Want to make ATP? You use sugar, largely glucose. When you have burned sugar to make ATP, you have a waste product to dispose of, carbon dioxide. Breaking down proteins to build new ones? You make urea, and you know you gotta get rid of that. A cell needs some minerals, where are they going to come from? How is each of the 10 trillion cells possibly going to get everything it needs, when it needs it? And get rid of what it no longer needs? Blood is the Amazon Prime, U.S. Postal Service, Waste Management, AT&T, Brinks, and the local sanitary district all wrapped into one. I want you right now to stop and think: When was the last time you pondered how absolutely wonderful your dog's circulatory system is? It reaches every cell in their body, all 10 trillion.

The need for a delivery system

On one level, this is a simple task. If you want to get materials out to every cell, simply drown them in it. Our model 30-pound (14 kg) dog has about 2 gallons (8 liters) of fluids, or nearly half its body weight in water, found in and around every cell. Water is a great solvent. Oxygen dissolves into it, so does carbon dioxide. Sugar and proteins can be carried in it. Urea will dissolve in it. Fats, with some extra effort, can be made to dissolve in it. Water is so essential to life as we know it, we have trouble imagining life without it on other planets. Every cell has water. Cells are bathed in water found in spaces between the cells. We also need to fight diseases and redistribute heat. There is an incredible distribution system that carries that life-sustaining water throughout the body. That highway of water includes miles (kilometers) of arteries and veins, several key organs like kidneys and hearts (yes, making it plural was a deliberate tease, read on). Those vessels are filled with a little over one quart or liter of blood in a 30-pound (14 kg) dog. The vessels include little pumps, valves, and a filtering system, including a way to get rid of waste products. The body has to be able to fix leaks in it (cuts, lacerations, and bruises), and to make more blood, since it wears out even when it is not dripping out on the floor. Let's start our tour of the circulatory system with the stuff of vampires: blood.

Blood

Blood is a miraculous fluid that just does not get enough credit. I hear people brag about how muscular their dog is, more often how beautiful the dog's coat is, or what great genes and pedigree their dog has. How about a little shine for the fluid that makes it all possible, blood? I want to hear you say, "Oh my, that dog must have some mighty fine blood to get a coat like that." Blood is most certainly not just water or plasma. Plasma is the base liquid, a mix of water and salts with proteins, waste products, sugars, fats, nutrients, antibodies, and hormones. A real witch's brew. A veritable treasure trove that does for the body what all those trucks on the highway do for cities: deliver absolutely everything a cell needs, and then take away everything it does not.

A major component of blood, like about half of it, is red blood cells. These are also what gives it that bright red color. The red is from iron, a part of the hemoglobin, which actively carries oxygen (O2) to the cells and carbon dioxide (CO2) from them. Each hemoglobin molecule carries four oxygen molecules, and in the cells hemoglobin trades those four oxygen for four carbon dioxide molecules. Each red blood cell has about 250 million molecules of hemoglobin, each with four O2 or CO2. So each red blood cell is carrying about a billion molecules of oxygen or carbon dioxide. That quart (liter) of blood in a dog has about 5 trillion red blood cells: 5 trillion times a billion molecules of oxygen or carbon dioxide is a really big number (5×10^{21} or 5,000,000,000,000,000,000,000). An average dog, if you can find one, has about 8 ounces, or half a pound, or 250 grams of hemoglobin in 1.5 quarts or liters of blood. Just to see if you are following, that means that of the 10 trillion cells in your average dog, 7.5 trillion are red blood cells! In dogs, red blood cells last an average of 133 days, so you have to replace about 0.75% per day, or 9 billion new red blood cells every day.

Blood is made in the larger bones, which seems kind of an odd place until you realize the insides of the bones aren't really doing much else anyway. Turns out, that is a pretty lame answer. In some animals like fish, blood is formed in the kidneys. Blood formation moved to the bones after animals ventured out onto land between 360 and 390 million years ago. The best hypothesis right now is that it has to do with protecting blood stem cells from the radiation in sunlight. In any event, the bones get a chemical messenger, called a hormone, from the kidneys that says "make more blood" and the marrow in the bones does just that. Red blood cells in mammals are an odd duck (which is a bird, not a mammal) in that, unlike other cells, they lose their nucleus and go about their business with no DNA to guide them. This lets the red blood cell squish into spaces it otherwise would not fit, carry more oxygen, and to adopt a shape that increases surface area to enhance oxygen transport, kind of like a jelly filled donut where the filling got sucked out, leaving a depression in the middle. No nucleus means no instructions for cell repair, so a blood cell only lives a few months and then has to be replaced. Veterinarians measure the hematocrit, or percentage of blood volume that is made of red blood cells, which is between a third and half (35% to 55%) in a healthy dog.

Blood also carries leukocytes or white blood cells, which are an important part of the immune or disease-fighting system. Veterinarians check these levels as well. Gromit had 5.2 billion in his last check-up; normal would be 6 to 17 billion, usually measured in microliters of blood. Since there are a million microliters per liter, and a liter of blood, the math is pretty easy. An increase in white blood cells generally means there is a disease problem, and too few means your dog won't fight disease well enough. Most of the white blood cells are a type called neutrophils, and these are important first responders to disease. They live about a day, so your dog is constantly making them, again in the bone marrow of the skeleton. There are also T- and B-lymphocytes, also known as T-cells and B-cells. B-cells make antibodies to fight bacteria and viruses, and T-cells fight infected cells of the host as well as runaway growth cells, called tumors. If you put 30 pounds (14 kg) of raw beef on your floor and left it there, by the end of the day you would smell it rotting, and in a week you'd have moved out. But to the bacteria, fungi, and viruses all around us, your dog is a warm mass of very tempting meat, and this immune function of the blood keeps it all in check.

Lastly, blood carries platelets, the ingenious leak-stopping system, kind of the plumbers of the circulatory system. Platelets, called thrombocytes, are fragments of large cells called megakaryocytes that live in the bone marrow, so they are not cells themselves. Just chips off the block set free to float in the blood. There are about 200 billion per average dog at any one time. Most of the time they are inactivated, but chemical signals from injuries will activate them, making them stick together, forming clots. Clots do two things: They stop the flow of leaking blood, a pretty important thing, and they actively summon the immune system, including the B- and T-lymphocytes, and actively inhibit bacteria. Not surprisingly, veterinarians also check the platelet counts. Gromit had 322 billion in his last check up, higher than average but the range is pretty broad. Too few, and clotting is ineffective. Too many, and you get clots where you don't want them, including in the brain and lungs.

Distributing blood

Distributing this wonder fluid is no small task. Like the water delivery system in your home, there is a series of pipes that direct the flow of blood. These vessels come in three types by function: arteries, veins, and capillaries. Everything hooks up to two main pumps in the heart, and a bunch of ancillary pumps out in the body. Wait, you must be saying, two hearts? Functionally the left half of the mammalian heart pumps blood to the whole body, the right half to the lungs. They beat as one, but they are functionally separate. Out in the veins, there are countless, or at least uncounted, one-way valves. Blood in the veins often has to fight gravity to get back to the heart, and is too far downstream to benefit much from blood pressure to move it along. Veins come equipped with these valves so that blood enters a segment of vein and the valve closes behind it. Then some muscle nearby, like the biceps in the arm, or any of those 600 muscles doing unrelated skeletal moving tasks, contract, which squishes the blood in the vein, making the blood move the only way it can, toward the heart to the next valve. And so it goes all the way back to the heart. There are some 50,000 miles (80,000 km) of blood vessels in your 30-pound (14 kg) dog, almost exactly the same length as the United States Interstate Highway System.

Classically we describe the system like this: Blood gets oxygen in the lungs, gets pumped out to the body, dumps the oxygen, picks up carbon dioxide, goes back to the lungs, and starts all over.

By now you know I am a big ATP fan, but honestly I never realized that until now. Energy is transported to the cells from the digestive system largely as sugar, so we will start our view of the circulatory system there. One glucose, in ideal settings, can yield 38 ATP in the complex cellular respiration cycle, the molecular accounting we make almost every introductory biology student memorize. But it is pretty stunning that in practice, one sugar nets about 30 ATP (that ideal 38 is rarely achieved in the real world). That is a lot of cell energy from each sugar. Each cell of the 10 trillion dog cells makes 68 million ATPs per second. Each ATP is cycled through to ADP, releasing energy in the cell, and back to ATP about 600 times a day, or about every two minutes. Again, noted earlier, that amounts to about the dog's body weight in ATP per day, but it is just a fraction of the dog's weight (about 0.06 pounds, or 23 g, of ATP in constant recycling). Ponder that a moment. Essentially all of the dog's energy needs, supplied by that daily dose of food, are ultimately handled in the cells by under one ounce or 23 grams of ATP molecules. Sugars, and all the other digested food products we saw swilling in the chyme in the intestines, are transported across the cell membranes of the intestine, where they enter the bloodstream. The blood moves from here to the liver where some processing and detoxification occurs, and then into ever larger vessels that lead to the heart.

The lungs and breathing

The lungs are light, foamy-looking bags with tiny air sacs called alveoli. A typical dog breathes 20 times a minute. My 15-year-old 30 pound (14 kg) Border Collie has taken something like 160 million breaths in his life, moving 24 million liters (or quarts) of air. That seems like a lot, and it is. He could have fully filled 10 typical hot air balloons had he tried, and with his hot breath, those babies would have sailed high. Air is drawn into the lungs because of the dome-shaped diaphragm muscle that separates the liver and other viscera from the heart and lungs. That muscle contracts, flattening, increasing the volume in the rib cage. At the same time, the muscles between the ribs contract, pulling the chest out. Air is literally sucked into the lungs.

Raise your hand if you like to breathe. You are exempt from this show of solidarity if it puts your cup of coffee or drink glass at risk. I am a big fan of breathing. I'd wear such a t-shirt if I found one. I hate coughing as it interferes with breathing. Likewise I hate congestion. I hate common colds, flu, and right now I hate the coronavirus named SARS-CoV-2, which causes COVID-19. I am getting a lot of writing done because in Minnesota, where I work, and Wisconsin, where I live, we are in what we call "lockdown." Prisons do lockdown. Ours is really just a "stay at home with our toys and distractions unless you really need to go out" order. I hate the coronavirus and the disease for two reasons. First and foremost, it robs people of their breath, and breathing freely is not something I take for granted, even though I have healthy lungs. I love to breathe deep, filling my lungs with pine-scented air, or maybe ocean air laced with a dash of salt. I live out of the city largely so I can have fresh air to breath. A few months ago, I had the flu (without testing being available then, we assume it to have been the flu). Every year I get a cold. Working with sneezy, coughing students will do that to you. When I have one of those diseases, I long for an uninhibited breath of air. When I am disease free, I really do savor easy breathing. Not every breath. I'd be quite distracted.

I breathe at rest over a dozen times a minute. I gotta get that delicious oxygen into my lungs and dump off that icky carbon dioxide, the final passage of my meals long-stored in my body. I can hold my breath, too. In my scuba days, two minutes was not that hard. How long can a dog hold their breath? The science on this is sketchy, because it is hard to test voluntary breath-holding when you do not know what is voluntary. There are anecdotes of dogs diving under water for two to three minutes, which makes sense as their physiology and ours are similar. How long can a turtle hold its breath? A lot more than two minutes. Maybe five? Ten? You who live more equatorially than we do in the northern half of the northern hemisphere are at a disadvantage here. We of the cold regions know turtles can be in lakes all winter, and our lakes freeze with a layer of ice over the top 2-feet (0.5m) thick. No turtle can tunnel up through that, and turtles don't have scuba gear. They hold their breath six months. OK, they cheat a bit. Their oxygen use as an ectotherm in near freezing water is so low they can supplement their oxygen by taking water into their mouth and their cloaca (it's close enough to call it their butt) and diffuse oxygen into blood and carbon dioxide out. Kind of like gills. I tell kids turtles breathe through their butts, which is colorful but a bit of a lie. That is the difference paid in energy, aka money for animals, to be an always-warm endotherm. We have to breathe every few minutes. Turtles can go months without a deep breath of pine-scented air into their lungs. As a complete aside to this tangent on my love of breathing, I am intentionally making offhand references to my favorite poet, Billy Collins, and his poem "Litany." Be a little liberal artsy for me and go look it up. Anyway, feed your dog every day. Mammals are energy hogs and that is why we breathe so much. You can skip feeding a turtle at the bottom of a lake for half a year.

The second reason I hate SARS-CoV-2…you forgot already I was on an anti-COVID-19 rant, for two reasons at that. The first was it interferes with one of my favorite pastimes, breathing. That was the last paragraph. I am no idiot, I hate that COVID-19 kills, and killed a friend of mine in the dog community who had our Wish's brother. I love breathing, hate these forms of death, but that is not the second reason why I hate COVID-19 because I think that is covered in the first reason.

My second reason is dog-related, so bear with me. Or at least the reason for this dog book. You have to know some science or you cannot navigate this world. You will be taken in by charlatans and ill-informed zealots. This disease highlights what happens when you ignore science. People in government and the general public have shown themselves to be only too happy to ignore science and medical professionals at almost every turn. We know a lot about this family of viruses called coronaviruses, and other respiratory infections caused by other types of viruses. We know how they kill and how they are transmitted and how quickly you have to act to stop an infectious disease. Despite that, the general public flocked to bizarre "cures" that killed many people, claimed all sorts of things that were scientifically impossible, ignored social distancing guidelines based on how far those droplets of virus can float (and 6 feet or 2 m is not an absolute, just a relatively safe distance), and put resources (aka money) into the wrong places. For years scientists had called for planning ahead and stockpiling supplies. This isn't rocket science! But even if it were, listen to your scientists, sure. More importantly, become scientifically literate yourself. Arm yourself with some science so you can make better, well-informed decisions. Not just on pandemics, which are thankfully rare, happening only every influenza season every single year, but on matters of dog health and well-being. There are so many cranks, so much misinformation on dog health out there. There are a lot of opinions with precious few facts or science. Learn the biology and you will learn to be skeptical of claims without asking, "What is your evidence?" "How did they test that against an alternative explanation?" "Does this sound reasonable"

So take a deep breath, relax, and continue to get your dose of science about dogs. Which also means I have just lectured those already investing in science literacy, you the reader, that you should be doing what you are, in fact, doing. My apologies. Seriously. Carry on. Back to our regularly scheduled breathing lessons. Breathe in, pause, breathe out. Repeat.

Air

To risk stating the obvious, air is a gas, blood is a liquid. A liquid, like the coffee in the cup on my desk, has a fixed volume but takes the shape of whatever container it is in, like blood vessels, hearts, and lungs. But when your dog is rolling around on the ground, turning the cup of coffee upside down, as it were, nothing leaks out. That is because the lungs provide a water-tight place for air and blood to mix. Air, being a gas, will fill whatever volume of space is available. If the space is huge, like outside the atmosphere, it spreads out and the pressure is very low. Pump it into a cylinder, like a scuba tank or fire extinguisher, or a party balloon, and the pressure goes up.

Air on Earth, where we spend most of our lives, is mostly nitrogen, 78% in fact. This is an inert form of nitrogen, triple bonded to itself, doing nothing for us but taking up space. The next biggest ingredient in air is what we use most, a highly reactive and toxic substance known as oxygen, coming in at 21%. Yes, I said toxic. Like other toxic ingredients, the dosage is essential. You can breathe pure oxygen at normal air pressures and be fine, breathe it under slightly higher pressure, like scuba diving, and you might die. It rusts metal. It oxidizes, facilitating fire. And that is what we need it for, to oxidize carbon chains from our food. Free radicals of oxygen contribute to cellular aging and death. So while it can kill you, go a few minutes without it and you are just as dead. Maybe you have done some math and added oxygen and nitrogen together to see that together they make up 99% of the air we breathe. Argon, another inert gas is about 0.93% (just less than 1%). What about carbon dioxide that we are hearing so much about with climate change? That is just 0.04%, a trace gas, which is why it is so sensitive to human activity. In my lifetime that has grown from 0.03% to 0.04%, and that small change is what makes all the difference in the world. The rest of the atmosphere is some really uncommon stuff by percentage, including but not limited to krypton, neon, and helium, which with argon are all very inert gasses on the far right column of the periodic table (which in my humble opinion is one of the most incredible of human inventions). There is also water vapor in the air, which makes for the humid summer days. Clouds differ: They are water in liquid form; air is all gas. Key point here is that air is mostly not oxygen, and we breathe it to get oxygen.

Air pours into the lungs via the trachea, a cartilage-ribbed tube that runs from the lungs out to the nose and mouth. The cartilage rings hold the tube open so it does not collapse like the inflator on a toy balloon. You can feel the trachea and its rings under your dog's head, at the top of the neck. Right, the Adam's apple is the top of the line for the trachea. The end of the line for inhaled air, the alveoli, serve to greatly increase the surface area of lungs. Here, with a freshly inhaled breath, the air has 21% oxygen and 4 hundredths of a percent carbon dioxide. Exhaled air has 16% oxygen and 4% carbon dioxide. The difference is all from cellular burning of carbon found in the food you fed your dog.

Lungs are rich in blood vessels. In the lungs, the blood goes from arterioles into ever smaller vessels until it is in capillaries, small enough that those red blood cells have to line up single file. Here the blood moves along the air sacs and oxygen diffuses in, carbon dioxide diffuses out. The blood turns from a dark red to a bright red as the oxygen combines with the hemoglobin.

Putting the respiratory and circulatory systems together

That must be what triggers breathing, right? Lack of oxygen? Nope. Turns out oxygen is difficult to measure. But the byproduct of metabolism, carbon dioxide from back at the mitochondria making that great ATP, raises the incoming air from 0.04% carbon dioxide to almost 4%. In the blood, coming from the cells, much of it is converted to carbonic acid, lowering blood pH. The body senses the buildup of carbon dioxide by measuring blood pH (how acidic it is), not the lack of oxygen. The blood, now oxygen enriched, flows back to the heart.

A roadmap

A brief roadmap of where we are going should help. Blood, lungs, and heart are all so intertwined. Instead of an organ-based description, let's first take a drive, one lap around the body as a blood cell carrying oxygen. That red blood cell is going to be our car, the blood vessels the road, oxygen and carbon dioxide the bags in our trunk (or boot for you Brits). There are a few towns we could stop at (organs) and two we must. So before we learn the parts and what they do, let's take a drive. Since it is a loop, we can start anywhere. We will start out in the bucolic countryside where traffic moves slowly on small, winding country roads. We are in the biceps of a left forelimb in a tiny blood vessel called a capillary. We stop at a nice country inn, take a selfie or two, drop off our bags of presents including oxygen, food, and the mail (in the form of chemical messengers), and we pick up some bags of garbage filled with carbon dioxide, ammonia, some salts, and urea, put them in the trunk, and start driving again. We also pick up or drop off jugs filled with water as needed in the area.

We follow this rural road for a while, which leads to faster country highways, and in no time we are on a freeway racing along at a good clip. The last highway we meet up with is the vena cava which gathers blood from all over the body, and it takes us to the big city, pumping with life. The heart. We enter a region of that big city, called an atrium, and get pumped past a big valve into the right ventricle (just another region of the big city) and that compresses and sends us really fast along an artery to the lungs. There we drop off the bags with carbon dioxide and pick up bags of oxygen. No tipping the porters who help. Maybe another selfie. Others waiting in line move us along, and soon we are driving down a large vein to the heart again but this time we are staying on the left side of town. We enter another atrium and that pumps us into the largest and strongest chamber of the heart, the left ventricle. That baby squeezes tight (good old muscle contraction) and that shoots us out into the biggest superhighway of them all, fastest speed limits, the aorta. There are lots of exits from this highway. If we go down an early exit we could end up in the head, a bit later in the kidney or hamstrings of the left leg. That is where we end up this time around, now on smaller rural highways and eventually on a small side street. We drop off our oxygen, pick up a few bags of carbon dioxide, skip the selfies, and begin our leisurely trip back to the heart.

The heart

Now for some details. We will start here at the place of highest blood pressure, the left side of the heart, which is the thicker, stronger side of the heart. When the heart compresses, blood is propelled under great pressure out to the largest artery, the aorta, and out to the body. This is the pulse from the heart we count. A small aside on fluid pressure in tubes to help you in a crisis. If blood vessels were inelastic like the water pipes in your home, blood pressure at the pump (heart) would be the same all throughout the circulatory system, including in the veins on the way back to the heart. It is not so because blood vessels have to be elastic (stretchy) so limbs can move. In dogs, and other mammals, blood pressure falls off so the veins have very low pressure relative to the arteries. When arteries bleed, you see blood pumping with each heartbeat. This is majorly serious and needs to be stopped now. Veins ooze blood, and normally this is far less worrisome, despite being messy.

When a veterinarian checks a dog's blood pressure, the surge of pressure when the heart's ventricles are contracting is the systolic pressure. We also measure the in-between-beats resting pressure, the diastolic. Canine blood pressure runs a bit higher than humans. Kidneys help regulate the pressure. The blood, now under pressure, moves out to the body. Some of it flows on paths to the intestines for more nutrients, some to the brain to feed that hungry organ, some to the kidneys to have waste products filtered out. Blood goes everywhere in the body. When an area needs more blood, like after a meal when the intestines are calling, the blood vessels dilate, or relax, and more blood flows there. When less is needed, the blood vessels constrict and the blood goes elsewhere.

Any given part of the body is getting blood constantly, but the whole volume of blood is not cycling with each heartbeat. The liver, brain, and kidneys each might get as much as 20% of the blood every minute, or on average a given drop of blood goes through the liver every five minutes, a little less often for the brain and kidneys. But that same drop of blood might not get out to the paws but once every 15 minutes. It will go through the heart on average 1,000 times a day or once every minute or two. Chance and need dictate this.

Blood is a window to your dog's health because it touches every part of the body. Our dog, Gromit, when he was about 2-and-a-half years old, had had a successful weekend in agility, with four first-place finishes. He was looking great, running well. My wife insisted something was wrong. He was peeing too often and "He just doesn't seem right." So we took him to the veterinarian, our friend, Brian. He did a quick check and said he did not see the obvious, a bladder infection, and other symptoms of diabetes were lacking. Likely the excessive peeing was from drinking too much water. Brian figuratively patted us on the head and politely said our dog was fine. I felt vindicated. My wife was not satisfied, and she looked at me and said under her breath, "There is something wrong. Do something." When in doubt, get a blood profile. I asked the veterinarian to run one, and he said, "Look, it is your money. Gromit is fine." Early the next day, Brian called me. You want those calls to be from a technician because that means everything is pretty much OK. The big guns only call when it is bad. Brian said to please bring Gromit in right now. We did. He did an ultrasound and found enlarged kidneys. The blood panel had shown elevated creatinine, a protein normally filtered by the kidneys. Kidney failure. More testing showed Gromit had leptospirosis, a relatively rare bacterial infection. The increased creatinine levels signaled a kidney problem. Enlarged kidneys confirmed kidney failure. What followed was a week of isolation and IV antibiotics and uncertainty if the kidneys would restart normal function. Terrifying, gut-wrenching times. Gromit is now 15 and doing quite well for a geriatric dog, thank you. All because of some suspicious activities, an insistent wife, an attentive veterinarian, and the miracles of modern blood tests.

Want to know how well the lungs are functioning? Look at oxygen and carbon dioxide levels in the blood. How are the kidneys doing at filtering? Look at some blood proteins like creatinine. Liver, thyroid, pituitary, and so many organs can be queried through blood. A typical canine blood screening includes, but is not limited to, counts and measures of red blood cells to check for amounts, the hematocrit. White blood cells are counted to make sure there are no signs of infection or cancer, but enough to keep the immune system up to par. Glucose is measured because sugar is so important to the cells, but too much might mean diabetes. Other proteins are measured to test for metabolic issues and liver and kidney functioning. Calcium levels can indicate tumors, or kidney or thyroid diseases. There are literally scores of tests available. Sometimes specific tests will be ordered to test for particular concerns. The creatinine levels in Gromit caused the veterinarian to want to see the kidney sizes. When red blood cells die, they are recycled in the spleen, or if the 2016 study from Massachusetts General Hospital in *Nature Medicine* is correct, the liver. (Theurl et al., 2016) Likely both. The hemoglobin is broken up to recycle the iron, and the rest becomes bilirubin, which serves no further function and is toxic. The liver dumps it into the bile it is making, and that in turn is dumped into the small intestine. Bacteria in the gut metabolize this, leaving stercobilin, which gives feces the characteristic brown color.

As the major infrastructure system in a dog's body, and by infrastructure think highways, sewers, power distribution, and emergency responders, all the things that keep a community running, the circulatory system is pretty darned important. We do our best to patch up leaks in it and keep it healthy. Our tour now moves outside the body to look at the protection systems that help keep the insides in and the outside out.

TOUR 7

TOURING THE EXTERNAL FORTIFICATIONS

Wouldn't it be simpler if we had all that DNA, all those bones and muscles, neatly tucked away in some nice, safe place where they wouldn't be damaged by all the assaults the world provides? It would, but you only get that as a developing embryo. After that, it is time to meet the cruel world, and off you go. Think about it for a moment. My dog's ancestors, alpha wolf male and beta wolf female in some pack somewhere, had to kill to make a living. Most prey don't take too kindly to that, so the environment assaults you at every single meal. While most others are a meal to you, you are also prey to some others, either your own species or other large predators. Mosquitos, fleas, and flies all attack for your blood. Outside temperatures vary from less than minus 40 (degrees C or degrees F, they are the same at minus 40!) to over a 105 degrees F (40 degrees C). It rains on you. Snows on you. You bang into trees and rocks, twist your ankle as you turn a corner too sharply. There is no ibuprofen to ease the inflammation, no morphine for the pain, no Benadryl for the itch, no antibiotics to keep those minor infections from going systemic, not even a stiff drink to offer stress release. How did anybody, any body, any dog survive that? Turns out, dogs are well equipped to face the warfare, the kill-or-be-killed world that is every day, every hour, of every non-domesticated organism. Their body is a fortress with the equivalent of moats, towers, and bulwarks.

Hair

Dogs shed hair. Some a lot, some a little. We have a magnet on our refrigerator that says "Our dogs live here, if you don't want to get dog hair on your clothes, stay out of our house." We prefer Border Collies with their black and white hair. That way, no matter what color clothes you wear, some of our dog hair will show up on you. If we don't vacuum every day, dog hair builds up in the corners of rooms, and let's be real, we don't vacuum daily. Doesn't even occur to us. After a few days with three dogs, the "dust" kitties of dog hair become more inquisitive. We find them venturing out into the middle of rooms. After a week, the dust kitties become large enough to become predatory, and we start to fear for our lives. Then, and only then, we attack back. Many of us bathe our dogs, buying shampoo with better ingredients than we use on ourselves. We comb, pull out burrs, preen the hair for ticks, stroke it to relax, and we scrutinize the coats of other dogs, always favorably comparing ours to theirs. Unless you show dogs. Then it is more like "How'd they get that hair so fluffy, white, with just the right lay?" Of course, we cover all that beauty with dog jackets to cover the hair to keep it clean and combed. Some people do. We don't. We prefer the more lived-in look for our dog's hairy coats.

Dog have hair for a couple of reasons, all relating to protecting them from the harsh realities of the world. Hair helps thermoregulate. Only two groups of animals evolved to keep their internal temperatures constant and at a different temperature than the environment: a small group of dinosaurs we call birds, and a cousin of the reptiles we call mammals. Hair absorbs the bumps and scrapes of moving about in the environment. In the wild, it also advertises danger — think skunk — or is colored to camouflage. It doesn't last forever, so it is on a replacement cycle. Now, with the 1960s Broadway song "Hair" from the musical of the same name playing in the background, let's explore our dogs' hair.

Form follows function. Hair comes in many shapes, colors, and growth patterns, controlled by a suite of genes. The origins of hair, and feathers for that matter, are a bit tough to discern. They do not fossilize all that well. Likely feathers aided flight before helping dinosaurs (birds) with insulation. An ectotherm like a turtle depends on easy heat exchange with its environment, and while scales protect it from wear and tear, they do not block heat conduction with the surroundings. Hair's original adaptive value may be tied to localized insulation needs, maybe the bottoms of feet in hot or cold climates. In any event, insulate it does. At its core, it has lots of air spaces trapped in a matrix of dead cells and a protein called keratin. Keratin is a double-stranded twisted protein that handles abrasion well and does not break easily. It is one of the toughest proteins there is, and it is hard to digest despite the acid bath of the digestive system. This is why cats cough it up, wolf scat is full of intact hair, and dead road kill is fully eaten, except for the hair. Those trapped air spaces insulate like a sleeping bag, or like the fiberglass and foam insulation in most homes. Wrapped around this core is a layer of dead cells, tightly packed together, which gives hair its strength and ability to stand up without breaking. There is a thin coating of keratin over the whole hair just for good measure.

Hair is not just a protein and dead-cell-based shaft. Each hair has a tiny muscle attached to it to change the position of the hair. That is what makes the ruff stand up on a dog trying to look bigger, or makes whiskers move around. Each hair shaft also has a nerve ending that transmits signals to the brain when the hair is involuntarily moved. You check that on your arm or head. Flick a hair, you can feel it. You do not feel the hair itself, since it is dead. It is the nerves at the base detecting the shaft movement. The base of the hair has a good blood supply feeding a cluster of cells that actively produce the hair strand. Each hair also has a sebaceous gland associated with it that secretes a waxy oil to lubricate the hair shaft. We wash hair to make it less greasy, or to remove that sebum that the gland produced in the first place, because we think that looks and smells better. Shampooing also strips positively charged hydrogen ions, leaving the hair with a static charge. Then we add back a conditioner to give the hair a more negative charge, chemically lubricate the hair, and soften it a bit. Just what the natural oils we washed away did. On average, wild hair on a wolf or coyote has a good balance of oils and doesn't feel too greasy, although it does get a bit aromatic in my experience, especially in the summer. Domesticated critters like dogs and humans select for hair traits that are not always in balance with the genes producing the oils. Your dog would be fine without baths, but the hair would feel coarser and likely too dry or too oily. How often you bathe your dog likely has a lot more to do with how you like the hair to look, feel, or smell, than it does the dog's health. Of course, if your dog gets too cozy with a skunk or rolls in bird droppings as Wish did a few minutes ago, a good bath is the only good solution unless you are willing to wait for all the hair to replace itself.

Hair varieties

The variety of hair "choices" in dog breeds is mind-boggling. There are dogs with long hair like Afghan Hounds and English Sheep Dogs. Some breeds have medium-length coats like Golden Retrievers and German Shepard Dogs. We have shorthaired breeds like Boxers and Doberman Pinschers. We even have hairless dogs like American Hairless Terriers and the Xoloitzcuintli. Dogs come in the wild type double coats easily seen in Collies and Siberian Huskies, or single short coats like Whippets, Boxers, and Bulldogs, or the single long coat of the Afghan Hound. Prefer tight, coarse curls? Try a Standard Poodle or Portuguese Water Dog. Soft, curly hair your thing? Maybe a Bichon Frise. Prefer that rough, lived-in look? Maybe you prefer a Rough Collie. Wire coats include the German Wirehaired Pointer and Airedale Terriers. Smooth-coated breeds include Great Danes and Bloodhounds. That was just texture! Consider the single-colored breeds like a Labrador Retriever or a Scottish Terrier. Some breeds carry two colors of hair like Dalmatians and Pointers. Basset Hounds and Bernese Mountain Dogs have three colors to their hair, called tri-color. Some breeds, like Border Collies and Australian Shepherds, come in smooth and rough coats, two colors or tri-colored. So much variety. The American Kennel Club in the United States (AKC) and the British Kennel Club (KC) recognize 200ish breeds. The United Kennel Club, also in the United States (UKC), and the Fédération Cynologique Internationale (FCI, also known as the World Canine Organization) in Belgium both recognize over 300. That is a lot of variety from one species. Remember back to the genetics sections on what is a dog, and what is a breed? Given that "breeds" are human-defined, not nature-defined, it is no wonder that organizations don't agree on how many breeds there are. I have no problems at all that we try to define a breed, I just like to repeat that it is a human-defined and segregated gene pool. No more, no less. I love my Border Collies, but I also love scores of breeds, and tons of mixed breeds (most of our dogs have been mixes of uncertain lineage, with strong presence of black and white hair). I think the plethora of dogs out there is a wonderful cornucopia of variety. It is also the basis of a lot of dog elitism, à la "My breed is better than yours." How about we try "My dog is different from yours, so I love mine best of all."

Hair grows. Its growth pattern varies. Seems obvious. Some hair grows to a fixed length and stops growing. That is called definitive hair. That is not the same as hair that grows for the whole life of the hair, which is called angora. If hair grew at an inch (2.5 cm) a month, and lasted on average three months, it would on average always look 3 inches (8 cm) long. That is not definitive growth, because each hair kept growing until it fell out, so all the hairs together just averaged out to 3 inches, with some strands longer and some shorter. Definitive hair is all the same length, unless it is new and just growing in. In humans, most hair is definitive except for the hair on one's head. That is angora. On a dog, most hair in most breeds is definitive.

Most dog coats are made of two obvious layers. The one you see is a colored, coarse hair, called **guard hair**, which serves to protect the main coat. These hairs tend to be long, thick, flat in cross section, strong, and coarse. They grow with a grain, or they lie in a direction. If you pet your average dog from head to tail, it feels easy. Go against the grain, literally rubbing the fur the wrong way, and it is difficult. In the wild, this facilitated shedding rain and ensuring sun protection. Guard hair gives most dogs their coat color and shape, certainly true in wolves.

Guard hairs lay over a shorter, far denser insulting layer called **underhair**. Like guard hair, this inner coat is also definitive hair. Underhair is soft, often 10 times as numerous as the guard hairs scattered in the coat. Each underhair is super-insulating and relatively easily damaged. Underhair is often drab in color. While guard hairs are far less numerous than underhairs, they make up most of the visible coat of most dogs. Guard hairs tend to be straight and strong. Most underhair is straight, too, but can sometimes be curly in the wild. Coloration in hair comes from a couple of pigments, one that does shades of red and yellow and one that does shades of black and brown. White and gray hairs are simply absent of or with less color pigments and with varying structures and density of air pockets. Note that a gray dog can be from gray hair, or a combination of black and white hairs. Our gray BC, Wish, is actually well-mixed black and white hairs despite looking mostly gray. This is called merle. Hair texture is also genetic, and it varies by how the keratin is used to make the hair. Thus each breed ends up with some standards for hair, and every dog is pretty much unique in its exact genetic makeup.

Hair patterns

All the variation we see in domestic dog hair such as growth pattern or color, is simple genetic variation for traits. It wouldn't hurt you to refresh your knowledge of genetics covered in Chapter 1, but you don't have to. It is not like I am going to stop by and quiz you. Probably. Over domestication history, we selected for combinations that pleased us or served some functional purpose. For example, if you breed out the undercoat, you get a single-coated dog like a Poodle, with coarser, tougher guard hair. Breed out the top coat, and you get a single coat of soft underhair. For the purists, "fur" refers to this softer underhair hair, so a beaver fur coat would have had the guard hairs shaved even to the underfur and would be mostly soft undercoat. You can still find the shafts of the guard hair scattered in, but they no longer stand out over the fur because they were trimmed. Water dogs need excellent insulation to dive into cold water, and were bred to have thick undercoats. Think Newfoundlands.

I find petting my dog to be very soothing, for me and presumably for them. I run my hand down their back, and I can't help but scratch under the chin and behind the ear. My fingers are in their hair, through their hair, and unconsciously I am feeling for familiar sensations. My dogs have different coats than yours, and each of ours feels a bit different from each other. Blindfolded I would have no trouble telling Beaker from Tattoo from Gromit from Blizzard from Wish from Cricket. Toss a Standard Poodle into that mix and it would feel worlds apart. Or an Afghan. Dog coats come in many versions. The hair has textures, different lengths, and colors. Let's look at the biology that causes that, because it sure isn't all based on your choice of shampoo.

Hair texture

Hair texture is genetically controlled, so breeds run common in texture. For example, hair can be straight or curly, wiry or not, short or long. Wiry coats are made of denser guard hairs that are twisted, giving a rough feel. They were originally bred to be almost an armor to protect the dog from harsh environments. Many people like them because they don't shed. However, all dogs shed. Wiry coats just tend to hold the loose hairs in place and they need to be brushed out. Single top-coated dogs really have a second coat of underhair, it is just very thin and reduced, so they are not really single coats. Texture and hair length can vary on different parts of the body, so you get tufts or beards. Classic wiry coats include Poodles and Fox Terriers. Multi-length hair on Border Collies show wings on the back legs and a classic ruff. Breed differently, and you get a Border Collie with a smooth coat of shorter guard hairs.

Hair color

Color originated in wild dogs to serve camouflage needs. Most domestic dogs still show lighter-colored belly hair. In nature, we call that countershading. It helps offset the shadow of the body, making it harder to see an animal in sunlight or bright moonlight. Genes govern color. There is a gene for how brown the hair will be, and shades of this come from how dilute the brown pigment is and how much air is in the hair shaft, so you can get chocolate brown, sedge, mahogany, liver, etc. Another gene regulates shades of red to yellow, where yellow is a fully recessive trait (which just means that if you get even one red copy from either parent, you won't get yellow). You mix reds or yellows with browns and vary the air pockets and the amount of pigment and you can get an enormous palette of shades of hair color. Another gene makes all of the pigments black. Now you can add in any shade of gray by diluting the black. Change the pattern of color in the hair shaft itself and you get sable hair, which is black tipped. Hair can be colored differently in patches over the body, think brown and black separations in Rottweilers, Doberman, and Dachshunds. If one kind of patch is white, it is usually called bi-color in the dog, although brown with black is also really bi-colored. Black and whites include Border Collies, but also Dalmatians. Brown and whites include King Charles Spaniels. Mix three colors, you naturally get a tri-color like that found in Collies, Shelties, or Papillons. Brindles show color variation in wavelike patterns. Saddle patterns present with a black patch over the back, as is common in many terriers and German Shepherd Dogs. Omit the hair altogether and you get a hairless breed like the Alunku, or mostly hairless like a Chinese Crested Dog. The variations seem endless.

This is not the book for an in-depth discussion of genetics covering which color alleles crossed with which other alleles give you what color. Whole books and lengthy college courses go into this singular topic. It provides endless fascination for some people. But we can easily look at the eight known genes to see what the toolbox has in it. The agouti gene, with something like five alleles or variations, covers the color banding in hairs and how the pigment is expressed in the yellow and brown varieties, or all black in the case of one of those alleles. Another gene, the B-locus or the brown/black gene, governs the production of an enzyme that controls the production of melanin. This gets you some of the brown to black patterns and shades. A third gene covers how dilute the pigment produced by other genes will be. Another gene covers color patterns on the face much like the agouti gene does for the body, giving you masks in some dogs. A fifth gene determines how dark black hair is and where on the coat black will show. This leads to all-black dogs or dogs with patterns of black. Another gene determines if the coat will be normal or merle. Merle is patches of reduced color in a coat. Our merle Border Collie has black patches, and also gray patches that really are black patches diluted with white hairs. Interestingly, this gene also affects eye pigmentation. People see our merle Wish and think she is blind because she has patterns of color in her eyes. We call them agate eyes because they look like those beautiful rocks we collect on the shores of Lake Superior while Wish persistently chases waves. On the other hand, eye color in Huskies like my first dog is unrelated to hair color. A variation on another gene can affect the merle gene. That variation is found only in Great Danes leading to harlequin pattern of a white base with black splattered patches. Finally, an eighth gene covers the white spotting on dogs made by several different alleles. So eight genes, each located apart from each other scattered over eight of the

39 chromosomes, each gene with multiple alleles or variations at the gene, leads to the cornucopia of color patters in domestic dogs. Where coloration is linked to unusual body shape like a bobbed tail, it is because the gene is on the same chromosome as the other and they travel together, only rarely getting separated in the crossing over of DNA in meiosis.

Diet affects hair, and better diets tend to show shinier and softer coats. All dogs continuously shed, just as you do. Those few hairs of yours in the shower drain are your daily turnover in head hair. You are shedding body hair, too. Don't go blaming your dog for all of the hair you find on the floor! Hormones can affect hair shedding, so many dogs blow a summer coat of thinner underfur in exchange for a thicker winter coat. Shedding is mostly genetically controlled, but unusual shedding in a given dog often indicates disease. Dogs who shed less are often called hypoallergenic, thought to reduce allergic responses. Actually most dog allergies in people are from dog saliva and dander, or dead skin. Most allergic responses are more individually unique to the dog, and not breed or sex unique.

You can plainly see that even in one breed like my Border Collies, you can get lots of variation. There are smooth coats and rough coats, variations in color patterns, two-colored brown and white or black and white that can also show as gray, and tri-colors. The pattern of spots and patches vary. I can easily tell each of my dogs apart, and I can clearly see that they are all or mostly Border Collie, and distinguishable from other breeds. With so much variation, there must be hundreds of genes at work, maybe thousands, right? Nope. Eight known and located genes cover coat color. There may be six more still to be found, so at best 14. Remember, that is eight sites on the DNA, but each site can have a number of traits, called alleles. Color gets really tricky fast because it involves so many genes.

Hair length and texture
Texture and length use another four genes. Hair length is determined by one gene with two alleles, short and long. If you get a short gene from both Mom and Dad, your hair is short. Get long genes from both parents and the hair is long. If you get one allele of each, the hair is intermediate. Long in one breed is different from long in another, so this only covers hair length relative to parental hair length. This gene can be expressed all over the body, or differently in different body parts. Another gene covers how wiry the hair is and if it is expressed in facial features. Get the wiry gene from both the puppy's mom and dad, you get coarse, wiry hair and prominent facial tufts of hair like beards and eyebrows on a dog; get it from neither and you have smooth hair with no hair facial features. One allele from one parent and not the other is intermediate, but still wiry. A third gene covers how curly the hair is. Get one copy of curly from each parent and the hair is very curly. Two copies of straight, and it is straight. One curly and one straight gives wavy hair. You could set up a matrix of hair length (three variations), wiriness (three variations), and curliness (three variations) and you would get 27 patterns just for hair texture. Just texture. Just three of the four genes for texture.

The fourth texture gene governs shedding, not actual hair texture. In the wild, puppies show a single undercoat of smooth hair that is not hormonally or seasonally shed. This gene covers whether that puppy trait is retained in adults (recall the longer discussion of neoteny in the first chapter). It also interacts with length and texture, making that 27-cell matrix of possibilities even more complex. A couple of other extra genes such as hairlessness, or a ridgeback, exist in some breeds.

Wild dogs were shorter-haired, straight and not wiry, with a wide variety of color patterns that fit local environments so the predator wolf could remain unseen by the prey. Variations from that are all mutations. In the wild, those mutations tend to be selectively removed from the population, either because the individual with the mutation is less successful at survival or it is less likely to mate. Wild dogs in colder climates were selected for thicker underfur. This explains why pelts from the arctic wolves historically were worth so much more than from wolves in the warmer southern places. Hair protected the dog from scrapes with trees and rocks, but also from biting insects. A thick coat of hair can even stop many bites from other canids getting through to the victim. Domesticated animals, including dogs, show great variation as we select and mix and match the various combinations. This is what keeps breeders in business, and is simultaneously the bane of their existence. They can get some consistent coats with interesting patterns with some unknown recessive trait lurking in the gene pool. That trait might not become expressed until some other blood line with that same rare recessive trait lurking in the gene pool is crossed, lands together, and is expressed. That leaves some breeders scratching their heads in disbelief. The good ones go digging to find out what happened, contributing to the endless supply of knowledge gained through generations of trial and error.

Skin

At its most basic, skin keeps the outside out and the inside in. By holding hair, it grows the layer we just examined that keeps abrasion at bay, shields from rain and snow, blocks the sun from burning the skin, and keeps biting parasites and predators farther from their target. Hair also gives coloration that aids in hunting. Skin is a lot more than just a base for hair. It holds the capillaries and larger blood vessels that regulate heat gain and loss, and carry immune agents to fight disease and heal wounds. Sure, it also keeps intestines from dragging on the ground, but really, muscles do the bulk of that. Skin protects the muscles from all that environmental damage.

Naturally, we need to start by looking at skin itself. In our average 30-pound (14 kg) dog, the skin covers a bit over half of a square meter, or half a square yard, and weighs about 3 pounds (1.4 kg). More in your Mastiff. Less in your Papillion. It has to be flexible enough to allow movement but strong enough to retain shape. If beauty is only skin deep, then beauty is between 0.02 to 0.2 inches, or 0.5 and 4 mm deep. Despite how thin it is, it plays a crucial life-saving role.

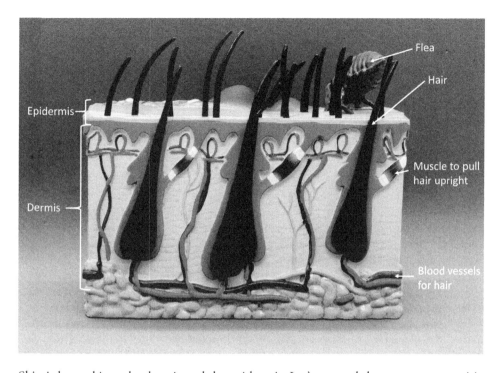

Skin is layered into the dermis and the epidermis. Let's pretend that you are a parasitic animal attacking your dog from the outside, gnawing your way in farther than a tick will go. First, you have to get past the hair. Remember, each hair is innervated, so the host will feel you wiggling your way in and try to stop you with a scratch of the nails or a nip with their incisors. If you get past the active behavioral defenses, you reach the outer layer of the epidermis. It is made up of dead skin cells that are heavily infused with keratin, making it tough and watertight. Skin is largely a waterproof bag. In order to lose water from it you have to sweat it out through special glands; otherwise you will pee it out or breathe it out. This layer is constantly being sloughed off. Any random epidermis cell lasts maybe three weeks. Your dog is shedding millions of skin cells a day; they rain off your dog and into your carpet, feeding a whole ecosystem of microscopic critters that you do not want to think about. It is this shower of cells that bloodhounds follow and track so well. Where skin is thick, like on the foot pads, it makes a really good shoe. Where it is thin, such as on the eyelids, it is only three to five cell layers thick. The lower layers of the epidermis are basically increasingly live cells with decreasing amounts of keratin. The epidermis has no blood vessels. It gets the nutrients and oxygen by diffusion from the dermis below it.

The epidermis covers the dermis, the layer of blood-infused, nerve-infested cells that you hate to cut into because it hurts. The dermis has pigment cells at the outer layer, giving dog skin its color patches (you can see these if you part the hair and look at the skin). In humans, this gives you your skin tone. Darker skin gives more sun protection, but in well-haired dogs, this matters mainly on the nose. The dermis has connective tissue, mainly the protein collagen, to give skin its elastic but strong shape. It houses the cells that color and grow hair and the nerves for touch, pain, itch, and temperature. Imbedded within and throughout it is a blood network that is opened (flushed) or closed through muscles in the small arteries called arterioles, allowing for dissipation or retention of heat. Variations in the tiny muscles attached to the base of each hair allow erecting the hair to make the fur thicker and hence more insulating, or to give you "goose bumps" when cold. See, your hair is trying to be a good insulator, you just lost most of the hair you needed because you are from the sweltering heat of the Rift Valley in Eastern Africa. Your dog has arctic wolves in its blood. At the base of the skin is a layer of connective tissue that glues the skin to the layers that surround underlying large muscles. There is often a layer of fat under the skin, too, that adds insulation, padding, and protection.

Skin has two types of glands. Oil, or sebaceous glands, produce sebum. This waxy, oily material lubricates and protects the skin and hair and has some antibiotic properties. Skin also has sweat glands that release a watery substance: sweat. Perspiration. Dripping sweat is a waste of water. Sweat works best in cooling by evaporation. Sweat also carries pheromones that give off unique smells and signals others of the same species, often as a unique identifier. In dogs, sweat glands are found mostly on their feet because that is about the only hairless place. This allows them to leave a scent trail of pheromones. It plays little to no role in cooling. I am about to delve deep into that, so let me repeat that dogs do not cool by sweating. You do. They do not. You are not a dog. They are not people. The crucial difference is that they walk around in a fur coat all day every day, summer and winter. You probably do not. Remember that our thinner-haired dogs still have the skin of those fur-bearing forbears. No sweat glands except on the paws. But also no warm protection on colder days.

Temperature control

Given the proliferation of air-circulating fans I see in dog kennels at summer dog shows, I want to delve deeper into the insulating role of skin, hair, and the well-built dog. Fans move air, which helps with evaporation of water. We humans sweat all over our bodies as a primary way to shed heat. On a hot day, even a small breeze feels great. To us. Dogs are well insulated, like a refrigerator. Their skin and hair insulate from extremes of heat and cold. Dogs are endotherms. They produce a lot of heat burning sugars to make ATP to stay alive. Recall that most of the calories (Calories if you are using the dietary measure) you consume are to feed your metabolism. Dogs are well insulated, so losing heat can be a real problem. Dogs have to spend energy to cool off in temperatures above 85 degrees Fahrenheit (30 degrees C) and spend energy to warm up in temperatures below 68 degrees (20 degrees C). This varies a lot by breed, so use it as a starting point for your dog's thermal neutral zone.

Any organism sheds heat through three means: radiation, convection, and conduction. Heat is constantly lost through radiation, so reflective sunshades for cars that block the sun's radiation also reflect radiative heat back to the dog inside, but way less than the sun's heat, so keep using them in sunny environments. Reflective foil jackets and survival blankets work the same way by blocking radiating heat loss. The primary way you (you the human, not you the dog if your dog is reading along with us) lose heat is convection, that cool breeze blowing across your skin, evaporating water directly off of your skin. When the liquid sweat evaporates, not when it drips off, but when it goes straight from liquid to gas on your skin, it takes away a lot of heat from your body. Heat can be directly lost by dumping off hot liquids like dripping sweat, drooling, and peeing, but it is not a lot and won't serve the need by itself. The process of vaporization in water, when water molecules move from liquid to gas, removes significantly more heat than dripping or drooling hot water can ever do, and it conserves water at the same time. Active evaporation is a great, efficient cooler. This is why you are covered in sweat glands and, even on a cool day, can sweat a pint (half a liter) of water. Naked skin with no hair equals lots of surface area for evaporation. Yeah you. It likely allowed humans to shed the extra heat that large brains generate or that we built up running miles and kilometers after prey on the savannahs.

Remember, your dog only sweats through areas not covered by hair in ancestral wolves. Since hair effectively blocks evaporation, dogs sweat through their feet. That accounts for little heat loss. Hairless breeds are no different. Our artificial selecting for different dog coat texture, length, and hair density did not include selecting for different placement of sweat glands. Hairy or hairless, dogs only sweat through their feet. Drooling accounts for some heat loss by dropping hot saliva out of the body. Mostly dogs cool through evaporation in their lungs. Think of that as internal sweating. The heat loss from evaporation occurs there, deep in the lungs.

Remember those dog crates with their fans blowing on dogs? These fans typically do remarkably little for your dog. They do make people feel like they are helping, however. Nothing like a good placebo. Except once you understand this, you can actually help your dogs lose excess heat with those fans you already bought. Fans don't cool air, they move whatever air is around them. Say it with me: Fans do not cool air, they just move it around. Blowing air feels cool to you because you are evaporating sweat off your skin. Not so for your dog. For an air-circulating fan to do much to help the cooling process for a dog, it would need to be deep in the lungs. That would hurt, those spinning blades knocking into the alveoli. Your dog has that covered already with their own air circulatory system. It is called panting, the rapid in and out of air unassociated with breathing. Rapid as in several hundred shallow breaths per minute. Fans outside the dog blowing hot air on the dog minimally aid heat-shedding abilities since the evaporation happens deep in the lungs. You feel better, but the breeze on the dog does very little to help.

Let's apply a bit of science here and find a way to actually cool our dogs using fans. Stop blowing hot air on your dog and blow cold air; that can help quite a bit. That puts colder air into the lungs where evaporation occurs, and that will help them shed heat. Take that nice fan you bought for your dog, and make sure it blows over something cool like a frozen 2-liter bottle of water, or a soaking wet towel, which through evaporation will cool, allowing cooler air to make it into your dog's warm lungs.

There are other ways to increase evaporative heat loss. Soaking a dog to the skin, and then exposing them to a fan does help as long as they stay wet, because the evaporation at the surface pulls hot water from the skin to the surface of the fur to evaporate. That is kind of like doing the sweating for your dog, right? But once your dog dries, the fan is not doing any real good anymore. The insulating hair blocks heat as well as cold, so shaving a dog does not help cool it unless you move into conductive heat loss, like putting a cool surface on the dog, such as one of those refrigerateable gel jackets or a cool, wet towel. More on that shortly. Shaving a dog actually makes lung evaporation less effective because there is no body insulation from the warm environment, allowing the dog to gain heat from the warm air around them. See, once you understand how heat is lost, you can choose a strategy that will help your dog.

Dogs also have longer noses than we do, which matters. Well, most of them do. I am not really trying to comment on your nose, as I have not seen it. This is about the dog's nose. If your dog does not, like a Pug or a Bulldog, listen up. The long noses are filled with a labyrinth of bones called the turbinates. Air going in or coming out of the lungs passes through this maze of bones covered in mucus membranes. Noses help condition the air, warming it on cold days and cooling it on warm days. It is easier to picture with cold winter air. Cold air can't hold much water, so it is dry. Air coming in on a cold, dry day is humidified and warmed by the turbinates before it goes to the lungs. On its way back out, heat and water are actively reabsorbed. Similarly, on hot days, hot air coming in is cooled to body temperature and then extra heat is expelled from the body when the dog exhales. Basically the nose via the turbinates handles the extreme variation in outside air, getting it to body temperature and humidity. Then it reverses the process as the air goes out. This allows it to condition the next breath. All this keeps the lungs from drying out and getting hit with a blast of cold air at each breath on cold days, and helps a bit with cooling on hot days. Dogs with reduced rostrums, i.e., short noses, can't do this as well, so exercise more caution on really cold and really hot days.

You might be about to point out that dogs seem to enjoy a breeze on their face and try to use that as evidence that a breeze matters. Dogs seem to gleefully lie by fans or stick their heads out moving car windows. Breezes do matter, but not much for heat loss, of that we can be certain. It likely goes back to the breeze's ability to keep flying and biting bugs off. Wild animals go to great lengths to get rid of clouds of biting mosquitoes or to avoid annoying biting flies. Just because your dog likes to stick their head out the car window, even to avoid biting flies, does not make that a good idea. A word on that. One insect in the eye at 70 mph (110 kph), and your dog can lose their vision. It will at least scratch the cornea. That wind also dries eyes from wind chill and dehydration, and grit gets imbedded in the eyes. Seriously consider dog goggles if you want your dog to do this. If you do want to do this, I think you are also ignoring the basic physics of vehicle accidents. You put your dog at great risk for ejection, and that is not as painless in real life as in a James Bond ejection seat. Every time I see a dog with their head poking out of a moving car or truck, I wish I could tell the driver to stop it now. Every wonder why you were told not to stick your hands and feet outside a rapidly moving vehicle? Think it is OK for a dog?

A fan that blows hot air out of a car does help keep dogs cool by lowering the internal car temperature, which is good. Caveat: Cars do not sweat. Even in a cool breeze, if they are closed up, the inside of a car will get hot. In fact, because cars do not sweat, the breeze really does not matter except if it helps expel hot air from open windows. Close the widows, and the breeze that feels cool to you does nothing to cool the car. Nothing. Nada. Cars are like small greenhouses. With closed windows, their temperature soars in direct sunlight, even on cool, breezy days (remember, the breeze does not matter to cooling the car). No amount of panting by a dog works in a car that is much over the dog's body temperature. The internal temperature of a closed-up car on a sunny day rises by 34 degrees F (19 degrees C) in 30 minutes, 43 degrees F (24 degrees C) in an hour. On a 70-degree F (21 degrees C) summer day (when the sun is high in the sky — this works less effectively on fall and spring days when the sun is closer to the horizon), all closed up, a 70 degree F (21 degrees C) interior temperature of the vehicle rises to 113 degrees F (45 degrees C). With outside temperatures starting nearer 100 degrees in the U.S. (38 degrees anywhere else), cars can become lethal to a dog in as little as six minutes (that is six minutes anywhere). Open vehicle windows allow heat to escape; however, smashing a window to help a dog that is not in heat stress subjects them to flying tempered glass, and you to a lawsuit. Is the dog comfortably sleeping, or is it passed out from heat stroke? Get a professional by calling a police officer before you choose to act. If you are parked at Hoover Dam ignoring all of the posted warning signs of hot desert sun, and you close your dog inside your vehicle, someone is likely to act on their own to protect the dog. Minutes matter. Be proactive by protecting your dog with opened windows that let heat out, sunshades that block solar radiation, or at least some clear evidence that you understand the heat risk to your dog with a sign on the dash that shows the time you left the car so people know if your dog was in there for very long. Most of us think of a dog locked in a hot car like we would a human baby. The law puts the dog at only slightly above a bag of groceries. When laws and human values do not agree, and people's ethics are in the mix, do not be surprised that people act. I most certainly am not calling for civil disobedience and car window smashing. Again, that can endanger a dog, too, with all that flying tempered glass. I am calling for dog people to be proactive protecting their dogs in the first place. Maybe take your dog home before you stop at the store on that hot, sunny day.

How many dogs die this way? PETA (People for the Ethical Treatment of Animals) says 100 per year in the United States; the American Veterinary Medical Association says maybe hundreds. Given how many dogs are left in cars in the summer, this seems like an incredibly low-probability event. Then again, if we are talking about my dogs, one death is too many. Don't do this!

Keep your dog cool in the summer, warm in the winter, and let nature do her work at thermoregulation. That means your dog needs a good diet of nutritious food and plenty of fresh, clean water. Water lets them pant effectively and lose heat through lung evaporation and some through drooling. A well-hydrated dog can tolerate more exposure to heat before they start to warm their internal temperature. Just because your dog is panting does not mean they are under great heat stress. Usually it means the opposite: All is well, and normal lung-based evaporative cooling is underway. But a drooling, panting dog with an extended and spade-shaped tongue is under heat stress.

In addition to radiative heat gain and loss, and convective heat gain and loss, all things get and lose heat through conduction. Conductive heat gain or loss is when a colder substance directly absorbs heat from a warmer surface with which it is in direct contact. Cold is not a thing. It is just the absence of heat. So cold does not move, heat does. Lie down on a cool floor. The cold does not move into you, some heat moves out. That is conductive heat loss. Put a cooling pad on your dog's abdomen where there is less hair, that cools the dog directly through conduction. Keeping your dog lean reduces fat, which insulates, and that mostly helps dogs because their hair does a better job insulating at freezing temperatures. Stop right now if you are about to say something like, "See, I let my dog have extra fat because their coat is so thin and they need the extra insulation to deal with heat and cold." Your logic is admirable but misplaced, as it ignores all the ill effects that being overweight carries, from heart disease to arthritis. If your dog has thin hair, don't compensate with a layer of fat; get an insulating dog coat. Dogs with shortened rostrums, or noses, like Pugs and Bulldogs, do not pant as effectively and therefore are not as good at shedding heat. Be extra careful with them.

Temperature extremes

A note about cold and wind chill. During the winter for us northerners, every weather forecast mentions the wind chill. Say it is freezing out. With additional wind, the air will feel even colder. But only to those of us who lose heat through skin evaporation. Wind chill affects us. Dry air on our skin evaporates moisture-sucking heat from our skin, and we feel colder than the ambient temperature. Wind chill does not affect your car or its ability to start in the cold. Your car does not sweat. Your dog does not sweat. Wind chill is largely immaterial to your dog. See, your dog actually evolved to survive quite well in heat and cold. I say "largely" because your dog's nose will be moist from exhaled air, and that makes the dog nose sensitive to wind chill.

Dogs can tolerate a body temperature a few degrees higher than humans. But once they get warm enough to overtax their ability to lose heat through panting, core temperature starts to rise. Signs of this can be subtle, but include excess drooling and a very extended and widened tongue that maximizes surface area for evaporation off the tongue. When it is hot out, slow down. Give your dog lots of water. Keep them out of hot places like hot cars. Feel the pavement; if it burns your hands it will likely burn your dog's feet. Soak your dog in cool (not cold) water. Place cooling gels or wet towels on their belly between the back legs. Likewise, but opposite, in the winter. Does your dog have thick foot pads? If not, their pads can freeze. Booties can help, but most dogs take a lot of training for those to stay on. Do dog coats help in the winter? Sure. Most normally coated dogs are fine down to well below freezing. Dogs with thin or absent undercoats (fur) need extra insulation.

Teeth and claws

Teeth and claws constitute two parts of active defense for dogs. Earlier, in our discussion about digestion, we saw how teeth play a significant role in processing food, and even serve as a generalized toolbox for dogs. A dog skull sits on my desktop, next to my computer monitor. I actually own hundreds of animal skulls that I use for teaching, and I keep a dog skull on my desk for the same reason medieval philosophers kept a human skull on theirs. It is called a *memento mori*, or a reminder of the inevitability of death. Those philosophers and scholars wanted to be reminded of the brevity of their own lives. I want to be reminded that my dogs will die too soon, and that each day is therefore priceless and precious. I cannot relate how many times I see that skull staring at me and think of Beaker, Tattoo, or Blizzard. Then I set down the work I am doing to go for a walk with one of my living dogs. For the record, I purchased this skull for use in dog classes. I could not bring myself to have one of my own loved ones on my desktop in skull form. And now I need to stop for a bit and take Gromit outside. He is nearly 15 and his kidneys are starting to give out. This paragraph reminds me that he is more important than this book. The book will wait. He will not.

That is not why I raise the skull here. For almost any breed or mix of dog, when you look at a skull, the large jaws covered in many sharp teeth stand out, particularly the canines, for which dogs in general get the genus name *Canis*, and the family name for all dogs, Canidae. Canine comes from the Latin for dog, and naming the most prominent dog teeth after dogs makes a lot of sense. There are four of these, two upper and two lower, one set on each side of the mouth. When a canid is taking down prey, the other teeth help hold on while the canines puncture deep. A nip with the front incisors might only grip hair, or bruise skin. Typically, to pierce the skin of whatever the dog is attacking, the canines will go in far. In the wild, canines damage muscles and split blood vessels. Add in the back and forth shaking motion of a dog's head, powered by large and strong neck muscles, clamped tight by huge jaw muscles, and you have an attacker that won't let go. Dogs evolved as pack animals. Let's say you are a 200-pound (90 kg) deer. A pack of wolves attacks. One or two of the wolves clamp down on you and you are no longer mobile enough to fend off the others because now you have 100-pound (45 kg) weights on your backside. It is not at all difficult to see the value of the canines both in procuring food and in defending against attacks. In wolves, the roots of the upper canines go way up into the skull, halfway to the eye sockets, deeper than the exposed portions of the tooth. Short of breaking, that tooth won't give way. It is made of bone and coated in enamel, the hardest substance a mammal makes, with a light core of keratin and the bone form called dentine.

Claws or nails on a dog are mostly to provide traction. Recall that, unlike a cat's, these are nonretractable. If your dog does not run a lot on hard surfaces, you know how quickly nails grow. A brief look at their structure will show how even well-worn nails can be sharp and provide a good last line of defense for a dog. Why last line? If a dog is flipped over and the belly is exposed, it is only the claws that are going to fend off an attacker. And they likely will. Animal attackers need to use their teeth, and that puts their face right up next to the defender's nails. The nails are at the far ends of well-muscled limbs, so they can hit with great speed and strength.

Nails have a pretty interesting structure. First, they are mainly composed of non-living keratin, the same super-strong protein that makes up hair. I have a general rule, ignored more than followed by the one in the house who selects our dogs: no black nails. It is so hard to see where to trim! If your dog has clear nails, or you have a friend's dog with them, take a few minutes to examine them closely. The nail grows in a curve. The topmost layer is called the unguis, and it is the hardest part of the nail, usually very distinct from the next layer, called the subunguis. That is made of a softer form of keratin protein. The effect of that partnering of a very hard layer with a softer layer means that the softer part wears faster than the harder layer, and that leaves a sharp edge where the two meet. That edge is what gives nails their grip and their value. Both of these parts are dead and without nerves. The inner part, the quick, is very alive. You can trim the dead parts to your heart's delight, except that for most dogs, the rest of the toe feels as if it is being handled, and many dogs resist that.

Ha. I just reread "…many dogs resist that." Our dogs used to place a sentinel on the nail trimming tools. Maybe they set an alarm. You could walk by the trimmer with no worries. So much as touch the tools and the dogs would disappear. Poof. If you could locate them, you would find them in the dark recesses of the house. After that, we had to call two linemen from the local high school football team to hold them down. You'd think we were torturing them. The dogs certainly believed it.

It does not take an expert to see the problem that develops. We want our dogs to do something, like accept having their nails trimmed. It is inherently challenging, as toes are sensitive, necessary to move through the woods effectively and snag that deer in the good old wolf days. We start with a difficult situation, they learn what it means, then they do what we would do: resist. We apply force, they resist more. This all spirals out of control. There is usually a better way, which once we figured it out, changed everything. Bribery. I mean training, but that is pretty similar. We made nail trimming fun with lots of cuddle time and treats (I still pay off per foot, and the dogs do not let me forget it). Over time, Blizzard got so that once you grabbed the tools of torture, he would follow you until you sat down, and then immediately crawl up into your lap. You trimmed his toes, and would start working on one of the other dogs, and he would try to climb up in your lap for an extra trim. That is what success looks like.

The base of the nail shows pink when viewed from the side, assuming you followed the no-black-nails rule of Lewis. The base is where the nail fattens or gets thicker, usually top to bottom. It is full of the cells that grow the nail, so it has blood and nerves. Cut into that and you get bleeding and a very sore toe. With a clear nail, you can usually avoid that, if your dog holds still, and that can be a big "if"! With black nails, you have to look for where the nail widens from top to bottom, best seen by looking underneath the nail (where the unguis joins the subunguis) and avoid cutting too far into that. You might wonder why the nails are so innervated. Like your fingers, it helps the dog know where their toes are and what the surface they are on feels like. Some dogs, like my dog Blizzard, love to get their nails trimmed and come running for the joy of being held and becoming the center of attention. Some, like Wish or Gromit, have histories that color the experience. Gromit has very arthritic feet, and Wish has several times broken a toe. To them, toe pain has left a lasting impact. They would not choose to let us trim their nails without a lot of extra training, or was that behavior modification? They do not seem to grasp that long nails are also painful to them and in the long run can damage toes and leg tendons. Logic and reasoning do not always work, and particularly painful episodes leave long-lasting impressions.

TOUR 8

INTERNAL DEFENSES:
THE IMMUNE SYSTEM

Help, my dog is under attack! There are germs everywhere. Literally everywhere. What to do? Prevention, then a generalized response, and finally call in the specialists. Think about how you care for a dog. You work to prevent problems including injuries and diseases. If they happen, you take general non-specialized action. Once you know the details, you use a specialist like a veterinarian if needed. You try to prevent a cut. If one happens, you stop the flow.

Why have an immune system?

You are sitting in a warm space, not, I presume, in a refrigerator or freezer. If you left a pound of steak or raw chicken at room temperature, how long would it be before it started to rot and decay? You measure that in hours. The smell would be noticeable in a day, and the meat would become unrecognizable in a week. Ever wonder why the same thing does not happen to you, your dog or, over a longer period, a living tree? After all, a tree can live to be hundreds of years old. But once it dies, it starts to rot. Quickly. In some measure, being alive means having an immune system that functions. Without it, one really is dead meat.

The immune system of mammals is the result of almost 4 billion years of evolutionary warfare. Even simple bacteria, the first forms of life, had to be able to fight off viruses and other bacteria. All living organisms have at least the first two parts of an immune system, a layer of prevention coupled with first-responding nonspecific defenses. As time passed, the attacks from would-be parasites grew more sophisticated, and so did the defenses. It has been billions of years of ever-increasing sophisticated attacks and defenses, an unbridled arms race. Mammals are a pretty recent invention, inheriting many traits shared with reptiles and even fishes. Your typical dog has some sophisticated tools at work all the time every day to fight a largely unseen world of viruses, bacteria, fungi, and even larger attackers like parasitic worms, ticks, and fleas. As if that were not enough, the immune system has to recognize when the body's own cells have turned traitor.

What occurs at the molecular level is complex and well-studied, but with much still to learn. We don't need to know all of the details here to understand the basic lines of defense. It will certainly help you understand what is at work all the time, why good nutrition matters, and what to look for when things go awry.

Bacteria are everywhere

Let's set the stage, or review the war zone. I first want to make it clear to you how common bacteria are and how worrying about them in daily life makes no sense at all. I am also not naive enough to think that all of people's worry about bacteria is rational or even needs to make sense to people. Bacteria evolved 3 billion years before vertebrate life. They filled the whole planet, from hot springs with boiling water, deep in bedrock, and certainly over every surface of the Earth and up into the atmosphere. The rest of life evolved buried in this carpet of bacteria, and could not have existed without being able to defend itself. Literally everything you touch is covered with bacteria; you have about 6 pounds (3 kg) of bacteria on and in you, and frankly, all but about 0.1 percent are harmless to you, your dog, and most of life. They are just doing their own thing, and (if they could hope) hoping to not be eaten by some protozoan or a slime mold. In fact, those harmless bacteria take up space and resources from the harmful ones, helping to hold the bad guys' numbers in check.

Think of the average yard of grass with a few weeds. If you sprayed a general herbicide on it, the grass would die leaving lots of space for weeds. Most of the time when you wipe things off with an antibacterial wipe, such as the now ubiquitous wipes at grocery stores for cart handles, you are killing the bacterial version of the healthy grass that crowds out the weeds. The anti-viral properties are sure nice, of course, especially with COVID-19 lurking about. But bacteria can double in numbers in as little as 20 minutes, so by the time you are done shopping with your "clean" cart, the bacteria have doubled a couple of times, and guess which grow fastest? The pathogenic ones. Face it, the world belongs to bacteria, and most of them are actually helping you, or are at least immaterial to you.

The average surface has something like 1,000 bacteria per square inch (150 per cm2), including your just-washed hands and the inside of the typical faucet despite chlorinated water. Kitchens have twice that. Your phone has about 25,000 per square inch (4,000 per cm2). And to be clear, the toilet seat you so worry about has only about 500 bacteria per square inch (75 per cm2). However, it is not the number of bacteria per area that you should be concerned about, because you are literally breathing bacteria as we spend this time together. It is absolutely the types of bacteria you should care about, and where the bad ones are most likely to be. Remember, most bacteria are good, benign to us, and occupying space the bad bacteria could otherwise occupy. Bacteria are common on your food, your dog's food, in active infections like wounds, or being generated by other sick dogs (or people), such as being around active kennel cough. If you are healthy, with a normal immune system, you could literally lick most surfaces and be fine. Your dog certainly is licking almost everything, and their immune system is no better than yours. The immune system is fighting attacks all day every day, and easily overwhelms the random pathogens. Where pathogens concentrate and start with higher numbers, that is where you have to pay attention.

For example, you do need to clean your kitchen after cutting up raw meat for your dog, because the pathogens that attack are concentrating on the now dead flesh that lacks an immune system. You need to wash up after cleaning that infection on your dog's leg, because it is loaded with pathogenic bacteria. You really don't need to worry about the random tapeworm egg (actually a sac of eggs called a proglottid) scattered somewhere and all dried up you encounter out on your walk; it is the concentrated fresh mass in a pile of feces from an infected host that you should watch out for. Choose your battles and recognize that most assaults on your dog are handled quite fine without you. We intervene on most pathogens we detect because a low percent of the time they cause great harm. Most doctors and veterinarians will tell you that left unattended, the body generally heals pretty well on its own. Not always fast, or pain free, however. Since the penalty for those few times would not be good, we intervene.

How the immune system works

Prevention, first responders, specialists. Prevention of infection starts with the hair all over your dog. Bacteria and viruses from the environment land there first. The hair itself, covered with the natural sebum the hair glands make, reduces bacteria counts.

Sunlight is a great sterilizer, so hair also serves to delay bacterial contact with skin, giving sunlight a chance to reduce their population. Prevention extends to the water-tight bacteria-resistant keratinized skin covering most of your dog. Most bacteria cannot get inside unless there is a break in the skin. Cuts and bug bites are common sources of skin breaks.

What about those other openings in the skin, the natural ones? Some of these guard the body by physically expelling invaders. Urine is a one-way flow that expels invading bacteria from the urinary tract. For what it is worth, if there is no urinary tract infection, urine is pretty clean. The gut is lined with mucus glands that help protect it from being digested in its own juices, but it also entraps and expels bacteria out the one-way path from mouth to anus. Wild dogs evolved eating carcasses, not just living prey. Dead foods quickly get bacteria. Dogs evolved particularly sensitive digestive systems to expel bacteria, either through regurgitation or by rapid expulsion out the other end of the digestive tract. Female mammals do in fact have an opening that is not constantly flushed, and it does become infected more frequently than other body openings. The body takes two defensive paths here, and they are similar to that used in the mouth. First, there is a host of benign bacteria growing in those warm, moist areas. These commensal bacteria take up the space other invaders would need. Typically, that colony is started — that is, infected — by the mother's licking of the newborn, because the host bacteria of the vagina and mouth are pretty much the same. The other defense is to keep the outer part of the area dry, because bacteria and fungi need moisture to grow. Most pathogens coming into the body have to get deeper than those openings to find a place to start. Venereal diseases in animals are inserted deep into the host body by external sources. Orally, most pathogens are killed by saliva or stomach acid, or attacked in the throat by the immune system in the tonsils, or in the airway in the adenoids in the back of the nose. The best prevention is to have healthy skin, which comes from a good diet and exercise. What can we do beyond that to help our dogs' immune systems? Clean up concentrated areas of pathogens like surface infections and feces piles. Prevent fleas and ticks with appropriate insecticidal collars, surface treatments, and oral prophylactics. While vaccines are a preventative measure, they work by engaging the third line of defense in the immune system, so I will return to them shortly.

Most immunologists separate the immune system into the cell-mediated response, such as white blood cells, and the humoral or body-fluid response that blood and free-floating antibodies provide. That makes a lot of sense if your goal is to understand the details of how the body makes those defenses. I am going to mix those two together and explain them in terms of first responses and specialized follow-up, looking at those two biologically based divisions together.

In some ways, the circulatory system is the key to first responses in the body. Like a road network, nothing really gets anywhere without flowing along through the bloodstream. Always present, always vigilant, are generalists such as platelets, white blood cells, and signaling molecules. When cells get damaged from an invading virus or bacteria or when they are physically ruptured by trauma, they release molecules that signal the invasion. Capillaries dilate in the area, increasing blood flow, while special white blood cells called neutrophils squeeze out of the blood vessels and attack invaders. The attack can take several forms. It might be that the white blood cells engulf or eat the invaders. Remember, viruses and bacteria are many thousands of times smaller than a blood cell: They might attack and kill the infected host cell. The response to the attack signals is immediate and overwhelming, with first responders attracted to the area of injury or assault. In addition to these cellular responses, there are chemicals floating in the bloodstream that adhere to invading forces, marking them for attack. There are molecules that interfere with a virus's ability to take over host cells. Basically, if an invader is recognizable as not the host, it is attacked by these generalists. Skin infections allow a good visual for this. Such infections become swollen and red because of increased blood flow and a generalized inflammatory response. Pus forms from the corpses of defending cells and attacked bacteria. Bacteria that get away from the zone of attack, often by being carried away by body fluids, are attacked at lymph nodes that are concentrated where limbs or the head joins the body. Other organs, such as the thymus and spleen, play a role in fighting these mobile attackers. This is an ongoing, daily process that happens in a mild background way, unless an infection takes hold. Those are the ones you notice.

In addition to attacking invaders, many host cells start to divide rapidly through errors in DNA or other causes. Some cell types, like skin, blood, and intestinal tissues are already rapidly dividing because they wear out fast and have to be replaced. If unchecked, these become tumors or cancers. Fortunately, most of the time that process also changes the molecular markers outside these cells, and the immune system attacks these as if they were invaders.

Many invasions that get past the other protective barriers, or that do not trigger effective first responders, require specialized cleanup. Here we have a system of responses specific to the invader. The first time such a specialist invades and evades immediate removal, the immune system samples the molecules on the outside of the invading cells, and manufactures specific molecules to mark the invader as foreign. The specific markers are called antigens. This process can take a few days while you feel ill. This is where those T- and B-lymphocytes, specialized white blood cells, come in that your veterinarian measures in a blood test. Besides active marking and attacking of learned invaders, these cells produce antibodies specific to the antigen, the marker on the invader. These are dispersed throughout the bloodstream; the antibodies grab on to the identified antigen, marking the invader for destruction by white blood cells. Some of the white blood cells retain this marker for a long time, creating up to lifelong memory of an invader. This specialized antibody-based response takes time to build up, often days or weeks. But once exposed to that known pathogen, later attacks are very quickly repulsed for as long as that cellular immune memory is retained.

Vaccines help the immune system

This same immune memory is why we vaccinate. When we vaccinate, we infect our dogs with either dead or deactivated invaders so our dogs mount a defense against a weak or already dead attacker. This can be done with an injection, a nasal spray, or an oral introduction. Once the cells learn that antigen, they might have it for life, or at least a long time. Some immunizations are once-in-a-lifetime, and some need to be boosted annually. Most commonly, dogs receive vaccinations to canine parvovirus, distemper, hepatitis, and rabies. These are deadly viral diseases, and vaccines not only protect the host, but by reducing the prevalence of the disease in the dog population, protect other dogs, often called "herd immunity" despite that fact that groups of dogs or people are not called "herds." Bordetella, or kennel cough, is an often-required vaccination for a dog who compete with other dogs. Canine influenza is a growing concern. For those of us who live out in the woods, leptospirosis now has a relatively effective vaccination, and Lyme disease vaccines are improving.

Timing of vaccination matters. Given too early, a puppy's immune system is still not functioning, depending on antibodies contained in mother's milk; the too-early vaccine won't be remembered. Too late, and a dog might already be exposed. Too many vaccines? There is no evidence that one can have too many vaccines in a healthy dog, as the immune system is assaulted daily anyway. A few deliberate affronts are lost in all the background noise. Still, some wonder about vaccine schedules and are willing to pay extra to have blood titers drawn. These measure the circulating population of immune system cells and antibodies specialized for a given disease. For example, I could have my dogs vaccinated for rabies yearly. Or I could have the veterinarian measure the blood titer for antibodies to rabies and decide when it falls too low and needs a boost. What is too low? Ah, there's the rub. Science can give you average amounts, and practice helps discern the titer below which it is better to boost, but it is a gamble. The higher the blood titer of antibodies, to a point, the better the odds of fighting the disease if it invades. What level of risk is the right amount? There are no guarantees. Some use this to argue that all vaccines should be given only after testing the blood titer. Others argue that with the lack of good data, we should vaccinate by timing. I suggest that instead of arguing we get better information. Pony up some money for research instead of imposing an opinion where facts remain thin.

Sometimes antigens, those markers of invaders, are close in molecular structure to other common substances. These common substances can trigger an immune response. Runny noses are an immune system's way of flushing out an antigen from the nose. Antigens cause histamine to be released, which causes swelling and itching. Itching can be a useful signal to the body to pay attention to an area, much like pain does. Like pain, uncontrolled itching can be maddening in its distraction and discomfort. Common misidentified invaders include pollen and some foods. Blizzard, my smooth coat Border Collie, used to get horrible reactions to spores from fungi. It was a reasonable response by the body: Fight invading fungus before it gets inside you. But it was an overreaction. An allergy. He scratched himself raw until we found out what the allergen was and could treat it with better than basic allergic response suppressors like antihistamines. There is some evidence that early exposures to many antigens helps mediate, or temper, the later immune responses to common allergens.

The best defense against diseases is a good diet and exercise. These promote healthy hair, skin, circulation, and immune responses. Get the recommended vaccines. Take your dog in for regular checkups from a veterinarian you are working with. Read multiple, well-respected sources. Be skeptical of many of the passing fads you see on the internet.

TOUR 9

THE DOG'S INTERNAL CONTROL SYSTEMS

When you really stop and think about it, thinking is an amazing thing. It seems relatively easy to explain that muscles contract to bend a leg to propel a dog forward in response to them smelling the treat in my hand. That requires no thinking for the dog. All it requires is chemotaxis, or orientation to a chemical signal. Some mysterious receptor thing in the nose signals FOOD! And the beast moves towards it. Even simple one-celled organisms can express this ability to orient to or away from a cue. Gromit, old as he is, catches the scent of a treat and pivots his head to look.

Vision is a tougher one to explain, but I will in this chapter. Getting a whole visual field from out there to make sense inside Gromit's brain, that is pretty complex stuff. It, however, is nothing compared to what has to happen once that brain starts weighing options. Do I keep chasing the squirrel or go to the food? What happened the last few times I went to the treat? Did they grab my collar and kennel me? Did they make it fun? Is that a bland treat or a really rare super treat? Does Tim look happy or angry as he is calling me over? Could I catch the squirrel on this surface at this distance? Even if all of those calculations happen at the subconscious level, like a professional athlete swinging a bat or catching a ball or cycling down a hill, or you driving a car, the brain has a lot to process. You could not do those things without a brain. But you also can do each of those without actually deliberately thinking about it. If you add in conscious thinking, how can we ever really understand behavior? Are dogs conscious (aware of themselves) or self-aware (aware that they are aware of themselves), with apologies for all of the true complexity I just glossed over, and forgive my doubts about the mirror studies used to test this. Dogs are not primates, so why would a mirror be a good test when vision is not their main sense of the world? Indeed, two recent studies show that dogs, being odor-oriented, do recognize self (Gatti, 2016 and Horowitz, 2017). I know you say "yes," and I say "yes," that dogs are self-aware, but science has trouble convincingly nailing down these questions for other species. Too complicated, you think. I respond with "If you can think it, we can probably figure out how that works." So we shall try.

Ecologists generally think in systems before specifics. Here this means that before we look into the brain, the eye, the ear, and the many other parts, we will look at broad systems of organization. Mind you (pun intended), we artificially organize how we talk about the systems, or how groups of functional units work tighter. I guess we think the whole is greater than the sum of the parts. The parts, and the ways they work together, were not developed in nature to be organized as distinct, so do not overly separate them as you read. They are functional toward survival: making successful copies of oneself. Mammals have two very different systems to control the body. You think about the thinking, nervous system. You should dwell a lot more on the chemical control system known to many — OK, not that many — as the endocrine system. Each has significant effects on behavior, but also on the many background activities of the vessel that carries the testicles and ovaries from one location to another. Each plays a role in health and wellbeing. The two do not always cooperate. Each is subject to disease and breakdown. Each can send you to the veterinarian.

Endocrine system

Evolutionarily, the endocrine system comes from modified nervous system cells. It is a body control system that uses chemicals secreted into the circulating blood to influence distant parts. These events are often tied closely to the brain's normal neural circuitry. See something scary with the eyes? Release adrenaline into the blood from the adrenal glands that hang out with the kidneys, and the whole body goes on alert, preparing for trouble. Endocrine control is more widespread than nervous system control, and longer lasting. For example, moving a leg is done fast, done now, and with no lasting impacts. Endocrine glands secrete chemical messengers, hormones, which exhibit control over a longer time and with more systemic effects. Many of these chemicals affect behavior, so it is easy to show that genes produce chemicals that affect behavior, which means that genetic influence on behavior has a clear mechanism. A few quick examples to convince you that chemicals affect behavior should suffice. Knowing that there is a whole scientific field called behavioral endocrinology might add to that. More widely known examples include the effects of estrogen on female sexual behavior, and testosterone on male sexual behavior. Oxytocin, found in some commercial pheromone dispensers for dogs, promotes social bonding. At least one study links aggression in juvenile male humans to testosterone levels. Leptin and ghrelin are hormones that decrease or increase appetite, respectively. (Dreger, et al, 2016)

Basically, the endocrine system consists of a group of organs scattered through the body that each secrete different hormones that cause different system- or body-wide effects. If one over-produces or under-produces a hormone, problems occur. Under-produce insulin, you get diabetes with high blood sugar. Over-produce it and you end up with too-low blood sugar and cells starve. The endocrine system has several major groupings, such as ones that control or affect metabolism; sex hormones, which affect mating; cortisol or stress hormones, which affect fight and flight systems, blood pressure and electrolyte balance; and blood sugar control.

This control system has glands, or discrete structures (often organs you have heard of but maybe wondered about, like the pancreas) or groups of cells, which secrete powerful chemicals directly into the bloodstream. Right here, this is where we return to the first words of this book. Testicles and ovaries. These are two very well-known endocrine organs that make gametes, as discussed earlier. But they each also secrete hormones that affect sex drive and prepare many body organs for bearing young. Estrogen, produced by ovaries, changes uterine cycling and is in turn influenced by hormones from the pituitary gland that signal the release of eggs. Testosterone, produced mainly by the testicles, increases muscle mass and bone density, determines penis and clitoris size and which one you get, sex drive, and some aspects of dominance aggression. Interestingly, this male hormone is not really that. It is not male-only. Females produce it in the ovaries, where it has similar functions, just at much lower levels. Likewise estrogen, the female hormone, is produced by both males and females, but in different amounts. Estrogen affects reproductive behavior as well as development of related female structures such as the uterus. Ovaries and testicles produce more hormones than just estrogen and testosterone, and they in turn are regulated by hormones coming from other glands. To muck it up just a bit more, there are chemicals in the environment that mimic normal hormones and therefore affect behavior and health as if they were produced by the organism itself. Most widely known is bisphenol, or BPA, a resin in many plastics that mimics estrogen.

That last paragraph so over-generalizes and so under-describes just those two leading organs and just two of their associated chemicals. I use that as an illustration to show

how complex the endocrine system is, because we would need a full book on it alone. You need to be aware that a lot of the steady-state behaviors and temperaments are influenced by hormones. One should ask how much this often-ignored system controls behavior, and therefore training and learning.

Endocrine glands

Let's take a tour of the main endocrine glands in your dog. You have the **hypothalamus**, a part of the brain that serves to link the brain and the central nervous system to the endocrine- or chemical-mediated body control. The hypothalamus has neurons that project into the pituitary gland, which dangles at the base of the brain. The posterior (toward the back) part takes brain signals in and secretes nervous-systems-oriented hormones like the feel-good oxytocin. The anterior (toward the front) part operates many interesting controls, including regulating stress hormones such as those produced in the adrenal glands, growth hormones, and lactation. Another is the **pineal gland**, responsible for serotonin, which regulates sleep, daily rhythms, and seasonal patterns. I am a morning person. This is likely controlled by my pineal gland. Others are late-night people. Why wouldn't our dogs be the same? Have you watched to see if your dog learns better in the morning, by day, or in the evening? You probably pick your training schedule on your work or personal rhythms. Likely you have not considered your dog's own biological circadian (daily) rhythms.

The **thyroid gland** is wrapped around the anterior or front of the trachea. Primarily it is responsible for regulating metabolic rates. Your dog is too hyperactive? You might need to check thyroxin levels. Too lethargic? Same hormone when under-produced. Hyperthyroidism is rare in dogs, but the hormone clearly affects activity levels. The **parathyroid glands** are nestled in the thyroid, but regulate calcium absorption. The **adrenal glands** sit on top of the kidneys, and produce cortisol, the stress hormone, under direction from the **pituitary gland**. In addition, they make adrenaline, so important in those fight-or-flight situations. While the pancreas has digestive functions mentioned earlier, it also secretes hormones that help regulate blood sugar.

Reconsider the testes and ovaries. A female in heat secretes hormones from her uterus, which in that respect would make it an endocrine gland, except these hormones are destined to be released to the outside world where it attracts males. Technically that makes this an exocrine gland function, as the hormone is released to the outside world. Hormones secreted outside the body that affect other beings, or act as hormones to others, are known as pheromones. Since pheromones show up in such products as electrical plug-in devices, sprays, and collars to reduce stress and encourage calm behavior, such as during storms, I thought you might like a glimpse at the biology. Back to sex and the pheromones the female produces that attract males. Note that I state "the female produces *that* attract males" and not "the female produces *to* attract males." Intentionality is difficult to discern. Even in an evolutionary sense, does the female produce the pheromone to attract a mate, or is it an incidental byproduct that males pick up on and use to find females who maybe had no interest in the males? And all of this is happening at the molecular level, so what leads to copies is more relevant than intentions anyway.

The finely tuned chemoreceptors in a male receive the signal. This activates its own endocrine system, putting it on high alert, and signals to the central nervous system to start tracking down that female. The male starts to move in closer to the female, driven by hard-to-control hormones. The brain cannot simply ignore these signals, nor is the body completely at their mercy. If another male enters the picture, also on the hunt for the female in heat, his central nervous system can override sex-driven myopia, redirect a release of adrenaline to prepare for a fight, and put mating on hold indefinitely.

Nervous system

This trip through the parts of the nervous system is intended to help you know the limits and capabilities of the parts and the whole, and how they go together. For example, if you know the basics of eye structure, you can understand what an eye can do and cannot do. This in turn will help you see the world as a dog does, which is not the same as how you see it. We do not really know how a dog perceives the world, or processes visual images in the brain, but current brain scanning seems to indicate, not surprisingly, that dog brains and human brains are structured the same, with the same basic wiring patterns. Humans add more complex processing, or so we think.

Like Rome, all roads lead to the brain. For all practical purposes, every sensory signal, if not silenced along the way, and every sensory organ, reports to the brain. We will tour the nervous system, but like those signals, we will end up in the brain.

We can think about the nervous systems by three main functions. There are sensors that detect things from the environment and send signals elsewhere, generally to the brain. The brain, mainly, processes signals and sends out signals to do something. Actions taken are mainly muscular, and the cells that control these actions are called motor nerves.

Another way to think of the controllers running throughout the body is to think of them geographically. The brain and spinal cord combined are called the **central nervous system**. The parts that feed into or out of these, all the sensors and controllers scattered throughout the body, are called the **peripheral nervous system**. The peripheral nervous system is broken into two broad areas, the voluntary and the autonomic. Dogs can control where they put their feet. You can train them to put their feet where you want. Gromit learned to raise his right paw high in the air whenever one of us asked "Who wants a beer?" People thought that was so amazing. The cue was "Who wants…" so he raised his paw for anything when asked; we used beer for the entertainment value. That is voluntary control. Voluntarily in the biological sense. Did I give Gromit any choices here? Not really.

The **autonomic system** covers the areas that happen behind the scenes. It covers internal organ control but is regulated by a brain structure called the hypothalamus. There is a whole wiring network (not real wires, but nerves and long neurons function like wires sending signals) for dealing with scary or aroused situations, called the **sympathetic system**, or for more calming activities when not aroused, the **parasympathetic system**. There is a third area of the peripheral nervous system that derives from the neural crest in the developing embryo; the neural crest is primitive brain country. It controls the digestive system where it resides. Some biologists call it the second brain, so maybe you really do think with your stomach.

There are sensors in the body that detect changes in the environment, known as input. Then we will look at the organ that processes all of those inputs, the brain. This is throughput, as opposed to input or output. Finally, we will look at output — which we can superficially think of as behaviors — but from a biological perspective. Sensors outside the brain, think nose or toes, send signals to the brain. The sensor that is doing the detecting fires a nerve. That stimulus is converted to an electrochemical signal. All of these electrochemical nerve impulses are the same at the cellular level. What differs is where the signal goes to. A signal from a pain receptor, once en route to the brain, looks just like a signal coming in from the eye giving information on light. Where that signal ends up in the brain makes all of the difference. If the signal is coming from the eye, it must be light. If you get hit hard in the eye, the brain sees a flash of light in part because that is what the signal is interpreted as, even though it was blunt force trauma.

All this is not intended to confuse you. The nervous system does an awful lot and reaches all areas of your body. It is hard to comprehend how complex that really is. Dog trainers and companions often talk about arousal state ("was your dog aroused or not" as a binary either/or choice) or talk about the brain as a pretty simple processor. Reward the activity, often with a food-based treat, and you get more of the desired behavior, reward less and it goes away or extinguishes. While this model worked well for B. F. Skinner and almost any student in an introductory psychology laboratory class, we now know the whole lot is far more complex than Skinner suggested. Rewarding a behavior works well most of the time, but when it doesn't, knowing what else might be going on is important.

Neurons

At its most basic, a neuron is a cell that is part of the nervous system. A single nerve cell, or neuron, can be quite large. For example, a neuron in your big toe extends as one cell all the way up your leg to your spinal cord. Bundles of neurons are called nerves. Sensory neurons detect signals or stimuli. Motor neurons send signals to muscles to do something. Interneurons connect to other neurons, often in the brain. Each is a neuron, and at this level, they differ in processing function rather than in their anatomy and physiology. As embryos develop, nerves (bundles of neurons) are laid down in predictable patterns that are common across mammals. The third cranial nerve in me does the same thing in my dog.

Earlier I described a general cell, comparing it to my office, which my wife now calls the "Gooey Room." I described the innards of the cell with some organelles like the nucleus, Golgi apparatus, and mitochondria. Neurons have all of these, but their action is all on the cell membrane, the bag that encloses the gooey room. Neurons set up an electrical gradient and send an electrical impulse. This electrical signal is definitely not like the kind that carries through a copper or fiber wire connecting your computer to some distant server pumping out movies or web pages. Those are electromagnetic signals. Every electrical signal carries a magnetic field; you can see this by placing a compass near a wire conducting electricity. A compass was a pre-GPS gadget that pointed north using the Earth's own magnetic field. Every magnetic field generates an electrical field. That is how you can charge your phone cordlessly. In fact, the two are one, and properly known as electromagnetic fields. They move along fast. Right there at the speed of light, 186,282 miles per second, or just shy of 300,000 km per second in a vacuum. For the curious, that is 670 million miles (just over a billion km) per hour. I guess it is that fast even if you are not curious. Can we agree that this is fast? In fact, nothing can go faster than the speed of light. It is the universal speed limit, part and parcel of the fabric of space-time. Neurons just aren't that fast. A nerve impulse, called an action potential, or the electrochemical signal that works its way down the cell membrane of a neuron, cooks along from as slow as 1 yard or m per second up to 100 meters or yards per second. That gives a range of 2 to 200 miles per hour (3 to 320 km/hour). Nowhere near the speed of light.

You might be asking why we biological critters use such a slow process for communicating in the body. Evolution works on past parts, and I can't find any evidence for organisms refining copper and putting wires into their own body (except for very recent humans), and you couldn't code for that with DNA anyway. In addition, in nature, signals going tens of miles per hour over the small body sizes we all have is near instantaneous.

All animals except sponges have neurons. Yes, sponges are animals, not plants. Typical neurons have tendrils that connect them to inputs from sensors or other neurons, called dendrites. Action potentials move along the cell membrane of these tendrils. These connect to the cell body where all the gooey room stuff is located, with the signal continuing out at the cell membrane. There are more fiber-looking protrusions out the other end of the cell body called axons. Signals go one way, from dendrites to the cell body to axons. There might be hundreds or thousands of dendrites collecting signals, but typically each neuron only has one axon. Some neurons need only a faint signal from one or a few dendrites to send the signal out the axon, while others require many signals. Some neurons make others more likely to send a signal, some inhibit the signal propagation.

Where neurons connect to neurons, you get a synapse. This is a gap in the wiring, a chance to modify the signal. An axon from one neuron might interact with a dendrite or the cell body of the next. If the signal is strong enough, little chemical signalers called neurotransmitters cross the gap, and restart the action potential along the next neuron. Neurons interconnect so one neuron might be connected to thousands of other neurons. All activity in the nervous system really comes down to this: Is there an action potential, how many are there, how is it (or are they) mediated, and what does that combination of neurons firing mean?

TOUR 10

A GUIDED TOUR OF INPUTS TO THE BRAIN — THE SENSES

The gray and white lump sitting in the darkened confines of the skull has to get information from somewhere outside, or it would get maddeningly lonely. What are the different ways the brain takes in the surroundings? Signals from neurons. How do those neurons get the signal? Signal propagation is not nearly instantaneous at the speed of light, nor is it some form of magic. There needs to be an intact physical cell connection from some sensor, like a touch sensor in a toe connecting it to a bundle in the spine, up some nerve to the brain, where the brain puts that signal in context with related signals and sends (or fails to send) out impulses to the body to do something, like move that toe. This can get pretty complicated, and might make more sense as we look at a few examples.

Eyes/vision

Since I already raised the issues of eyes and seeing, and since primates (you and I) are visually oriented critters, let's start our tour of the senses there. At one level, an eye is a sensor that takes ambient or available light and focuses it on a sensor surface. The sensor surface sends signals to the brain for processing to create a visual image. The brain also tosses in other related information from memory and other sensors. My dog sees the food in the dish, smells it, and associates memories of feeling really good when that stuff goes into the mouth. So he eats it. Cricket, if she sees a new food, will puzzle over it, looking from different angles, sniffing, and will eventually take the new food into her mouth and carry it away where she can lick it and test it over and over. Our other dogs always just eat and skip all the preliminaries. Same sensors, different processor.

Eyes are roughly spherical balls of living material that develop from embryological skin tissue and from brain tissue. If you were to start on the outside of the eye like a beam of light and work your way in, you would encounter the first layer of the eye, the conjunctiva. This tissue layer moistens and feeds the outer layers of the eye, and is easily scratched and hurts like crazy. Why? Pain makes one recoil, and moving away from whatever is scratching your eye is usually a good idea. I used to wear soft contact lenses because my supposedly near-spherical eyeballs are more football-like. I am rather nearsighted. Every once in a while, when pinching out the soft contact at the end of the day, I would discover that I was in fact tugging on the conjunctiva and not the soft plastic contact. Poor technique. Ouch!

Next we pass through the cornea, the outer lens that gathers light. We cruise into an anterior chamber where the iris sits. This structure, the pupil, can open wide to let in more light or close to a small hole so the sensors in the back of the eye are not blinded. There is a bit of interesting physics here that if you grew up in the old film-camera age you might well be aware of. Likewise, if your eyes are getting older, like past age 40 for most, you can readily test this. Light focused through a small hole has what is called a large depth of field. That means that things both near and far can simultaneously be in focus. The larger the hole or aperture (lower f-stop for you photographers) in the iris, the narrower the distance that can be in focus. In a brightly lit area, the pupil is small, and you can focus on words on a page and some scenery in the background at the same time. In a dimly lit space, if you focus on something 6 feet (2 m) from you, things closer and farther away will be out of focus. This will be key to understanding dog vision, so keep it in mind.

Pupil shapes vary in the animal kingdom, and this tells a lot about the ecological role of the critter carrying that eye. Small round pupils work great for day work and give a wide range of light adjustment. Pupil slits rather than holes help open the eyes maximally, letting in lots of extra light. In predators, the slits are oriented vertically, which seems to maximize the ability to use low light at near distances when closing in on prey. Prey animals, like sheep and deer, have horizontal slits for pupils, which seems to help detect low light movement at a distance along the horizon. Movement out there is rarely good if you are prey, so you don't need good distance focus, just a sense that something is coming to get you. Back to our round pupils and our lens system. We focus our light into a small circular area (the fovea centralis) centered on the retina, but dogs focus the light along a more oval shape, oriented horizontally. Many fish have the focus area positioned such that the light from above is what focuses on their retina. This makes sense since their danger comes from above.

Anyway, past the pupil you hit the main focusing lens. It is a flexible lens held in place and changed in shape by a ring of muscles. Flexible, at least when you are young. We post-40-year-olds see the impacts of a lens that flexes a lot less. Bifocals or reading glasses are likely in your future. These tiny muscles change the focus of the lens so that you can see things up close and far away, adjusting that depth of field. Now the light passes through a large, jelly-filled chamber and strikes the sensors in the back of the eye. Here the visual image is changed into a chemical-mediated action potential message to the brain for processing. Got that? An eye simply converts photons of light to action potentials in neurons for your brain.

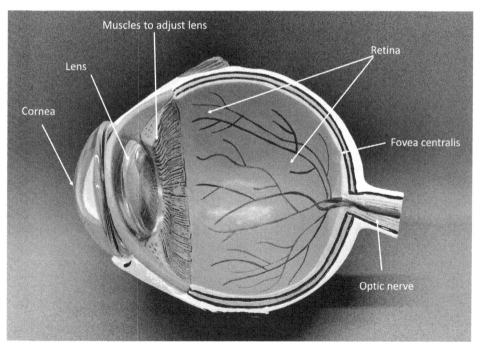

To be clear, you see with your brain, not your eyes. Repeat after me: "We see with our brains, not with our eyes." Again. This will also help you later when you realize how piss poor the memories of things you saw really are. You can trust your eyes. Don't you dare trust your brain. Eyes gather and focus light. If I fitted you with glasses that inverted the world so everything appeared upside down, after a week or two of wearing those lenses, your brain would figure it out and flip the image back so it was right side up. No big deal, because you see with your brain, just like you feel touch with your brain, and you smell with your brain. Another example: Each of your eyes has a blind spot where the optic nerve leaves the eye. You generally cannot see that you have this because your brain hides the blind spot with whatever else is around it. Close one eye. For this example, let's assume you close your left eye because nine out of ten of you are right-handed. If you are of the sinistral set, feel free to close your right eye and do this with your left hand and move left where I say right. Actually, either group, lefties or righties, can do this with either eye so just start with your right one, OK? Left eye closed. Right hand in a thumbs-up position like the emoji on your phone. This will work best if you have a blank wall as a background. Stare at some convenient point on the wall, a smudge, a mashed insect, or a very small dot. Have your right hand at arm's length and place your thumb between your eye and that point on the wall you are staring at. Now slowly move your thumb to the right, staying at the same level of where you are staring. Stare at that point, not your thumb. Very soon your thumb will disappear, but your hand will still be visible, so long as you keep staring at the fixed point on the wall. If that does not work for you, draw a dot on a piece of blank paper. Put a nice thick plus sign about five inches (12 cm) to the right of it. Close your left eye. Stare at the dot with your right eye. Hold the paper at arm's length. Slowly bring the paper closer to your nose. The plus will disappear when it hits your blind spot. You don't see that in daily life because your brain ignores it, and it does not matter because you are constantly moving your eyes and head so the blind spot does not stay in any one place for very long. You see with your brain, not your eyes. Optical illusions work the same way. Even when you know what is going on, your brain is easily tricked.

The sensor field of the eye is the retina. It is made up of cells called rods and cones, and the cells differ in structure and molecular makeup so with a microscope you can tell them apart. Rods are very light sensitive, and they signal only presence and absence of light in shades of gray, so they offer no color distinction. They are so light sensitive that they are great for seeing in darkness, but by day they are all overwhelmed, blinded, by the daylight, and of little help. Cones come in a number of versions, and different ones are activated by different wavelengths of light. For a human, we have three types, so we can distinguish the three primary colors of red, yellow, and blue. All of the colors we perceive with our brain, millions of hues, are the brain interpreting the signals from three different cone types. There is no way to know if one brain perceives a color the same way as another. All of what a normal cone detects in a fixed wavelength is pretty much the same, so if we have healthy eyes, we all send pretty much the same signals to our brains. This means we would all call that the same color, maybe blue for example, but there is no way to know how one brain sees blue compared to another. In fact, there are some interesting optical illusions that imply we do not all see color the same way. One on dress color made the internet meme rounds recently. If you have a genetic defect, and end up with only two functioning cone types, you are called colorblind. Say the red cones are not functioning: You cannot distinguish red from green. It is not that you don't see a red or green object; a red or green object is not invisible. They are just signaled the same because you lack functioning red cones. You would easily distinguish blue from yellow.

Dogs have lots of rods, good for seeing at night. They also have two kinds of cones, like most mammals. These see blue and yellow. As an aside, I bet you did not know that was why we colored the book cover the way we did. Our three-cone system is rare, found only in a few mammal groups. A dog's brain gets signals the same way a red-green colorblind person would. Let's be clear, colorblind is a misnomer. One is not blind, and in this example, a red object is not invisible. Red just comes in as one of the shades of gray or blue or yellow depending on tone. Two-color vision is really useful in nature. Distinguishing blues and yellows works great in low-light nature. In nature, there is not a lot of red that a dog needs to see. No stop signs. Sure, the sunset is likely less dramatic. Red-green colorblind friends of mine are better at seeing birds and other camouflaged animals than I am, so it may be that being dichromatic (two cone types) is better for hunters than three. Dogs were hunters. And don't start thinking, "We are number one, we are tri-chromatic!" Mantis shrimp have up to 16 cone types. No, I do not know why; likely it helps find food or mates. Evolutionarily speaking, that is a great cop-out because almost everything is for food or mating, or both.

The take home here is red does not contrast well with green for dogs. Dark red will appear black, light red will appear gray. I have a friend who wears a black top with red sleeves when she runs an agility dog, she says so her dog can see her arm positions better. To the dog, it is all black, given the shade of red she uses. Another uses a bright red toy when he plays fetch, so his dog can see it better. A third uses an orange Frisbee when she tosses to her dogs. Another an orange tennis ball. There are apps out there that convert a smartphone image into what a dog sees. Dogs do not see red. To them, orange minus the red is yellow or green, depending on which orange you have. Red against grass is gray to black against green. Throw in shadows, and red looks like a shadow. Orange against grass is a shade of yellow, which can be good contrast, or green, which is bad, again depending on hue. Yellow on black is much better. Yellow next to blue is the best contrast for dogs. In addition, dogs only have about 1/10 the total number of cones that we do because they are packed with night vision rods. Dogs have lots of rods in their fovea centralis, so they focus extremely well in the dark. It also means shapes and patterns are likely far more important than the color involved since the rods in the focal point don't discern color. They also have a reflective layer behind the retina, the tapetum, which increases night vision. They can see in about 1/6 as much light as we can. They rule the night, but they do it by sacrificing daytime color distinctions that we make. At night, we huddled in our caves or treetops and slept, hoping nothing saw us because we likely would not see them unless the moon was bright.

Our fovea centralis, where our lenses focus light, is almost all cones, because we evolved to work in the light. Having rods in that center area, which don't work well in the day, would give us less visual acuity and diminish the ability to distinguish small differences. But at night, those cones do not work. They need a lot of light to activate. We see adequately in low light, except when I stub my toe, but without good focus. Go out into the countryside far from the city where it is really dark, but not pitch black, or go into a darkened room with a tiny amount of light. It will take 15 or 20 minutes of no light for your rods to recover from blinding headlights, room lights, or daylight. Look around you. You won't see color. If you focus on a star or the smallest dot of light you can produce, it will disappear because it is sending its light to your fovea centralis, where there are not any rods! Look just slightly away from that star or point of light, and it will be visible again. Pretty cool, but this has a point. Our senses are adapted to what worked best for our setting in the millions of years we evolved, not always in our current settings. Dogs also did not evolve in cities or on farms, so their parts are optimized for different situations than ours.

Dogs can see things far away. How far? What is the farthest item you can see? This is a trick question. You see with your brain (repeat that again), so you can see anything that projects onto your retina, and only that. Really, you can only see as far as your retina. If you know where to look in a dark sky, you can see Andromeda, a neighboring galaxy. It is 2.6 million light years away, or at the time I am writing this it is 14,931,708,431,500,830,490 miles away. Andromeda is getting closer to us at the rate of about 100 miles (160 km) per second or 360,000 mph (580,000 km per hour)! It is not the distance of the object; rather it is the brightness of the object and the eye's ability to focus that limit what one sees.

Distance does matter, but here the distance is from the eye to the rest of the brain. It takes about 100 milliseconds, or one tenth of a second, for the image in your eye to get to the brain and get processed. What you see as now was really a tenth of a second ago. You simply cannot see the present. This is philosophically interesting, but at highway speeds it is life-changing. If you are driving at 60 mph (100 kph), you travel 8.8 feet (2.7 m) before your brain has processed the information it saw. At 70 mph hour (110 kph) it is 10 feet (3 m). Be careful how close you drive to another car! For a dog, a prey animal running 25 mph (40 kph) will travel almost 4 feet (1.2 m) before the brain can process the information. That would never do to catch anything but an already-dead prey item. The brain has to calculate speed, estimate trajectory, figure out where the mouth is relative to the eyes, and grab that prey or that ball or that Frisbee. Catching prey that are evading to save their lives is a lot of neural processing. Processing takes time. With prey living now, and the image being old, one has to learn to anticipate. This is all very profound if you give it a millisecond of thought.

When I go to the eye doctor, I get a set of numbers. Let's say the doctor says I have 20/20 vision. In the metric world they say 6/6 vision. Use that and sound European. Or Indian. Or pretty much any place outside the U.S. It means I can see clearly at 20 feet (6 m) what an average human sees at 20 feet (6 m). 20/200 (6/60), closer to what I am, means an average person can see clearly at 200 feet (60 m) what I have to be 20 feet (6 m) from to see. Thankfully, I have glasses to correct my nearsightedness to 20/20 (6/6). My dogs, if they are average, see the human equivalent of 20/80 (6/25). They need to be 20 feet (6 m) from something an average human could distinguish at 80 feet (25 m). They are better at detecting movement than we are, which has to do with how the retina is wired. Lateral or side-to-side motion in their eyes triggers the brain at lower thresholds than our eyes. A single dog eye has a field of view that is a tad wider but essentially the same as ours, which is 135 degrees. Eyes like ours, which are set facing forward, have a combined field of view of about 190 degrees. A full circle is 360 degrees so 180 degrees is half a circle. Dog eyes on average, and this varies widely by breed, are set about 20 degrees off the center line, so they see a wider field of view, about 250 degrees (270 is ¾ of a circle). A typical dog looking forward has vision extending back to their shoulders. Our vision overlaps more, which is how we detect depth or distance. Our eyes overlap a lot more than dogs, so we have a wider arc of 3-D viewing. Dogs have a wider arc of overall vision.

Lastly, and I have by no means exhausted the subject, dogs' eyes sit a good 4 feet (1.3 m) closer to the ground than ours do. If you want to see what a dog sees, start by getting down on your hands and knees. If you have a smaller dog, belly to the floor, please. The world looks a lot different there. Tall weeds now block your view. Low fences and couches are the same as tall walls are to us. What lurks behind that? We see over it, no worries for us. For your dog it is unseen terror or opportunity. When I lie down on the floor, my dogs go nuts with glee, rolling on me, jumping on me, tugging at my ball cap. It is play city to them. Move my face above theirs, and they see me very differently again.

There is a great, if a bit dated, article in the *Journal of American Veterinary Medical Association* from December 1995 entitled "Vision in Dogs" that I highly recommend. I so love the summary statement that I will quote it in full. "Compared with the visual system in human beings, the canine visual system could be considered inferior in such aspects as degree of binocular overlap, color perception, accommodative range, and visual acuity. However, in other aspects of vision, such as ability to function in dim light, rapidity with which the retina can respond to another image (flicker fusion), field of view, ability to differentiate shades of gray, and, perhaps, ability to detect motion, the canine visual system probably surpasses the human visual system. This has made the dog a more efficient predator in certain environmental situations and permits it to exploit an ecological niche inaccessible to humans." I think this is a great listing of differences between dog vision and ours. It concludes not by finding that one version is better than the other, but that they allow different ecological roles. It reminds me that the question, "Who sees better, a dog or a human?" is all a matter of perspective and evolutionary history. I love it.

Ears/hearing

When we think ears, we tend to think hearing; that will be the first focus. The ears are also where balance is sensed, unrelated to hearing, but using some physically adjacent structures crammed in next to the ear and derived from the same embryological tissue. We will cover that, too, but hearing first. Eyes are sensors optimized to detect photons of light. Ears detect physical motion of air or water molecules: sound. In a vacuum, they are not much use because there is no medium to propagate the sound. "In space, no one can hear you scream." The movie "Alien" got it right with that tagline. One of those geek pet peeves. If a spaceship near you explodes, it would be silent, as space is a vacuum, so there are no air (or water) molecules to move to set up a vibration or shockwave for you to hear or feel.

You can feel vibration through your whole body, so in some ways the whole liquid bag of enzymes that is your dog is an auditory detector. Ears are where that is done best. Like the eyes, ears have a device to focus the incoming energy. In the eye, that was the cornea and lens. In the ear it is the external ear or ear flap or pinnae. Dogs can generally rotate theirs about, which helps locate where the sound is coming from. The time delay (actually a phase shift, but it really does not matter here) of a sound hitting one ear before the other lets one detect the direction. Ears are offset ever so slightly vertically, as well, giving some ability to detect up and down differences. Sound travels far faster in water than air, about 4.5 times faster, so in water it is harder to distinguish sound direction.

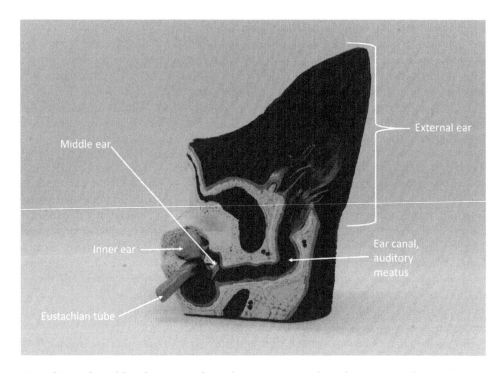

Sound is gathered by the external ear, but now it needs to be converted into a nerve impulse. In the eye, that happened directly at the retina as light triggered nerve cells. It is a bit more complex in the ear. First, sound is amplified in a series of mechanical steps. The eardrum picks up the air vibrations. It is articulated through three bones in a sequence from eardrum to inner ear: the hammer, anvil, and stirrups (or in Latin for the medical types: malleus, incus, and stapes). These bones slightly amplify the sound by about an additional 1/3 because of the way they interlink. However, these bones collect sound from the whole eardrum on one end with the hammer and concentrate it onto a small area on the other with the stirrups, increasing the sound by about 18 times. Interestingly, but not surprisingly, there are a couple of muscles attached to the bones of the middle ear that can reflexively help muffle sounds that are too loud. The eardrum covers the whole ear canal to gather sound, but the three bones need to be in air to vibrate freely. That would create a pressure differential inside the head, making the ear less functional, so there is a small tube for equalizing pressure, called the Eustachian tube, that connects the middle ear to the throat. Often when you get a head cold, that tube gets blocked and you have trouble equalizing your ears. You also feel the value of that little tube when you use an elevator, fly in an airplane, or dive underwater.

The last of the three bones as one moves inward, the stapes, sits on a small membrane window on a liquid-filled organ called the cochlea. The stapes moves back and forth there, setting up vibrations in the inner ear that are detected by nerve endings. Think of the cochlea as a long, straight tube, but know that in a good space-saving manner, it is actually coiled up. Where sounds hit the nerve ending varies by frequency of the sound, so it allows a dog to differentiate frequencies (which control pitch). Because prey moving through vegetation make a lot of high-frequency sounds, dogs can hear a higher pitch than you can. Dogs' hearing covers roughly 30 hertz (cycles per second, not rental cars) to 50 thousand hertz. Humans hear roughly 20 hertz to 25 thousand hertz. A piano serves as a good illustration. If you wanted it to cover the whole range a dog hears, you would need to add 48 keys to high end for dogs, the last 20 of which would be un-hearable to humans. Lots of things like motors make sounds too high-pitched for humans, and our ability to hear high sounds greatly shrinks as we age. Vacuum cleaners sound horrific to most dogs because of high-pitched sounds we cannot detect, so we just think they are loud and miss many of the sounds a dog is hearing. Dog sound amplification is better than ours, too, so they can detect sounds about 4 times fainter than we can. Their world of sound is far richer than ours.

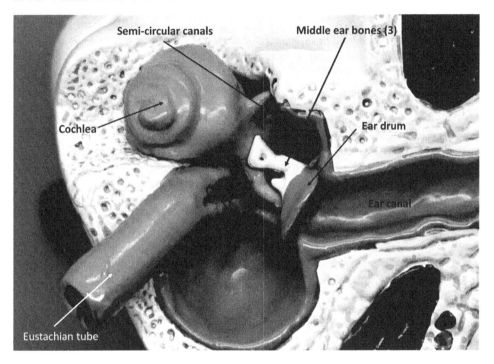

Ears use an intricate linkage of bones to set up vibrations in a liquid where nerve cells can pick up the movements and convert them to brain signals. If the liquid movements did not come from sound, one could use the same structures to detect other signals. Evolution did just that. The inner ear has some physically adjacent neighbors using the same liquid in a tube movements to detect body position. It is difficult to be sure, but some embryological comparisons suggest sensing body position evolved before sensing sound location rather than the other way around. I cannot imagine how you could use that information in any way whatsoever, but I thought it was interesting, and I wondered which system plagiarized the other.

Balance

Balance is a complex result of one's brain integrating visual cues from the eyes, proprioception — or body position signals using peripheral sense touching and a sense of where limbs are — along with a sense of acceleration. Acceleration normally is gravity, which pulls you downward, but if you spin around, your body feels the pull outward. I think we all underrate this unless we get vertigo and feel dizzy. Suddenly we think this is hot stuff. So let's repeat a bit of why this is so complex. One's brain, nestled inside the bony vault of the cranium, cannot detect anything on its own. It is rather dark inside the recess of your brain. No street lighting. Two separate eyes are constantly sending complex visual images that need to be interpreted. All over one's body there are sensors sending in information about where each part of the body is and what it is encountering, be it slippery or sticky or hot or cold or…. Each finger has thousands of touch sensors. Every muscle has stretch receptors so one's body knows positions.

The number of signals entering the brain each second is unimaginable. Each signal is either amplified, passed along, or ignored, in real time. My dog can see a squirrel, then leap over fallen tree after it, note a change of direction in the squirrel (corners and climbing being their specialty), pivot when landing, and start in a new direction. What really gets me is how quickly that neural network in the head adjusts to never-before-encountered situations. Wish, able to run and climb and jump and scramble for over a decade every day, hour, and minute, tore her CCL. That is the ACL in humans, a ligament that holds the femur from sliding too far forward on the tibia. She blew out her knee. That leg barely held weight for the two weeks we had to wait for surgery. She adjusted to the new normal of a bum leg en route from returning with the Frisbee that she caught when she tore her main ligament holding her tibia to her femur. Picture that. She lands and turns, Frisbee in mouth, and her CCL tears completely, so her right knee is now unstable and the leg that has supported her always and without fail for 11 years does not function correctly. She ran back immediately, with no pause in the action, Frisbee in mouth, ready for another throw, without using her now mostly useless leg. How can a brain adapt so fast to a wholesale change in the body, its balance, its locomotion in an instant? Why didn't she just collapse in a quivering mass, like she does when we put a winter boot on her foot? I cannot fathom it at all.

Balance, or the sensory sensing of equilibrium, or knowing which end should be up and keeping it there, is primarily detected by a series of liquid-filled loops located in the inner ear sitting right on top of the cochlea. These are analogues to the accelerometers in your smartphone. Your smartphone has electronic devices that measure movements so it can do things like turn on when you lift it up, or record your movements as you walk. Your inner ear can do the same using nerve endings tipped with a tiny crystal at their ends, detecting relative movements of the crystals in the liquid. Picture yourself in a car with someone else driving. When they make turns or rapidly brake, your head tries to keep going the same direction it was, compliments of inertia. They turn the car sharp left, your head feels like it is pulling to the right. Your head on your neck is like the crystal on the hair. These tubes are like long buses or trains full of people, able to feel changes in position by detecting the heads bobbing.

Two loops, one in each ear, are vertical and oriented in line with the ear-to-ear axis. A second vertical pair faces nose to the back of head. The third pair lies horizontally. With six loops, three to an ear, you get a 3-D view of your own motion. These loops are the semicircular canals, and they make up the vestibular system. The location on the cochlea is not coincidental. In many ways, this set of liquid-filled tubes works with the same mechanism as the cochlea. The balance and hearing systems evolved together. When the movements are in the cochlea, the brain interprets sound. When they are in the vestibular system, the brain detects changes in orientation.

Balance is obviously crucial. One use of all this information, one I overlooked my whole life, is that your body has to keep track of its position to allow your eyes to stay locked on some image. Lose your sense of balance, and you cannot read or walk while looking at a fixed object. Your eye wanders as if it has a mind of its own. The balance system in the inner ear is essential in part because it sends signals to the muscles of the eyes so they can react and keep things in focus. But your eyes also help you keep balance. Try standing on one foot with your eyes open, and then with them closed, and please be careful not to fall over. In a fascinating way, eyes help the brain interpret balance, and the three pairs of loops in the inner ear help your eyes lock on a target so you can keep your balance.

This system of nerve endings in liquid tubes has a third use in addition to hearing and balance. There are two more otolithic (literally "ear rock") organs next to the cochlea. These detect acceleration, and that is not the same as body position. Body position is which end is up, and where up is, whereas these detect if one is starting to move faster or slowing down. All of these organs are physically located together, and send the same kind of nerve signal: action potentials. However, the signals are interpreted differently depending on their source. A vibration in the cochlea is perceived as sound. A vibration in the semicircular canals is position. A vibration in the otoliths is a change in motion. You can be in a completely dark room and know which end is up and if you are falling. For what it is worth, if you ever get to go up in space like an astronaut, you will not be free of gravity as it appears. Gravity certainly reaches there as it reaches further to the moon and holds it in orbit and on beyond. In orbit, you are actually falling. Constantly. But you are falling so fast that you keep missing the Earth and going round and round. After a bit of time, your brain will start to reinterpret the signals and you will experience it as if you were just floating, going nowhere. Meanwhile you keep falling at 5 miles (8 km) per second. Sound goes at about 1 mile per second. Pretty cool, right?

Touch/feel

Light is detected with eyes and lets you see the world around you. Vibrations in the air are sensed with the ears so you can hear. Position and movement are distinguished in the inner ear. However, without being able to sense the surfaces a body is in contact with, our ancestral dogs would lose a great deal of information they need while chasing rabbits for dinner. Is it slippery out? Did I just bang my leg against a rock? Is it hot out? Is that snow or sand? Is that rabbit in my mouth and OK to eat? Skin is loaded with sensors that detect temperature, chemicals, pain, and touch. They work in various ways to detect the environment, but they all turn that into an action potential and send that up the nerve to the brain. Always, the perception of the signal happens in the brain. When someone says, "It's all in your head" they are right. It doesn't make it any easier to ignore an itchy bug bite, however.

Run your fingers through your dog's hair. That feels different than running your fingers over a hard table or in your dog's mouth. With your eyes closed, you can feel a nose and a nail and easily tell them apart. There is a clear survival advantage to being able to detect your environment. In fact, if you lose your sense of touch even temporarily as numbness, you are at much higher risk for injury. There are several types of touch receptors that send signals we interpret as vibration, a light touch, or pressure. Damaged skin has detectors that send a pain signal. That is why a cut hurts. The cut body part is signaling the brain, "Be a little more careful, and maybe send a little help here." A burn, a cut, and blunt bruise pain are all signaled the same, with the same type of detector, but somehow the brain can tell them apart. Some of these touch receptors detect stretch in a muscle so you can perceive how far you have moved a limb. Temperature sensors in the skin and in the mouth detect changes in temperature from the base body temperature. They seem to work via changes in proteins that initiate the action potential in the neuron. In other words, they are made of temperature-dependent proteins that change shape as temperature changes, and a neuron detects those changes and launches an action potential. That all sounds pretty straight forward, but it is anything but that. Dogs can detect subtle changes to the texture they are walking on, but there are not an infinite array of texture detectors, just four or five. Yet that allows grass to feel different from carpet.

What is pain, really? Pain is just a signal (action potential in a neuron) like pressure or heat or cold moving from sensor to brain. It is a thought, no different than a dream or an image of a swan on a lake. Unless I am mentally unstable, I can ignore the voices, the images, the smells. But not the pain. How does the brain do that? How does it make a pain signal so irresistible and the sweet smell of clover so ignorable? Each is just an action potential in the brain, but the ones that make a difference in survival get priority. Cue the amygdala. More on that in the next chapter.

Brain signals move fast, but you can measure the time delays. Your brain can compensate for that. If something touches your foot and hand at the same time, your brain will perceive the touches as simultaneous even though one is farther from the brain than the other. A brain can use other cues to tell if that is one touch or two separate ones. Was the touch light, a tickle, or severe? Here's the other kicker. Gromit is lying on the floor at my feet right now. The skin neurons do not know he is asleep, so every neuron from every hair is sending signals about what he is touching. His brain is ignoring them. Sounds of me typing are still coming into his ears but are ignored. I reach down and touch his face and his eyes are open in an instant. Millions of signals are coming in all the time, largely ignored, but still coming. Right now, stop and think about your feet. Without looking, you can tell if you have shoes on. Those touch cells have been firing all along doing their job, yet your brain selectively ignored them. Your brain can put the different touch signals together and tell you without your looking where your feet are, what parts of your body are covered in clothes, and what the relative temperatures are. Pain is a great defense mechanism and gets immediate attention even if you are asleep. Certain sounds will immediately awaken Gromit. The sound of a food bag rustling. The feel of me taking a step near his head. A pair of structures in the brain, one on the left and one on the right side, the amygdala, constantly monitor signals, sorting the relevant from the less significant. Pain seems to get attention because it is so necessary for survival. Ignore pain and you can die. Ignore the feel of shoes on my feet, not so much.

Chemoreception/taste and smell
Smell and taste are really the same sense: chemoreception. Literally, this means receiving chemicals from the environment. As primates, we rely on sight for much of what

we do, and a large portion of our brain is devoted to visual processing. But all mammals are pretty good at the sense of chemoreception, or chemical detection, or as we always call them, taste and smell. Most of what you think of as taste is actually smell, and the two really work pretty much the same way. Next time you are eating something tasty, pinch your nose shut. Loses a lot of its taste, doesn't it? That's because you no longer smell it. Dogs are superstars at chemoreception. How far away can they detect a smell? Ha, tricked you once with that before, didn't I? We smell with our brains, not our noses. The chemical has to get into the nose or into the mouth, so the distance is zero. But smell molecules can waft in from very long distances indeed.

At a molecular level, different chemicals trigger different neuron types. It is a lock and key kind of a deal where certain shaped molecules fit into certain shaped receptors and trigger that neuron, or fail to, depending on the fit. These neurons are scattered on the tongue and in the back of the nose (where the smells that you thought were taste waft up from the mouth). The cells on the tongue only do a rough job protecting against dangerous foods like bitter poisons. Humans have maybe 500 types of chemoreceptors. Dogs are understood to have 1,000, although some scientists say they have 20,000 different types. There is not complete agreement on how different a receptor has to be to be counted as distinct. Confused? Let me use color to clarify, since most of us have that sense, and we are rather poorly attuned to our senses of smell. How many colors are there? Three, the primary colors of red, blue, and yellow; all others derive from them. So there must be other derivative colors. How many? I say 64 because that was what my box of Crayola crayons had when I was in school. Now they come in boxes up to 120. My computer monitor displays 256 colors. But we see 1,000 levels of dark-light and about 100 levels each of red-green and yellow-blue from the cones. That would be millions of colors. If you look into an eye, you will only see three kinds of color receptors. Long story short: Looking at cell receptors might not be the best way to distinguish differences in a sense we really are worse at than dogs.

Let's look at humans and our 500 types of receptors. Like our eyes with three types, likely these receptors respond to different concentrations and mixes. Combinations of chemicals coming in and combinations of receptors firing give us those complex smells that we perceive as unique: pine pollen or freshly cut grass. Some chemicals can be odorless but still send a signal, like many pheromones. Smells are also closely associated with memory. We remember smells and we remember memories associated with that smell. Oddly, when I smell bread baking, I still immediately remember a sermon a friend preached his first year out of seminary, where he described bread-making at length. I have no idea where that happened, nor do I recall anything else about the sermon, or even why bread was part of it. But baking bread makes me think of that memory. The yeast smell also makes me think of beer brewing, which makes me think of the many pubs I have been to. Bread really is wonderful, but I digress again. Those 500 chemo receptors in humans were thought to mean we could detect 10,000 smells, but recent work suggests we might be closer to a trillion. Dogs would be far greater than that because they have more types of receptors. If so, if we can detect a trillion smells, but only 10 million colors and about half a million sound tones, this would imply that smell is a lot more important to humans than we thought. We know it is to dogs, so let's look there.

Smell needs to be detectable as unique, and is measured in concentration or strength. Consider that you can take clothing worn by any random human, give the article to a trained dog to smell, and they can remember that smell and track that unique individual. Bloodhounds have been known to follow a trail for over 100 miles (160 km). They can detect minute differences in concentration and potency, or recency. With that ability, they can tell which way to go on a trail. Think about it for a moment. If I am walking along a trail, I might cover 100 yards (90 m) in a minute. A trained dog could sniff around on that trail, and let's say the dog walked the whole 100 yards (90 m). In that 300-foot span the dog would detect which end of it had the more recent scent, and therefore what direction I went, even if I laid down that trail hours before. Usually they can do this in a few feet, not 100 yards. I would have crossed that 100 yards in one minute. So the dog detects a one-minute time difference in scent concentration and picks my scent out from all of the other competing scents. Explosive-sniffing dogs at the airport can pick up a trillionth of a gram of chemical scent in a large room filled with many bags containing coffee, dirty laundry, and the smells of all the places the bag has been and the many hands that have touched the bag. Friends of mine have trained dogs to find the specific species of turtle I studied. Once trained, dogs can smell the differences in blood sugar of a diabetic partner (actually detecting ketones released in the breath when blood sugar changes). They can be taught to sniff out certain other diseases, including cancer. They can sniff out electronics, such as banned phones in a prison. No, dogs are not perfect scent detectors, and they can be fooled. Ask anyone who has trained for nose work or field scent trials. But they are astoundingly good pursuit predators that use scent to detect prey at a distance, sound to get closer, and sight to close the deal.

Other senses

Sight, hearing, taste, smell, and touch. We covered all of the five senses. Whew. Except, who ever said there were only five senses? No, I am not referring to the unscientific sixth sense of something supernatural. The five-senses count goes back to Aristotle, and he has been dead for years now. Like 2,300 years. We have learned a bit since then. You have a sense of balance, which works using touch detectors in the inner ear, but also incorporates vision. Likewise you have a sense of velocity or acceleration. Do you call that a new sense, or a combination of two already covered ones? Skin has touch sensors, but we now know pain and temperature receptors are different from touch, and there are even several kinds of distinct touch receptors. Your bladder and other muscles have stretch detectors that tell you muscle position (proprioception) and the sense or urge to urinate. Hunger and thirst are also senses, but are poorly understood. Likewise you and likely your dogs have the sense of time or chronoreception. Scientists like me would add in here that senses of magnetism and electric fields are known in some other species and could be in dogs. I am not (yet) convinced by the study of dogs orienting to defecate. There are interesting situations caused by a genetic mutation where some people have an extra cone type and can detect four primary colors. Some other people have synesthesia where two or more senses blend. They can taste colors or see sounds. It all seems reasonable when you remember that each is just an action potential and the brain has to decide at an unconscious level what the signal means.

TOUR 11

HOME BASE: THE BRAIN

When I was new as a biology professor, there was this new field called neuroscience. The discipline led to a rapid change in our understanding of the biology behind our sensing, perceiving, and acting on the world around us and how the brain puts it all together. Neuroscience continues to make unbelievable discoveries, as we will see as we look now at the brain, the organ in the body where essentially all the signals from the nervous system eventually end up.

When I wrote about the liver, did I need to get all philosophical? No, I did not. Did I need to explain my biases when I covered bones, the very foundation of an organism's structure? Nope, not then, either. If a person gets a kidney transplant, do we think they are a different person? No. Start to cover the brain and now we are treading on dangerous ground. Ancient Greeks believed thought and spirit were located in the heart, and we still use a heart to signify love, even though we now know emotions are perceived in the brain. Ancient Egyptians, when making mummies, gave the heart special treatment. The brain, they scooped it out through the nose and threw it away. Today we get all squishy when we talk brains. No one gets surprised if I compare a dog's heart to a human's. Mammals are mammals. The mammalian heart is pretty much a mammalian heart. Sure, a mouse's is too small to move my blood, and I could climb into a blue whale's heart, which can weigh over half a ton. Same valves. Same layers. Same cell types. Understanding the brain is different. It is not just neurons and connections. It has memories, and it evaluates and weighs ideas that are not physical external items. It can conjure up fantasies and imagine what never was. Maybe, however, it is just neurons and connections and our sense of reality is an artifact of biology, an unintended consequence. See, we are getting squishy. We do not separate the brain from what it is to be "us" or to be "Gromit." The brain seems to be so much more than its parts.

All the current brain imaging shows that a dog's brain functions and its neural pathways are laid out in tracks that are the same as humans. When I was a wee lad in undergraduate biology, we were taught over and over how special we were, how our brains set us apart, how that brain gave us moral superiority. Even then, I felt like we were missing something important. All the evidence is that my dog's brain is pretty much as versatile and complex as mine at most levels. Not at all of them. I am sure we will find some really important distinctions. Most of the brain research involves humans, because we can tell researchers what we are thinking and feeling. My biology teachers told me that until it was proven otherwise, I should assume all animal brains were as simple as reptile brains, incapable of higher thought. I have since become convinced through research as well as observing dogs closely for decades that we would be wiser to assume that the similarities outweigh the differences. My descriptions of brain functions generalize what we know about dog brains and offer links to what we know about humans.

None of that, however, is a claim by me to give rights for dogs that are equal to humans. I am not primarily a philosopher or ethicist, nor am I devoid of ethical considerations. My vegan and animal-rights friends argue that my position means I have to extend all human rights to dogs, as if rights go with brains. My hunter friends argue the opposite. They say rights go by species. My friends doing research involving mammals seem to prefer to not talk about it at all because it would affect their results, and maybe their willingness to do what can be very important research. To be clear, brain function or species is not how I view rights. I am much more geographic or relationship-oriented in my view of rights. I see a homeless human, blessed with a great brain, and it breaks my heart. I might give them a dollar, and make some additional modest donation to shelters and food pantries. If my dog shows a wisp of discomfort on his plush bed, he is off to the veterinarian. I give my dogs more rights than I would give most any person, not because they are dogs or not, or have brains or not, but because they are directly in my family. Nothing more complex or nuanced than that. I do not think the fact that dog brains seem to be pretty much like ours from a biological point of view tells me much more than just that. If brains are what matter to our ethics, then do you give smarter people more rights than less intelligent ones? Really, we aren't going there in this chapter.

I do wonder every day about just how perceptive dogs really are. I worry about humans who bore their dogs to insanity with inactivity and repetition. I worry about our failure to recognize mental health problems in dogs, just as we fail to treat them as equal to other health problems in people.

OK, we got that out. Let's look at the brain.

Physical layout

Unlike the heart or bones or muscles, the physical layout of the brain is difficult to discern. First off, it is a soft, gelatinous structure that cannot be studied well (dissected) unless it is chemically fixed. This changes it to a tougher, waxy texture but also adds all kinds of anomalies. Early brain studies did this, and it was useful in identifying areas of the brain, locations that could be named, but revealed only a poor idea of what those parts did. In fact, often the only way to know what an area did was to find someone missing that part, say from a brain lesion or accident, and see what was going wrong. That required you finding someone with a problem and working with them until they eventually had the courtesy to die so you could see what part was damaged. So much of the rest of the body is "this part sits here and does this" that any unique area was given a name and a perceived function.

Then there was 1990. Before that, we were poking around in the dark with no flashlight. After that, spotlights, laser beams, and a whole new world. That was when functional magnetic resonance imaging (fMRI) became known to the scientific community in a paper, and soon thereafter at a major MRI conference in San Francisco. MRIs had only been around for a decade, and this new kind with the "f" in front of the name revealed more than just structure. Functional MRIs show brain activity. Pre-1980s, there was just no good way to look at the brain without actually opening it up and poking around in there. Since the brain has no pain receptors, researchers could numb your skull and skin, cut open a hole, and stick in thin metal probes. Then they would ask you things like, "Can you feel this?" You would hope never to hear the surgeon say, "Hmm, this looks interesting." Sounds barbaric, but that was an improvement over not being able to do anything at all. With MRIs becoming available in the 1980s, things changed. MRIs have giant magnets, and through some really cool technologies, they can use the water molecules in soft tissues to take what looks like an X-ray. X-rays use DNA-damaging ionizing radiation and are best for imaging hard tissue like bones. But now, boom, soft tissue in 3-D with computers using revolutionary software so one can look at parts from every angle. The f in functional MRI, or fMRI, refers to the ability to use an MRI to measure the metabolic activity of what it is imaging by measuring blood flow. Active, functioning parts of the brain use more energy, and so they get more blood. In fact, your dog's half-pound (230 g) brain uses about a fifth of all the energy used by its body.

I have had MRIs of my brain, so they can confirm I do in fact have something up there, much to my friends' surprise. You lie on a narrow bed, and they stick your head into a large circular opening in a huge electromagnet. In the old days, your whole body went in to a grave-sized opening and you felt pretty enclosed. Because at the time they were looking for a tumor in me, I could not help but think "casket." The technician says, "Now hold perfectly still" and you hear enormous banging and clanking and thumping. Your reflex is to want to look at the noise. You fight it. In case you were wondering, my brain came out OK. The doctors got images of my living tissue at work, no hole in my head needed. Over time, this ability allowed us to map brain functions in humans. Look at a picture of a farm, certain parts of the brain light up. Look at a picture of a pretty person, your choice of gender or lack of gender, and another area lights up. Food, another area. It showed us how simplistic our view of our brain functioning was. By now, you gotta be thinking, "So what does this have to do with me and my dogs?" Everything. Give me just a moment more.

Functional MRI allowed researchers to move beyond anatomical studies from MRIs to functional work on living brains. So far, nothing allows us to actually map the 100 trillion synapses in the brain. Another source says over a quadrillion synapses. However, lots of good human data was coming in. It wasn't long before other researchers saw animal applications. By 2005, there was published work on rats. In 2015, dogs made the big time with a paper entitled "Functional MRI of the olfactory system in conscious dogs" (Jia et al., 2015) for work done at Auburn University by Hao and others. Using positive reinforcement and ear plugs, they trained dogs to sit perfectly still but unanesthetized through all the magnet banging in the confined spaces. Now several labs are doing this, mostly with Labrador and Golden Retrievers, and Border Collies so far. Yep, labs are using Labs! The studies on mammals in general, and dogs in particular, show a distinctly mammalian brain with the same basic structures lighting up at the same times. Pleasant food lights up the same areas. Negative images light up similar areas. Our brains and their brains, as long as they are mammals, act pretty much the same. Do we think the same way? Heck, I don't even think the same way as my wife or my siblings. That is where the divide starts. We will return to it in the section on behaviors. For now, let's take a squishy walk through the gelatinous brain.

I want you to think of the brain like a city, with the roads as neurons and the water lines and sewer lines as the circulatory system. I say to you, "Take me to where the government control of the city is." You take me to city hall, but you point out another building where the state offices are, another for federal IRS, a dozen others for federal mail, scattered police stations, fire departments and, well you get the idea. Where do supplies come in? Rail yards, airports, and every street. Functioning is diffuse, scattered around, integrated and connected. So it is with the brain. We can point to areas with primary responsibilities, but those are connected through neurons to other areas that impact them. Take one example. You tell me my dog is coughing. My brain has to engage language functions so I know what you said, and each word has associated other images, like the time I coughed so much I thought I broke a rib. The part of my brain involved in emotions rolls in because this is my dog, not your dog, so I care more. I listen to see if I agree with your diagnosis. I am already planning ahead. What if I need a vet? What if it is kennel cough? Didn't we get the vaccine? I try to remember. Is it some random dog, or is it Wish, who gets these weird cough-like spells anyway if her collar or leash presses on her throat? There is no one, singular part of my brain for Wish or memories of her. No Wish Central. Wish thoughts, memories, and associations are scattered. Complex, sure. Do we fully understand it? Absolutely not. My point is that while I walk us through the structures of the brain, I want you to remember that there are lots of areas every memory associates with, and the more there are, the easier it is to remember. That will be the core of behavior coming up.

Interconnecting neurons

Even primitive critters like earthworms have brains. Brains are centralized areas for neurons to gather and interconnect. If the gathering is small, say 15,000 neurons, we call it a ganglion. We have these scattered about our bodies, with 20 pairs of them along our spinal cord. As does your dog. The human brain has maybe 16 billion cells in our cerebral cortex (higher thinking area of the brain). Our closest relatives, chimpanzees, have around 8 billion. Dogs have under a billion, but still twice as many as house cats. This puts dogs similar to raccoons and lions in cell numbers. All this according to a fascinating graph and numbers filled article in a 2017 *Frontiers in Neuroanatomy* paper comparing carnivore brains. Each neuron can have thousands of connections, so having billions of neurons is great and complex. We cannot well imagine what that does to one's cognitive abilities. Not everyone agrees that counting neurons is the best measure of intelligence, but it sure beats using methods that layer in cultural biases like standard written tests. Most dogs just eat those or pee on them, adversely affecting their score.

That should illustrate my core point. We know some of how brains work; the parts are the same, but the sophistication and size are worlds apart. Think of the complexity differences between a computer from a decade ago and one from today. For the younger set reading this, look at what your current smartphone does compared to five years ago. It has more ability, way more sophistication in function. I would posit that my dog loves and hates, is happy and sad, and has all of those basic emotions that I have. However, our brains have the capacity to imagine worlds that do not exist and to write about them and create technologies to achieve them, and likely the thoughts my dog is having are more built around eating, sleeping, and checking the pee-mail next time we are out to see if the neighbor dog is in heat yet.

The brainstem

Many functions of the brain are basic, needed by all vertebrate life, and things you don't want to have to give much thought to. When is the last time you consciously controlled your heart rate? If it required thinking about it, what would happen when you fell asleep? Those functions are handled by the brainstem. I am going to skip naming all of the parts. So here, for example, the lowest part of the brainstem, where the spinal cord leaves the neck and enters the skull, is the base of the brainstem, called the medulla oblongata. Cool set of words. Fun to say. But we are going to generalize here like we did before with other body parts. The brainstem is easily recognizable on any brain diagram because it looks like a fat extension of the spinal cord. In some sense, that is what it is. Or think of it another way: The spinal cord is just the part of the brain that extends outside the skull all the way down the back. There really is no dividing line inside, just the geographic boundary of the skull. Some very basic activities occur here in the brainstem, like keeping the beat of life (heartbeat), breathing, swallowing, eye movement, that sort of thing. If you count the spinal cord as part of the brain, as I do, and I may be the only one who does, but without a skull you have little way to draw a line there, then it also covers reflexes like your knee-jerk reflex. There are a dozen cranial nerves every human or canine anatomy student has to memorize that go to places like the ears (auditory nerve) and the face (facial nerve), and 10 of these come out of the brainstem. The brainstem is kind of a nexus or hub that lots of pathways pass through or originate in.

The cerebellum and the cerebrum

Two big blobs come off the brainstem, the cerebrum and the cerebellum. Really? Couldn't they have used more distinctive and distinguishable names like "the higher functions center" and "motor control central"? That is what they are. Cerebellum first. This easily-seen structure of the brain is located in the back, closest to where the spinal cord enters the skull. It handles fine motor skills of the paws as well as posture, balance, and coordination of motor functions. In the cerebellum, the left side controls the left side of the body, the right covers the right. These are heavily interconnected to allow coordination. I have a friend, let's call her Sue, whose dog Yeoman showed some gait abnormalities when Sue met Yeo at a shelter, when one of them was just under six months old. Sue's vet ordered an x-ray only to find half the dog's cerebellum was missing. Mostly her dog was normal for its life. How? There is so much about the brain still to learn.

In front of the cerebellum, and coming off the anterior part of the brainstem, is the cerebrum. It is large in mammals. The cerebrum has a huge groove or valley down the middle, dividing the left and right side. The sides split out some brain functions. In general, the left side of the brain controls the right side of the body, and the right covers the left. Let's stop right here for a moment. In the 1960s it became popular to think of being "left-brain dominant" or "right-brain dominant" and to assign things like analytical ability to one and creativity to the other. Often gender was likewise assigned. Too often that was used to make people of one gender think they were superior to another in analytical or creative thinking. The only problem with that way of thought is that it is inaccurate. Wrong. Demonstrably so. Functional MRI scans and other methods show this is not at all correct. It is still a popular idea, but brain anatomy and function do not support what many people want to believe. In fact, beyond a few examples, the side differences tend to be geographic body control, not thinking, which scoots back and forth across the brain all over the place. Language is left-sided, but the context of language seems to be more right-sided. This brain-sidedness is called lateralization, and most species show it, so it must offer some advantages. As I noted earlier, 90% of humans are right-handed. If handedness were not important, you would expect half to be lefties and half to be righties. Dogs are this way, half lead left, half lead right. We are not sure why most species show a preference, nor yet can we say why dogs don't. More properly I should say that experts disagree on which explanations are best supported by the data. We just have trouble with the details, but beware of the common, gross oversimplifications like "My dog is right-brained, so he is more emotional." He might be more emotional, but current science shows it is not due to the sidedness of the brain involved.

The cerebrum has several lobes with some specialization each. The back lobes are the occipital lobes, left and right, which are heavily involved in vision and language. The side lobes, or temporal lobes, are heavily associated with visual and verbal memory (language and recognition of what an object is) and interpreting others. Parietal lobes are the next most anterior, and process inputs from other brain areas and help organize them. The most anterior lobes are cleverly called the frontal lobes. They coordinate higher-level thinking like problem solving, planning ahead, making decisions or evaluations, paying attention, and some more motor skills, and the vague thing called personality.

Ventricles and meninges

The brain has some empty spaces called ventricles. OK, they are empty of neurons, but full of a specialized body liquid called cerebrospinal fluid. These ventricular spaces are continuous with spinal fluid that goes all the way down the center of the spinal cord. It gives some impact protection to the brain by absorbing shock and provides an isolated area for the immune system in the brain. This isolation helps protect the brain from chemicals and invaders in the blood, known as the blood-brain barrier.

Wrapped around the brain are three layers of tissue called meninges that make a sac around the brain directly beneath the skull. The outer layer is tough and fibrous, the middle layer is more like the rafters in a roof with a spider web network to add space and cushioning. The innermost layer, up next to the brain and spinal cord itself, follows all the contours of the brain, sticking tightly to the outermost parts of the brain. That's it for protecting the soft gelatinous numero uno organ of the body. All you have protecting your brain is a layer of hair, muscles that primarily work the jaw but cover the skull, bone, the meninges, and then the brain itself. Pretty well adapted to handle a dog running full tilt into a tree or getting kicked in the head by glancing blows from hooves. A direct blow can still kill. If you put that dog brain and its wrappings in a car hurtling down the road at the evolutionarily-never-experienced speeds of 40, 50 … wait, you go 80 miles per hour (65, 80, 130 kph)? What if your car runs full tilt into that tree, what is making up the deceleration difference from a dangerous 20 mph (32 kph) run into a tree versus the lethal speed of the car's sudden stop? Dog seat belts and collapsible kennels help absorb the blow. Don't leave home without them. Drive defensively, because those restraints only help some, and your dog deserves to keep their brain intact.

The wonderful interplay of it all

Let's take a break here to revisit a main point. There are dozens of structures I can name. Most of them have vague functions like "relates this area to that" or "coordinates signals from this region to that." The main point, the salient point is that the brain is all interconnected, with each neuron having thousands of connections to many parts of the brain that somehow coordinate and relate and associate signals coming in from various areas. Those signals are the action potentials described earlier that propagate along the neurons. At each connection, or synapse, there is a chemical mediator that can stop or alter the incoming action potential. It is this super-complex web of connections that matter. Interfere with the synapses and you affect brain function. Mess with a connecting area, like the corpus callosum that connects the hemispheres of the cerebrum and you get other problems. Muddle the circulatory system sending oxygen and sugar to the brain, other problems. Throw in the electrochemical interfaces where the brain connects with the chemical endocrine system at the hypothalamus and pituitary, and you get other issues. Now throw in memory, history, and other associations that affect how the brain treats information. It should be clear that behaviors are complex and we cannot treat them as isolated events. Is my dog ignoring me because he has past bad memories of this trick I am training, or is the body chemistry off, or the brain chemistry, or a portion of the brain is not associating this perfectly, or because the brain is paying more attention to something in the background, maybe a smell or sound I cannot detect?

Let's look at an exchange I just had with my wife that helps illustrate why I am presenting all of this. It also shows how difficult her life is living with a geek like me because this was exchanged as texts. This morning's weather was predicted to be freezing rain starting between 6 and 7 a.m., and her dog agility trial walkthrough started at 8. She decided to go in early. Seems obvious and simple. My text to her was along these lines:

Do you ever stop to think how complex that was? You had to take information about the current conditions of the road, imagine what the roads would be like based on past experiences projected forward, layered with memories of driving on icy roads and the incredible stresses that still places on you, evaluate all this in terms of timing to get to the 8 a.m. start, weighted against not going (Ha, like that was ever really an option!), and then go. Going means driving, which involves lots of motor skills so trained and ingrained into you that you don't think about driving while you control this metal box between two lines 8 feet apart on a paved surface… Then you take Wish out to a course she has never seen before. She had to learn what each obstacle requires and follow a path you signal with subtle shoulder shifts she had to learn to read, adding experiences so that when she sees you over there and this obstacle is over here she needs to do a particular thing, all at full speed, without tangling her feet in the weaves or the tunnels, ignoring all the smells and sounds and sights of other dogs and people milling about. You increase her motivation, but she had innate drive, too.

The text, of course, had abbreviations and language short cuts that she would infer, but you cannot because you don't share the same history. See how complex our days are?

Now I'd like to dabble in reality a bit. There is some solid evidence that in humans, at least, imagining can be as useful as physical practice, since muscle memory is not really in the muscles, it is in the brain. Based on empirical evidence, time spent vividly imaging running an agility course, or moving about in dance or freestyle, or throwing a Frisbee, or handling a dog sled or doing other physical activities, once you are good at them so you can vividly recall experiences, can be as effective as physically doing the activity itself. Imagining actions won't burn calories or produce endorphins, but it allows the brain to rehearse. Once the signal is in the cerebral cortex, it appears that the brain does not distinguish if it came from the motor cortex where you did the action, or other parts of the cerebral cortex where you imagined it. Likely that works for your dog, as well. We cannot force our dogs to think about a given topic, but I have to believe they replay a good squirrel chase, or a wild Frisbee catch in their own brains, rehearsing the steps. Ancestral wolves that did this would have had a definite survival advantage over those that did not, so it seems a likely path to develop. It also means that reality to our cerebral cortex may be a bit fuzzier than we like to think.

TOUR 12

BIOLOGY AND BEHAVIOR:
OUR MESSIEST TOUR

If you want to start a good argument, get a bunch of dog trainers, veterinarians, and behaviorists together in a room and pose the classic nature versus nurture question: Which impacts behavior more, genetics or the environment? You can do the exact same thing with a room of biologists, neuroscientists, and psychologists. Bring your popcorn. Stay out of the line of fire and watch the fireworks. Oh, wait, you are one of these groups? Well, this is about to get really interesting. Can you really train a Greyhound to not run after a squirrel? Or, to go right to the fireworks: Can innate aggression be controlled? On this tour I want to examine a couple issues that I hope, in my role as a biologist, I can shed some light on. Please know up front that this is still an unresolved issue that will likely have a very complicated and nuanced answer. There are data to support a wide array of opinions, and it is always difficult to scientifically test statements with "always" or "never" in them when the exceptions are slight and hard to measure. Anyone with all of the answers lacks all of the evidence. But that does not mean it is not worth a stop on the tour.

Can one override genetically driven behaviors?

The canine brain can, with training, learn to control hormonal and other instinctive programmed responses. Most responses. Some responses. To what extent? Both dogs and humans are influenced by hormonal drives. Both have brains that are complex enough to learn when it is OK and when it is not OK to follow the chemically induced behavior. Hunger, the drive to eat, is driven by the hormone ghrelin, produced in the stomach. Without training, a dog responds to the hunger drive hormone by eating. Place food in front of a hungry, untrained dog, and it will eat. Now. With gusto. With training, even a hungry dog can learn to ignore the hunger drive and wait for permission to eat. Which is really in control, the brain or the hormones? Wait long enough, such as starvation conditions, and the hormone will override the brain. But in normal circumstances, the brain can control most hormones, at least for a time. At least it seems so now. This works on other hormonal drives. I teach college students. I make it very clear that hormones do not ever excuse behavior, be it hunger, aggression, or sex. Hormones influence, but with training, most can be controlled. Maybe all. There are clearly some individuals who, even with the training they get, cannot control hormone-induced behaviors. Could they with better training? Hormones influence dog aggression. How much? Can it be controlled?

We need a quick timeout on vocabulary here. To an evolutionary ecologist, material in the brain (thoughts, induced actions, etc.) are either innate (genetically based) or learned, or some interactive combination of the two. You are either born with it in your genes, or you learn it from the outside, or you figure it out inside. Training is the act of directing that learning, as opposed to self-discovery. Based on corrections offered to my talks, I would surmise that in much of the dog training world, the terms are not used this way at all. Training generally seems to be used to refer to taking a neutral or nonexistent action and getting more of it. Behavior modification is an approach used on existing behaviors to get them to stop or change. I am absolutely certain I am being too simplistic, but I am not interested in explaining training or behavior modification as the dog training world knows them; there are a bazillion books on that and it seems scores of operating paradigms. My experience is that many biological scientists have difficulty talking to trainers and behavior scientists about training because they have different terms with different nuances. These are often driven by the school of thought or methodological paradigm they use. Not good, not bad, not unique to this field, just is.

We often lump behaviors irrespective of what their source is. For example, I frequently hear talks about how to train dogs out of fear, aggression, depression, or lack of attention span without distinguishing if those come from genetics, are learned from past situations, or are caused by disease or poor nutrition. So if I ask if you can control my dog's fear aggression, the answer probably depends on the cause. To really test that, I need a controlled experiment for each cause, treatment, and variation in breed and age and…Hard facts are hard to get here.

The word "control" I just used is another problem. I am asking a basically biological question: If a dog has genetically influenced behaviors, how much of these can be attenuated or amplified through environmental (non-genetic) means? Which is stronger, learning (broadly defined) or genetics? Does brain disease override both? We also need to note, as we venture into this space, that the science-based answer on this is difficult and imprecise. Just one example: I hypothesize that all genetically influenced behaviors always can be overridden (say any aggression can be trained out of a dog). That is logically impossible to test. I would have to test all dogs at all levels of aggression. Any dog not trained out of aggression could be blamed on the training (my use of the word training here). But you can easily do the opposite. I hypothesize that no dog can be trained away from aggressive acts. With a bit of effort, you could easily prove that statement wrong. "Always" in this example is impossible to prove because you cannot try all training (or behavior modification) on all dogs, especially if your measure of success is aggression against humans. There is a pretty hefty ethical problem with experiments that puts live humans at risk. In addition, while aggression is a prime problem in dog behaviors, I care as much about OCD, pursuit instincts, fear, depression, and hunger.

Just yesterday, a dear friend called me. He is a medical doctor and asked me, "How much of dog genetics can be overridden with training?" His son bought a beautiful pit bull mix, and the good doctor feared for his grandchildren based solely on breed. I asked him, based on his years as a medical doctor, how much genetic behavior could be trained out of people? He paused, said that the science isn't there. Likewise with dogs. I would love to be able to say that with this amount of training we can override that amount of instinct. I do not think the answer is clear, despite having people on both sides of the argument insist based on their experience that it is.

Let's use aggression again. Let's say I train a dog, and like at least one place I saw, guarantee for life that after my training your dog will never be aggressive enough to hurt a human. My first response, having had a fearful dog, is what about aggression to other dogs? That seldom gets recorded in the medical databases, so we have only spotty records. And there are no records for the number of near misses from drive-by looks and snarls. Or, let's assume my training or behavior modification works and we get rid of the visible aggression. If it is genetic, is it sitting there like a time bomb waiting to go off, or is it really safely locked away? The biology says instincts are strong, and written into genes because learning them takes too long and results in unsuccessful offspring. Brains are pretty powerful. Can they override instinct? Sure, in many cases. I get the urge to steal your food but I don't. I can delay my gratification. Does that mean that all people or dogs can learn that? Does it mean that instinct was just weak in me?

If I had the answer to this, I would be in a very different line of work. For over three decades I have had open scholarly debates with psychologists and trainers on this matter. Unfortunately, the debates are pretty fruitless as the data are still in question and the question is really a whole array of questions hiding behind the labels of nature and nurture. It is a core question that gets at the ethics of incarceration in people, euthanasia in dogs, incarceration in dogs, and execution in people. No wonder we have such strong opinions on this. Likely the reality is going to be too non-absolute for our desires. It sure appears to me that the answer is that some or most hormonal behaviors can be control-led some or most of the time. How unsatisfying is that? You want to know "Can this behavior, right here, be affected now, with reasonable training?"

Can learned behaviors be unlearned?

Let us not forget that I have been focusing on brain control versus hormonal con-trol. We also know some unacceptable behaviors are simply learned, without genetic involvement. Maybe most. Can those really be unlearned? How completely? We also know brains suffer physical damage and disease. Can a behavior that results from such organic tissue changes be overridden? How much? Try. That is the best I can do for now. Try, but be careful of your safety and that of others who might be less attentive to the dog and their mood. I have seen really good behavior therapists work miracles, and I have seen the results of dog attacks where miracles were not worked, either untried or unsuccessfully tried.

Answering the impossible question

Watch the literature, be skeptical of any extreme claims, demand evidence, and require more than one study that shows whatever it is you want to believe. There are many good books, a few really great teachers, and a world of literature on this. At its core, it so ties to ethics that they seem inseparable to me. If I start with all dog lives matter, I will push really hard to try to save every dog, even the psychopaths. If I start with the position that any injury to humans is intolerable — either because of the value of humans or the recognition that dog-caused injuries and killings lead to local controls on breeds and dog cohabitation — then I push hard to eliminate aberrant canine behavior (perhaps by eliminating the canine). I hope we can all recognize the complexity of the situation even if we do come at this from many different deeply felt starting points. It really is a life-or-death question without enough real biological answers to help much, complicated by varying ethical positions, enormous variation in individual dogs, incomplete data, and sometimes unhelpful or overly simplistic media reporting. The media rightly wants clear answers to report, and we just don't have those all of the time.

But you want answers right now. Sorry, the science is not there. My doctor friend wanted to know right now what I advised about his grandchildren. I advised what he has done thousands of time for patients who wanted solid answer to "Can I beat this cancer?" or "What is the best way to deal with...?" You balance the risk and the rewards. Risk tolerance is individualistic. I would be far more willing to take a personal risk than to impose it on you, or a child, or my dog. The risk goes both ways, however. If I assure my doctor friend that the dog is safe, I risk physical injury to a child exposed to a breed known to have guarding instincts. Or I risk making a child ever fearful of dogs if I say, based on no previous individual behavior, that this breed is dangerous when many individuals are not. There are some pretty good (not perfect) assessment techniques out there (see Sternberg, 2016), and excellent dog behaviorists who can professionally help evaluate dogs and their behaviors. We assessed our dogs as puppies and regularly throughout their lives. No guarantees, but information to help evaluate the odds. Every time I drive a car, I risk maiming a child or hitting a loose dog. I reduce the risk by not texting while driving, not drinking and driving, and by being very vigilant while driving. At the least, you ought to identify the risk levels and work to reduce known hazards.

Can all behaviors be controlled if there is enough high-quality training? That is a fascinating and as-yet-unresolved biological question. We cannot tell, for example, if a great trainer could take the most felonious dog and retrain them. There are network programs that imply that you can simply and easily train away any bad behavior in any dog. I do not buy it. Maybe with medicine added, but I am still skeptical. Normally found biological variation leads me to believe there will be extreme exceptions. How many? I do not know: 0.1%? 1%? 50%? Can we save them all? How far are we willing to go to retrain? It brings back images of the movie "A Clockwork Orange." Go look that up, but I am not recommending the movie. Odd thing, that one.

Reality is that even if all dogs or humans could be retrained (or modified) with expert, perfectly applied technique or drug, these are in short supply and never available all day every day, and certainly not for free. Individuals vary. An average dog can be taught an awful lot, on average. What do you do with the individuals who either cannot control their behaviors or be taught to control those behaviors? I had a dear friend who rescued a dog. My friend is an excellent trainer with a lot of experience with the breed she adopted. She spent months of unsuccessful training or modifications to behavior. The dog still bit her hand several times, regularly took up very aggressive positions to her kids, her husband, her, and her other dog. Eventually she had to give up on the dog, as it was destroying her family. With more research, she found out this dog had a history of such behavior in two previous homes. The rescue believed all dogs deserved a home, and that mindset almost ruined a family.

Does every dog deserve a good home? You asking me? Sure. So does every person. And dogs all deserve good brain-challenging education, love, and access to medical care. Is that realistic? I don't see how.

I recognize that this issue so divides the dog-loving community, and now more than ever as we have so increased the value of dogs to humans. When I was young, most people barely medically treated their dogs. The cost of a new dog was free, and the cost of medical care was not. As people, we moved from a mostly agrarian people to urban. According to the U.S. Census Bureau, the percent of urban dwellers in the U.S. exceeded 50% for the first time in 1920 in the North, and in the South in 1950. Dogs in the U.S. moved from disposable tools (to many people) to indispensable members of the family. Looking forward, I would urge you to consider breeding and selecting dogs for positive genetically-influenced temperament and behavior rather than genetically based good looks. That won't resolve the problems of today, but it would reduce this dilemma in future generations.

In each case, endocrine glands interact with other glands or organs, including the brain. They co-regulate and affect each other, and often affect every cell in the body. The endocrine system gives widespread control affecting many organs at once. When we talk about dog arousal behavior, we often think it starts with visual stimuli or maybe sounds or smells that get the nervous system alerted. Arousal is not the same as stress, but I see the two equated in places in the dog community. Arousal is a physiological state of heightened sensitivity to certain signals, a firing up of the sympathetic nervous system, and it does not imply sexual overtones of arousal. Stress can be a type of situational arousal or a chronic condition associated with a particular suite of hormones that impart life-saving focus in times of danger. Arousal can be used to enhance learning, while stress hormones reduce the ability to learn. The best learning occurs when your dog is not stressed, but is aroused and paying attention. Recognize the difference in the biology of what is described, and worry less about if we all use the words the same way.

As a teacher, I cannot expect exams to teach much, because the room is full of stress. To get students to learn, they have to see some reward. Likewise, I can use fun, activity, and food to arouse my dog and enhance training. When the dog is stressed, I can only hope previous training will help me mange the situation. Through the hypothalamus, new system-wide chemicals like adrenaline can be released, which keeps the body aroused. Endocrine function is not on and off like the nervous system. It is also context-specific. Adrenaline can play a role in arousal, but also in fight-or-flight stress. Because the endocrine system ties directly to the nervous system, we can often forget that many behaviors are being chemically driven or influenced by the endocrine system with little to no nervous system involvement. Body control, or behavior, is a pretty complex topic.

How do you get past all those absolutely incomprehensible, complex interactions? I sit in absolute wonder at it. Do you need to know how a car runs to drive it? No, but it helps if you hear a strange noise and can run through possible failure points and decide if those are likely important or if you can safely continue on. Do you need to know all of the brain parts to teach Wish a new trick or to take her for a walk? No, but it helps if something goes wrong, and that knowledge can be used to make you a better trainer. For example, knowing that behaviors are linked to so many past associations increases the need for consistent good environments, positive experiences together, and maybe the option to be a little more forgiving when you don't get exactly the behavior you wanted. Much of our work with our dogs builds on our relationships with our dogs. Our dogs' brains associate us with emotions and events. If I am mainly disappointed in my dog, it shows. If I am a source of joy and fun, my dogs will associate that with other things we do. One tiny example. I call Cricket to "Come." Every time she comes to me, no matter why I called her, it has to be a joyful event, even if I pulled her off of some garbage she got into. Coming to me has to be positive because immediately coming to me without hesitation could save her life. On that day, I don't want her brain trying to figure out if this will be fun or not as the moment of contemplation could at worst be lethal.

Understanding consciousness

Gromit runs agility. Wish herds sheep. Cricket dances freestyle. All of them chase Frisbees and rabbits. Dogs can be incredibly active. But they sleep more than half of their lives. We sleep a third? Why? You won't find a definitive answer here. Predators, including humans, get largely uninterrupted sleep. Prey like moose and deer, ever vigilant, sleep in short intervals of a few minutes. Dolphins, which might otherwise drown if they slept, can have one hemisphere of the brain sleep while the other stays alert, and then they trade off. But sleep we all do, except for shrews and a few other oddities. We do know some things about sleep. Rest gives time for the body to catch up on tasks like filtering blood, digesting food, and healing damage. It conserves energy, important in the wild when you have to search for and acquire every meal. No quick stops at the fast-food for takeout. Lack of sleep impairs memory and learning, so it plays a role there, too. From an evolutionary perspective, clearly sleep is essential or it would not get so much of our time, leaving us remarkably vulnerable.

Is any of that brain control conscious? Let's dispense with all the important philosophical considerations and moral valuations of consciousness, as this is mostly a science book. Also, because of the wonders of neuroscience, we now have some ideas about the biology of consciousness.

Consciousness involves actively experiencing what is happening in the world around you. When you sleep you are not experiencing the world. You are unconscious. You are not dead and can be easily awakened. Even in sleep, parts of the brain are on alert. Most neurons of the spinal cord and cerebellum are transactional, feeding signals along paths forward to the brain or from the brain to the body. The cerebrum has many, many, many, many, many feedback loops: opportunities for putting conditions on activities of the brain or adding nuance to signals. Most of this happens in the white matter, or the outer layer of cerebrum. It seems to happen most in the non-frontal lobes of the brain. Damage to the frontal lobes affects planning and appropriateness of behaviors, but not how one experiences the world. Even in humans, we still are not sure what brings on consciousness or exactly what it is, or at least we cannot agree on what it means. Most scientists argue that we cannot measure it very well in ourselves so we cannot measure it in other animals. Note that there are scientists who spend their careers doing just this, and they would definitely take issue with what I just wrote. Such is the nature of science: We use facts and experiments to make convincing arguments, and very few areas of study have all scientists agreeing on anything.

Maybe we should just use the definition of being sentient or aware. Nope, still vague. And it is binary, implying that you are or you are not aware, but there are shades of awareness. I can drive or walk for miles, a very conscious act, and be thinking about my dogs, and have no idea how I got where I am. Was I conscious? I was not aware of the world around me. But I must have been; I never crashed or tripped. Are there shades of consciousness? Honestly, the amount of value I personally place on any being is unaffected by whether or not they are sentient or conscious. But if consciousness is a measure of problem-solving, memory, and context, then mammals have it. Whatever consciousness is.

Voluntary versus involuntary behavior

How much of what you do in a day is consciously controlled or influenced? Much of what we think is voluntary behavior is not, and our brains do a lot that we are unaware of. Current estimates put unconscious activity at 90-95% of what the brain does. Even conscious activities are not always controllable. If they were, I would weigh 15 pounds (7 kg or just over 1 stone) less by simply choosing to. I wouldn't ever say the stuff I blurt out in class if I had complete control. If it were all voluntary, brain damage or disease-induced behavioral changes could be fixed by simple instructions. If that is true in us, do not be surprised if the same applies to dogs. Indeed, we seem far more comfortable talking about behaviors in dogs that are innate or genetic than we do in humans, so let me reverse this and say that since we know some behavioral tendencies in dogs are genetic and beyond their control, don't be surprised to find that in humans. Remember, unlike dog breeds where we often keep genes pools separate with lots of paperwork, humans swap genes all over the place. Elizabethan morals aside, we humans are a promiscuous species and we have rarely made long-term widespread attempts at keeping breeds.

Border Collies were bred to do some pretty important herding functions where being obsessive about the details mattered. A herding dog cannot just ignore one of the sheep off by itself. They have to get every last one. We bred retrievers to sit quietly with us in confined blinds to aid us in hunting, but not until called for, and then with great abandon to go get a downed bird. They are excellent at hanging tight and relaxing as well as very energetic play. We have identified genes for sociability in dogs, and we can select for that. Shout outs for The Functional Dog Collaborative and their podcast and website. Check them out. They are where I hope the future of dog breeding goes. Sociability is the genetic, temperamental focus of dogs on people, as opposed to socialization, which is a trained response to people and the human environment. Can we completely train over those genetic temperaments? There is not a complete biological answer yet, but certainly it is easier to train away aggression in a dog starting with less-aggressive tendencies, and easier to train tricks in a dog starting with more curious or investigative temperaments.

How genetics control or influence behaviors at the molecular level is not well understood. We saw earlier how genetic traits also have environmental influences on them. So, too, for genetically controlled behaviors. Genetic traits might be heavily influenced by the environment, like body size, but studies of identical twins show even pretty basic genetic expressions are impacted by learning and the environment. Wish and Cricket are closely related, sharing ¼ of their genes. Remember, that is a quarter of the genes that vary between dogs. The overwhelming number of genes are identical in all dogs. We see basic temperamental similarities in sociability, for example, in each. Other dogs we have raised with them at the same time in the same environment showed very different traits consistently throughout their lives. Gromit is far more aloof. Blizzard was as people-centered as a dog can be, except that he had a pretty low threshold to elicit his WTF-is-going-on mode, which the professionals called fear aggression. Genetics influence canine behaviors. They set boundaries. They are not the sole decider so we have to train. We do know some pretty interesting basic mechanisms, and they are most useful in training dogs.

The (brain) chemistry of learning

Return with me to our ancestral dogs some 20,000 years ago. Their physical environment would be constantly changing with weather, time of day, movement or even migration of prey, fires, and seasons, as well as nomadic or sedentary humans in the area. It would be useful to have a base set of behaviors and tendencies that could be adapted to changing times. For example, in a social group species like dogs, it would not serve well to be genetically programmed to follow whatever dog you first see at birth, like the imprinting found in geese. That lead dog won't be around in a few years, so then what would happen? Learning allows one to adapt to new circumstances. Genetic behaviors set the foundation that learning builds on.

Learning at the molecular level inside the brain, inside the neurons, maybe at the synapses, involves drugs. Good drugs. Strong drugs. These drugs are often neurotransmitters, found in the synapses between neurons. They also have systemic or whole-body and brain effects. Studying drug addictions and other kinds of addictions has helped us learn about the built-in molecular reward system for behaviors. Studies of stress show us the other side, the negative reward structure. We do not fully understand these systems, and the public has glommed on to them and oversimplified them. I am likely to do the same to drive home a few points, but I hope not.

There are a few well-known feel-good recreational drugs that imitate the feel-good hormones and neurotransmitters in your body. The naturally occurring ones you and your dog both have include but are not limited to dopamine and serotonin. Something that works out well causes a release of these drugs, and/or endorphins or oxytocin. Those provide a feel-good response, a chemical reward, which causes one to repeat the activity to get more of the feel-good chemicals. After a few repeats, dopamine starts being released in anticipation of the act, giving some of the good feeling even without the act. Often, it seems, this anticipatory hit can be better than the rewards of the action itself. I sit, you give me a treat, it feels good satiating some hunger and releases endorphins (naturally occurring opioids) which makes me want that food. Dopamine is released, driving that want, so I try some activities I just did because I don't yet know if the treat was for sitting, looking at you, or the car that drove by at the same time. Repeat it enough and I develop a minor addiction to that activity because I get opioids for it, and eventually even in anticipating it. Clear, well-timed cues help me see more quickly what I did to get that release of opioids.

Many of us have heard of things like a runner's high, where a runner gets enough endorphins from that physical activity that they sacrifice all else to keep getting that high every day. Any addiction will do it. An addiction to opioids themselves short-circuits all the mess of actually having to do the work. I get a burst of dopamine learning new things, likely because that was what I was rewarded for early in my life, or at least what I thought I was getting rewarded for. Those who know me say I am addicted to learning, which is now my job, which makes me a workaholic. Get addicted to that, you get rewards. Get addicted to alcohol, your body suffers and you get socially ostracized. Get addicted to sports, and you play all the time. Get addicted to dogs, oh yes, I just went there. Dog enthusiasts get dopamine hits anticipating their next dog activity, then they do it, and they (we) get rewarded chemically again after doing it. I wonder how much difference there really is at the extremes between passion and obsession about a dog activity and other obsessive behaviors like alcoholism and obsessive-compulsive disorder. Like any of these addictive behaviors, there is a lot of safe middle ground. I love a beer or a glass of wine, but that does not make me an alcoholic. My psychologist friends say that the only real distinguisher between a healthy passion and an addiction is how it interferes with other healthy aspects of life. If my dog obsesses about squirrels when he sees them, it may be healthy. If he cannot do anything but look out the window or chase phantom rodents, that is a problem.

Dopamine and serotonin have become so popular, there are people with jewelry showing the molecular structure, like the woman at the grocery checkout. I asked, "So are you a chemist?" She said, "No, why?" I replied, "Because you have a chemical structure as a necklace." She said, "Yeah, dopamine. My spirit drug. I don't really know what it does but it makes us all feel good." Like anything, good to a point. Rats given free access to dopamine will forego eating and sleeping to self-medicate. Too much of almost anything is not so good. All this to say that while you are getting addicted to your dogs, they are getting addicted to you and to the activities you are teaching them. When skipped for a day, some dogs mope. Gromit, 15 and arthritic, will walk around the house with an insistent bark until he has had his Frisbee fix for the day. Take care of that, and it has to be from me, then he settles down until the next day. It has to hurt his joints, but the dopamine drive supersedes the pain and release of stress hormone. The dark horse is cortisol. Again, a caution about oversimplification, but it can help us see some generally applicable information. Cortisol is released when the body is under stress. Evolutionarily it functions in the sympathetic system of fight or flight. There is a whole network of nerves in the peripheral nerve system that suppresses nonessential functions and reroutes blood and attention to allow an organism in an immediately dangerous or potentially dangerous situation to fight for its life or get out of Dodge. In what is perceived as such a crisis, blood is shunted from digestion to the muscles. We develop tunnel vision. Muscles prepare to act and often exhibit extra strength. Hearing enhances.

This is all great stuff in short doses when your life is on the line. It is an aroused state, but has the opposite effect from an aroused state from dopamine drive. When given too much cortisol, or low amounts for long times, many negative physiological results occur. Bodies subject to chronic cortisol exposure, usually from ongoing stressful situations, show fatigue, sleep issues, increased aggression, tissue damage like arthritis, digestive problems, and attention issues, to name just a few. The body learns to avoid those situations that release a lot of cortisol, or suffers chronic cortisol level issues.

The same activity in different contexts can elicit dopamine or cortisol. When I get in front of a group of people to give a talk, I am already pumped for the dopamine released in anticipation. Afterwards, I am high from the euphoria of being on stage. To most humans, that is one of the most feared and stressful situations, pumping out cortisol, leaving the person fatigued, irritated, and relieved to be done. Racecar drivers get chemical highs doing what elicits all the signs of PTSD in my wife, driving fast under adverse road conditions, weaving in and out of traffic. Does your dog associate the sport or activity you so like with rewards, joys, and dopamine? Or does it elicit stress and worries of failure (if I can use the word "worries")?

Sociable dogs are those who carry genes for orientation towards humans. They are the descendants of those who self-selected to be around humans, who could read them closely and know if they were friend or foe. Dogs as a group are extremely good, some researchers say the best besides humans, at reading human emotions and attitudes because that was what was selected for. Take agility as my current example. If I was stressed every time I went into the agility ring (and I do experience stress in that situation, so I don't ever do agility), my dog would sense that. I would be emitting scent-based hormones and showing stress and fear. My dog would pick up on that. If my dog underperforms and does not get a reward for the event, more cortisol is released by each of us. If I am pumped and excited and positive, my dog would sense that, and if they are rewarded during the run with successful execution and afterward by me, then positive addictions form. Of course, what happens when I reward a bad run? There is a balance there that varies by dog, where the event has to be always fun and rewarding, without signaling that a bad portion of a run was the desired outcome. Evidence is pretty strong that the longer the time between event and reward, measured in a few seconds, the harder it is for a dog to associate a reward with an event. If my dog hits a bar in an agility run and 10 seconds later sees me disappointed at the end by the run, the dog will not think "Oh, that darned bar." They will associate disappointment with the run itself or with me.

Therein lie all the complexities of behavior. Actions are responses to a lifetime accumulation of memories of rewards, including the chemical releases associated with them and the anticipation of them. Behaviors are compounded by the intended and unintended associations of negative events and memories. Performances are complicated by the brain's attention to the task at hand versus the distractions in the area, the relationship of dog and person, which layers into this, all built on a foundation of innate or maybe disease influenced tendencies. Do my behavior-oriented reviewers a favor. They wanted this paragraph in bold, with flashing letters. The publisher did not have flashing letters as a type-face option, so maybe you can just reread it.

How far can dogs go with learning? Chaser, my hero in the Border Collie world, learned 2,000 words and probably simple noun/verb sentence structure (Pilley, 2014). Watch any freestyle dance to see how many complex behaviors can be chained together, often with emotion. There are literally thousands of books, videos, seminars, and presentations on dog behavior and training. I ask you to remember the biology that lies underneath learning, the mental health issues that we largely share with dogs, and the extreme importance of good training and behavior modification and use all of that to help you sift the good from the bad, and what will work with your dog, and what won't. Sorry, no magic lesson or potions here. At least we do have places to start our look for answers.

TOUR 13

KEEPING YOUR DOG
HEALTHY

The main reason for this book is that you really can apply your knowledge of biology to enhance your relationship with your dog, your vet, and other care providers. I will give you some examples, in case the point is not yet evident. In addition, now that you know basic functions and parts, you can see how they vary through time. Hence a brief look at puppies and older dogs.

Gromit is nearly 15 years old. He is really not the same dog he was as a puppy or as a 7-year-old. He is not just less playful or energetic, he is different inside. The average Border Collie lives 12 years, so he is getting up there. He is very stiff when he gets up from his naps, and the length and frequency of said naps has increased substantially. His feet are enlarged and his hips less flexible. When I look into his eyes, they are cloudy. He can't hear the rustle of food dishes. On the plus side, thunderstorms no longer bother him. His nose has never worked better. Daily, he demands Frisbee time from me no matter how many walks we have had. He still jumps for the Frisbee even despite throws kept low to protect his joints. He seems to just want to jump. Too often the disc smacks him in the head or he grabs at the wrong place or time. He rests after about 10 short throws, and then we do it again. That box checked, he can get on with his day. Sometimes I just stare at him.

Gromit was our transformational dog. He moved us from being dog owners with other foci in our lives to dog people who build their lives around their dogs. We pick our cars based on how well the crash-resistant kennel will fit. We selected our house because it had enough land to set up a huge fenced running space. The first substantial work on our house was to build a barn for dog agility practice. My wife changed her career from environmental education to a dog-centered training business. I added dog research to my academic portfolio and incorporated dog biology into my class examples, much to my students' delight. All of our dogs come with us on trips, including field labs. Gromit changed our daily focus and pulled us into his world. Our time together is growing very short. So much of what I learned, so much of what I write here, is what I learned the hard way, and wish I had known all along.

Gromit came to us as a rescue, like almost all of our dogs. I didn't understand what subtle ways behavior could be genetically influenced because I did not know anything about his lineage or his siblings. Over the course of his life, he has had a pretty typical run of dog medical issues. Many times he cut himself running through the woods. He had skin tags, testicular cancer, leptospirosis and associated kidney failure, arthritis, Lyme disease, and now seizures that began a few days ago. He is mostly blind from operable cataracts and inoperable clouding of the vitreous humor. He has arthritis, maybe from the Lyme, but also from over 14 years of being a very active dog, and a common form of arthritis is from wear and tear. He has had ticks. He has had many gastrointestinal irregularities, and a bladder infection. Way too soon, he will die. Before him, Beaker had tapeworms as a puppy. He had a severe bout of painful and bloody diarrhea from giardia. Wish added to our medical knowledge with face and leg lacerations, some of which required stitches, and a repeatedly broken toe. This week, she tore her CCL, as I mentioned earlier. She awaits surgery and two months of physical therapy. Tattoo added vestibular (inner ear) problems to our experience. Beaker and Blizzard both died from cancers. Tattoo and Gromit required us to manage pain and make judgments on quality of life. Knowing dog biology has helped me keep them alive longer, and helped to let them thrive as they lived their lives. It has never helped me let go or say goodbye. My hope is that the information in this book will help you enjoy your dog more, marvel at their complex but graceful bodies and minds, know what to watch for or ask about when you suspect illness or injury, and make your time together just a bit better.

From puppy to old age

The biology I have covered so far applies to any aged dog. They eat and digest. They breathe. They have genes and cells. They use muscles and a skeleton to get around. Hair defends the puppy as it does the adult. However, pre-natal puppies differ from new-born puppies, which certainly differ from adults, especially geriatric ones.

Puppies

Except in unusual breeds like Alaskan Klee Kai, which at least to me looks like a puppy version of a Husky, it is not difficult to tell a puppy from an adult. Same with humans, right? Keeping a puppy healthy is not the same as keeping an adult healthy.

We need to start where I left you off in the first chapter, after the sperm and egg meet up. Ponder, if you will, that in all mammals, there is no guarantee that the whole litter shares the same father. Sperm from different matings (or dads) can hang around the oviduct in the female at least a day or two, years in turtles, not that you asked. You can be confident that all of the puppies share the same mother, however. Embryology is fascinating, to be sure, but not a stage most dog owners see. The single cell with the 39 chromosomes from dad, the sperm, joins the much larger egg with its mitochondria and 39 chromosomes, from mom, and you get a full set of 78 chromosomes. This can be thought of as Cell One, which copies its DNA in a process called mitosis, and divides in half. Two cells. Each of them doubles to two more each making four. Then eight. No, I am not going to do this all the way to 10 trillion, but that is what happens. Along the way, cells specialize into three layers called endoderm, mesoderm, and ectoderm. Endoderm makes brains and nervous tissue, including the retina of the eye. So cool. Mesoderm makes most of the muscles and organs inside. Ectoderm makes skin. Layers fold, divide, move about, and structures come and go because of evolutionary baggage. That is when we see gill slits from fish stages in our past and…really let's get to the puppy, right? Do pause for a moment, and think about the difficulty of getting a couple of dozen identical cells in a ball to differentiate into tissue types, then organs, and have parts end up in the right place. I really wonder that any of us come out with the right number of fingers and toes. Besides, what is the "right" number, anyway? Those variations are all that allow long-term species survival in a changing world. Remember, also, species don't care about survival. Those that make copies show up in later generations, those that do not make successful copies do not. There is no evidence or even any conceivable mechanism that would allow a species (a big group) to care about anything unless they communicated broadly via social media. Most species lack Facebook, Twitter, Instagram…I show my age picking those examples.

Mammals give live birth, except for three species from Australia and New Zealand that lay eggs. Embryos go through all that cell dividing stuff and eventually a young 'un pops out for the rest of the needed growth. From an evolutionary point of view, the developing embryo is a parasite in the mother, taking resources from her, sometimes challenging her immune system, leaving traces behind. The placenta, that organ that connects the embryo to the mother to get much-needed oxygen, and to dump off waste and carbon dioxide, is made of tissue derived both from the embryo and from the mother. After giving birth, some fetal cells remain in the mother and have been found growing in maternal tissue in the heart, liver, and brain.

Mammals don't produce newborns that are sexually mature adults. Can you imagine a human carrying a baby for 15 years? There are lots of interesting variations in mammal species where embryos delay development for up to a year so they are born when food is more available (look up delayed implantation — Mustelids are pros at this). Embryos are also born in varying degrees of "doneness." On one end, marsupial embryos crawl out of the vagina while very tiny with only their front arms well developed, crawl up into the marsupium or pouch, and reattach and finish most of the development that other mammals do inside of their moms. At the other end of the spectrum, you see animals like horses and deer that give birth to precocial young. These are well developed, and can walk within hours after birth. They are usually prey animals, and it behooves them to be ready to run, or at least walk, before some predator strolls along. Gestation in Mom for them is close to a year in horses, seven months in deer. Size matters. Elephants gestate 22 months, and pop out ready to roll.

Many predators take a different path. Lugging around a half dozen parasitic puppies can put Mom at a real disadvantage. Extra weight slows her down and makes her less maneuverable. Better to get the puppies out sooner and bring them food, let the puppies finish in the den rather than in the mother. Dogs are closer to the unbaked side at 60 days. We call that being altricial. Puppies are born blind and deaf, and spend the first couple of weeks rapidly developing systems that in precocial offspring happen in the womb. Eyes finish forming, the middle ear develops, the heart finalizes closing off valves between sides and now routes blood to the lungs, that sort of thing. In fact, the eyes do not even open for around two weeks and would be damaged if they were opened early and exposed to light. In many ways, in most ways actually, this is still embryo development, just in a den instead of a uterus. Unless you are a dog breeder, or you have a dog whelp puppies at your house, you never see this. The average litter size in dogs is a half dozen puppies, with lots of variation from breed, as well as individual variation and luck of the sperm on that trip.

The next couple of weeks after birth, out to a month postpartum, is time for muscle building, learning to walk, connecting the brain to the outside world so it learns that what it sees, hears, and feels is what is going on around it. This is also a time of feeding, drinking a lot of fat-rich mother's milk to provide the nutrients and immune molecules needed to protect the new puppy.

Published stages of development are, let me just say, all over the place. I wanted to say that they were poorly developed, but that is incorrect. Each is well thought out, but based on different criteria. These stages, after all, are human-defined. It is continuous growth in nature. The American Animal Hospital Association in 2012 published Canine Life Stages Guidelines that can help us see the stages of development. See what I did there? I skipped all of the food giants' descriptions of puppy stages, and all of the animal behaviorists' sources, and went to a hopefully more objective source. Dogs grow continuously, so as biologists we often speak of neonatal, juvenile (pre-sexual maturity), adult (sexually mature and fertile), and post-reproductive. You can add in geriatric in domestic species. In the wild, being geriatric generally means you are food for another. But we humans like to divide stages up, so the cutoffs are somewhat undefined. Because what I am about to do is arbitrary, I want to be able to cite AAHA instead of Mark and Mary's Better Dog Care Site (no such site exits, I made that part up).

For AAHA, the puppy stage is defined as the entire time from birth to reproductive maturity. It covers the whole time of development, puppy teeth, transition to solid food, and lumps them together. Let's tack some milestones on those first parts, recognizing we have bred in a lot of variation in different dog lines, and individuals all vary. Puppies get their baby teeth, the 28 small sharp teeth, starting at about 4 weeks. Puppies generally are weaned off mother's milk in weeks 5 or 6. I am often asked why puppy teeth are so sharp. One speculation is it makes it painful for the mother, forcing her to wean the puppies. That would seem to lead to selection for puppies with less sharp/painful teeth so they can get a free meal longer, so I am skeptical. Puppies are generally separated from their moms and find their new homes between 8 and 12 weeks. Puppies start to explore the world around them, and usually there are a lot of efforts to socialize the puppy at this stage. Data on this are mixed, and to argue against doing that without data would get this book burned, so let's just admit that this is what is done. The adult teeth replace the milk teeth between 15 and 30 weeks. Domestic dogs reach sexual maturity as early as 6 months and as late as 2 years, generally less than a year. This is a heavy cell division and growth stage, so puppies tend to eat protein and energy-rich food in their first year. Pre-sexual maturity is all about growth and strengthening and socialization and learning. It is also the time that lots of genetic problems become apparent, because the systems are new and growth puts a lot of stress on them.

Sterilization

Time out for another fight, but this time there are some interesting biological data to support some of the newly emerging positions on sterilizing dogs. First, should you sterilize (spay a female, neuter a male)? This is not a science question, so this one is worthy of a good fight as you will have no data to support your cherished opinion. Science can ask how to sterilize, and what are the effects of sterilization, but it cannot experiment or gather data on if it is ethically or socially acceptable. Since the answers affect puppy development, I place this section here. But I argued with myself about putting it way back in Chapter 1, or at the start of this puppy section. Apologies if you would have chosen another location. That slight digression was to give you time to gather your weapons.

Some people argue that it is unethical to sterilize, and indeed in Europe it is becoming socially unacceptable to sterilize. Many people want what is "natural" for their dogs. Natural, however, would be undomesticated freedom. Too late for that. Maybe I should say that many want their dog "unmodified." I can't argue with that. If, however, you claim that one should not sterilize because the dog cannot choose to do it, I would respond that the dog did not choose to become domesticated, to live in my family, to have as family members other dogs and people in my household, and cannot actually be given the option to select to be sterilized, either. Choice involves knowing more than one side of an equation. We quickly anthropomorphize our dogs, assuming they would think like a human and choose accordingly. In a pack setting for wolves, most do not mate. Do they even think of mating the way we do given that most would never produce puppies? You will choose for them either way. Own it. But do not bully others to your opinion and decision. Talk, persuade, and consider that the dogs we humans domesticated tens of millennia ago to be our tools are in many cases now living in our houses as full-fledged family members. What was OK to do to domesticated cattle may no longer apply now to our once-pets, now family members. I accept that times are changing, but I do not accept that dogs get to choose when they cannot know the choices. Either way, we choose.

I am currently still in the camp that says dogs are domesticated cohabitants, but there are too many in the world and I make life and death decisions for them without any ability to consult with them. This includes, for me, a preference that pet dogs be sterilized if there is no intent to breed them. Believe you me, if I could, I would seek their counsel and consent. I admit that I am troubled by that paternalistic approach, and it tends to cut out (pun intended) really good genetic dogs in favor of those less discriminating or controlling. I give this only a few sentences here, but this is a deep and profound question and I feel incredibly unequipped to address it as my opinions are changing over time. I will point out that the reason rescue groups and humane societies promote sterilization is to reduce the huge number of unwanted puppies who suffer and die from neglect. That is a real, population-level biological issue. There is also a lot of convenience to having sterilized dogs. Females in heat attract uncut males, menstruate, and might bring an unexpected litter to your family. Males who smell a female in heat can be a challenge to control. Yes, you can learn to control many males, and easily manage females in heat, but it is an added challenge that most people new to dogs are ill-equipped to consider.

I fully appreciate those that say it is unfair to sterilize because the dog never gave permission. I agree that the dog never had a chance to consider sterilization because you cannot communicate that complex thought to a dog, so maybe if you did offer that clearly to your dog, the dog would choose it. Either way, you are choosing for your dog. Don't think for a moment that the choice side alone should decide this. Personally, I am not a fan of unnecessary surgeries, so I would not remove dew claws, because they stabilize feet. I would not crop ears; I like the unaltered look. I would not dock tails; they give balance. I do not judge those who do. I think in the grand scheme of things, I am going to judge you by how well you care for your dogs, how trim their weight is, and how you adapt to their needs. I can overlook a little mutilation along the way. I have friends who are anti-cutting of any sort. I see their point. I have friends who think minor cosmetic surgeries are OK. I see their point. I have no friends who think dogs are just property and we can do as we please. Unacceptable to me. But they are out there. Globally, by far, that is the dominant position.

So let's assume for this paragraph that you want to know when you should sterilize a dog from a biological perspective. I'd like you to have some biology to add to what is normally just a who-shouts-loudest fight or a default to whatever others tell you. I am not saying you do want to sterilize, or that you necessarily ought to if you are knowledgeable of the repercussions of your choices. Especially if you are new to the world of dogs, I am a much bigger fan of making life easier for you and your dog and sterilizing. When you are a few dogs deep, I want to see you wrestling with the many tough choices you make for your dog, and wishing you had known more with your first dog.

Turns out there is a growing body of biology to guide your sterilization-timing choice. Hormones affect behavior, and there are behavioral risks to early removal of gonads. Hormones are very powerful, and spaying/neutering before the adult hormones have a chance to impact physiology also carries measurable health risks. The data so far seem to indicate that if you are going to remove gonads, wait until sexual maturity, or even later, until growth stops. We shouldn't be surprised. Testicles and ovaries are evolutionarily what the whole organism is about. Stopping development without the hormones those impart is bound to have significant, adverse effects.

In male dogs, waiting until the growth plates in the long bones (femurs and humeruses, tibias and ulnas) fuse leads to stronger legs, and a less leggy-looking dog. Early cutting leads to increased vulnerability to physical impacts, especially in performance dogs, and increased risk of many cancers. Would I avoid adopting a pediatric neuter? Our dog Blizzard was a spindly-legged model of the effects of pediatric neuter from a wonderful rescue group, and he died young from cancer. I can't prove that his cancer was causally related to the early neuter, but the odds are in favor of it. I wouldn't trade a day we had with him. Wonderful dog. I would not choose to neuter a dog so young, did not choose that with Blizzard, and all things considered would not choose another pediatric neutered dog. But I am also far enough along in my learning that I can manage behaviors that arise in unsterilized dogs, which allows me to make a much later permanent decision. I understand why rescue groups do this, and why you might choose this for a dog, especially early in your time with dogs. But I would not personally recommend it.

Female dogs spayed early have reduced risk of mammary cancer and pyometra, an infection of the uterus. Can't happen if you remove the uterus. On the other hand, you can sterilize a female dog by just removing the ovaries and leaving the uterus. No one said this would be simple. Studies are starting to convince me that the best option for a female is to allow one fully developed estrus cycle allowing estrogen to make its mark before spaying. That requires noting the first estrus; it is not always visible. It also requires keeping the female away from uncut males for several weeks. Others recommend waiting until after the second heat since the first one can be a less active hormonal situation. Some vets recommend keeping the ovaries, so hormone patterns remain normal, but removing the uterus so that the female is not attractive to males and cannot get a uterine infection. Many veterinarians still recommend removal of both ovaries and uterus since ovaries can develop ovarian cysts. I think here you are going to have to do additional research to finalize your conclusions because the studies are still being done, and many vets refuse to leave the ovaries. You see, it is not so simple. Biology is nuanced, and laced with your ethics and your ability to manage situations. We let our last female dog have a full estrus before removing her ovaries and uterus. On the next dog, I think I would like to leave the ovaries intact if the early studies support that.

Geriatric dogs

Now we pass over the normal adult dog, because that is the stage your dog will spend most of their life in and we spent most of the book on, and what the next sections really focus on with veterinary care. At some point, your dog will go from adult (full grown sexually mature) to mature. This is, according the AAHA guidelines, from the middle of your dog's life expectancy to the last 25% of the dog's expected life. This is too arbitrary for me, and nothing biologically distinct is happening. Old age, by itself, is not a disease, it is the passing of time. Your dog is just getting a bit older, past their physiological peak, but still active. By the by, "life expectancy" means the average expected life. Half of all dogs will outlive that, half will die before that. Border Collies live on average 12 years. By AAHA standards, mature for a 12-year life expectancy is from 6 to 9 years. Your dog will soon become a senior even if they are a puppy today, as time flies. Senior, the last 25%, for my BCs is ages 9-12. Geriatric is anything over 12 years in a BC, since that is the average breed life expectancy. Gromit, are you listening to that? He is approaching 15.

Biologically we want to look for the aging diseases. Any system can fail, but odds increase as more time passes. Osteoarthritis comes from wear and tear on the joints. Muscle tone and fitness declines such that dogs sleep or rest more, and play or work less. Vision clouds, often with cataracts. Hair grays. Teeth damaged by wear and tear break or have to be removed.

So how old is my dog in human years? They aren't humans, so why ask? I guess because it is fun. Find the life expectancy of your type of dog, and use the AAHA percentiles if you need labels. I will show you how shortly. If you do not want to calculate based on life expectancy by breed, there are many charts out there with dog size compared to age in years that relate to human years. I find those misleading on many fronts but easy to use. Pets.WebMD.com has a popular and easy-to-use chart. Let's consider my 11-year old Border Collie, Wish. Wish weighs 27 pounds. On that chart, she is 65 years old in human terms, nearing retirement. On the AAHA percentiles, she is 92 percent of the way to the average life expectancy (11 years old/12-year average BC life expectancy), a senior dog. OK, I buy both of those. She is not the spring chicken she once was. She runs in agility, dances freestyle, goes on 10-mile hikes, and is very active all the time. When she tore her CCL, we asked ourselves if we should fix it. Surgery is not cheap, and comes in three prices ranges from expensive to if-you-have-to-ask-you-cannot-afford-it. The priciest option is the least invasive and has a shorter recovery time than the middle price. For Wish, the least expensive option means she will likely never run again. By age and chart, maybe I say it is time to retire and go the least expensive route. That would be reasonable. By her activity level, she could return to sports with the most expensive option. She is past her prime for certain, she is not winning like she used to, but she clearly loves to run, even on three legs as we await the most expensive surgery. No, we do not let her do it. Treat the dog, not the age chart. Surgery is in a week.

I still like the AAHA guidelines, as they force you to consider average breed longevity. Look up your dog's breed. Adams and her team published a paper in the *Journal of Small Animal Practice* (2010) that lists breed average ages based on over 15,000 dogs. For all dogs, the average was 11.25 years; use that with a mixed breed. For the more common breeds, Bulldogs were the lowest at 6.25 years, and Great Danes and Shar-Peis at 6.5 years, At the other end of the life expectancy scale, we find Cardigan Welsh Corgis made 16 years (Pembrokes average 12 years), Irish Terriers at almost 15 years, Toy Poodles at 14.5 years, Cairn Terriers at 14. There is a lot of variation, both by size and breeds themselves. Once you have the average for the breed, or dogs overall, use the percentage scale the AAHA uses and you will have a good idea where your dog is age-wise.

Health and veterinary care

Depending on your lumping or splitting of categories, about 10 or 12 dog issues make up most of the visits to the vet. In no order, these include changes in appetite, vomiting, and diarrhea; dental issues including bad breath; bladder issues; coughing and respiratory issues; soft tissue damage including cuts and bruises; limping and joint issues; skin issues such as itching, hotspots, and skin lumps including infections; ear issues; and changes in behavior. While my intent with this book is simply to show you the delightful biology of our best friends, there is a pretty close correlation to dog biology and veterinarian visits. One visits the veterinarian when the biology is not working the way it evolved to work, be it because of trauma or disease. Each of these represents changes from normal, so they require knowing what is normal, not just for dogs, but for this dog at this age with these other specific conditions.

Breeds, cancer, and death

I would love to simply list the breeds most likely to die. That is easy. All of them. Or I would love to simply list the 10 breeds most likely to get cancer. Easy to list, hard to do correctly. The problem is lots and lots of dogs die every year from unknown causes, so we incorrectly identify the causes of death and incorrectly estimate cancer rates. Some cancers are easier to find than others, so we over-identify those types. Some breeds are more likely to die of accidents, and while they may have cancer in them, they are recorded as accidental deaths and do not count toward cancer. One should not infer from this that the data are not out there. Just that you have to take them in carefully. Cautiously.

Let me give you an example. A pretty interesting study done in Sweden by Bonnett and others in 1997 showed interesting breed specific results. (Bonnett et al., 1997) The highest risk breeds (and most prominent cause of death for each) were in order of highest risk first:

Irish Wolfhound: tumor

Bernese Mountain Dog: tumor

Great Dane: gastrointestinal disease

St. Bernard: locomotor system disorders

Newfoundland: heart disease

Greyhound: locomotor system disorders

Dobermann: tumor

Boxer: tumor

Giant Schnauzer: tumor

Pomeranian: trauma

Drever: trauma

Basset Hound: tumor

Cocker Spaniel: tumor

German Shepherd Dog: locomotor system disorders

Fascinating. But they list the top three to four causes for each. Looking at them grouped, the picture is even more complex! An updated work in 2005 with a different approach, a larger data set, and far more details about specific causes of mortality, with some different results. (Egenvall, et al., 2005)

Dobson, in her 2013 review article on cancer in dog breeds, ignoring other causes of mortality, like many studies, found skin tumors to be the most common. (Dobson, 2013) They are much easier to see, obviously, so they get diagnosed a lot. She found these 10 breeds as the most likely to die from cancers: Irish Water Spaniel, Flat-coated Retriever, Hungarian Wirehaired Vizsla, Bernese Mountain Dog, Rottweiler, Italian Spinone, Leonberger, Staffordshire Bull Terrier, Welsh Terrier, and Giant Schnauzer. Is it that simple? Dobson's paper is 24 pages long. Cancer comes in many flavors, and different breeds have tendencies for different types of cancer.

PetMD on the internet has a list of cancer-prone breeds. Based on their survey of professional experience in the United States, they list these nine: Rottweiler, Bernese Mountain Dog, Bouvier des Flandres, German Shepherd, Great Dane, Labrador Retriever, Bichon Frise, Boxer, and Golden Retriever.

Short lists like this greatly oversimplify the issue of which breeds are healthiest. On the other hand, knowing breed probabilities for what mix or "pure" set of genes you already have is a pretty useful first step in knowing what to watch for in your dog. Likely to die from trauma? Watch out for accidents. Cancer? Which type? Watch for symptoms. Again, know normal in your dog so you can recognize abnormal.

Bacteria can infect any part of the body, and therefore any symptom or change you note could be an infection. Probably not, however. Bacteria are everywhere and can be anywhere. If you ignore an infection, sure, over time the body will most likely eliminate it or isolate it. However, doing so can leave lasting damage. A simple infection can become isolated and chronic, causing ongoing pain or discomfort, or might attack heart valves.

Often, I think, we overlook that, except for schizophrenia, dogs seem susceptible to all of the mental health issues we humans have. These don't show up on x-rays, but often are no less chemically caused than diabetes or allergies. We just seem to think the brain should play by different rules. It does not. You need to watch for common signs of mental illness. Unfortunately this list overlaps with lots of other medical conditions, such as attempts to escape or non-playful hiding, compulsive licking or chasing, decreases in playfulness, destructive or aggressive behavior, diarrhea, sudden weight loss or loss of appetite or thirst, excessive shedding not at season changes, cowering, reduced social interactions, increased sleeping, trembling, or vomiting.

Uncontrolled growth of normal cells, also known as cancer, can occur in any cell type and manifest anywhere in the body. Potentially any symptom could be caused by cancer or an infection, but most likely is not. You need to note symptoms, changes from normal, but not leap to diagnosis without proper testing. Similarly, not every symptom requires an immediate run to the emergency clinic. How much do these symptoms interfere with daily activities? How rapid was the onset? You see, every day is different, so an astute observer can find something to worry about every day. Millions of years of evolution in a world with no medical help pretty much weeded out most crises that occur inside the body that need absolute immediate fixes. Relax, observe, think, take notes.

Skip that last sentence about relaxing if there is severe bleeding or extreme difficulty breathing. Without air to the lungs and blood to move the oxygen around, you have only minutes. Poisoning can cause a break in circulation or breathing, and likewise treatment ought not be delayed. Otherwise, relax. Even severe diarrhea won't dehydrate your dog in minutes, and a twitch in the shoulder might not need anything at all.

Finding the right veterinarian for you

Now, while everyone is healthy, find a good veterinarian. Be proactive and find one you can trust and work with. They are easy to find and most veterinarians are excellent. I took care of an elderly woman for two decades. She had Golden Retrievers. Her veterinarian was a favorite former student of hers. To keep my elderly friend happy, he gladly let her visit every time one of her dogs had any indigestion. Her dogs were always overweight. This veterinarian never mentioned that to her. I specifically asked him why he had not raised the topic. He said he wanted to keep my friend happy. That might be the veterinarian you want. However, for me, I want a veterinarian who is straight up, who offers clear advice and explains the biological mechanism behind it. This also may not be your choice. Maybe you want a veterinarian who is accessible, friendly, and doesn't waste your time with explanations. There are as many veterinarian types as there are personality types. Most can adjust their style if you are clear to them about what you need from them. All of them should be good at diagnosis. None can read minds, yours or the dog's.

In the wild, and through most of domestication when dogs were merely tools, any dog that showed pain or weakness was attacked, discarded, or eliminated. Showing pain was strongly selected against. That means that if your dog is showing pain, they have to be in pretty severe discomfort. More panting than normal, unless it is pretty warm out, is often a sign of pain or discomfort. Increased heart rate without associated activity can be pain-induced. Yelps when moved or touched are obvious signs of pain. Resistance to normal touching or petting is a subtle but similar clue. More sleeping than normal, decreased appetite, or lethargy can all be symptoms of pain, and pain is a symptom of an underlying problem.

The vet visit

A typical veterinarian visit involves a team, although at smaller clinics the same person might do everything. A receptionist will set your appointments, greet you when you come in, and let the team know you have arrived. A veterinarian tech will get your dog's weight, discuss symptoms with you, and fill in the chart (digitally or on paper). That chart, that record of information you give to the technician, communicates to the veterinarian why you are there, and is reviewed before the veterinarian enters the exam room. Be clear and completely forthcoming here, do not "save it for my vet so I don't bother the tech." The walls in vet clinics are often too thin. I have heard people describe things that they did not tell the tech. That information would have helped the veterinarian prepare and diagnose. A few vets have told me that some people tell the technician different (or made-up) symptoms "to make sure the vet will see me." The more credible you sound to the technician, the better you communicate for your dog. The more clearly you can communicate, the better. If you can't, don't be afraid to say so. Sometimes all you have is "My dog is not acting right. I can't put my finger on it, but it is not OK." That matters, and is way better than made-up symptoms. In any game of "Telephone" the messages get blurred in the telling. You still have to pay attention and make sure the veterinarian heard what you said to the technician. Your information is crucial to an accurate diagnosis. The veterinarian will ask questions, do a physical or check-up to the degree that the symptoms require, maybe order up a test or two, and help you understand the next steps. Most vets I know wish people would raise financial limits early in the discussions, as that often dictates a different course of action. Someone will give you a bill and then you are on your way.

You do not need to go to a large clinic to get great care. One of the absolute best veterinarians I ever worked with was in a very rural part of Vermont in Newfane. I had called a local large clinic in Brattleboro when Wish cut her face on a sharp edge of fence while herding sheep. I could see the muscles, the zygomaticus minor most likely, but it could have been the levator labil superioris, the muscles in the rostrum area that lift the upper lip. I am sure you were thinking the same thing, right? A local clinic, just 10 miles from where we were, said they would not see us if I were not a regular client. I don't live in Vermont; I was there to give dog biology lectures. Sure, dangling skin and exposed muscles are not a life-threatening emergency per se, but I can't stitch that up myself (actually I can, but I lack the drugs to numb the pain), the wound needed cleaning, and we would need antibiotics. I also could not tell if there was any particular risk to the eye. I am sure they were a great clinic, but they offered no referral and no help. I presume their local clients love them, and that is who they chose to focus on. Their website sure made them look popular and responsive to needs. Such was not my experience.

The next closest open veterinarian was 40 miles away. The veterinarian on duty at West River Valley Veterinary Services answered my call herself, said she would gladly stay open for me as she was about to close, and invited us in. Since the clinic was 40 miles away by gravel road, over a few mountain streams, and through a cute covered bridge, she had to wait an hour for me. When I got there, the veterinarian, Tara, greeted us as we came in. She had called one of her techs to come back to the clinic. Tara gave a careful exam, asked enough questions of me to make sure my story checked out, and clearly explained what she was going to do. All the while, she talked lovingly to Wish, cleaned, stitched, and dressed the wound. Tara offered follow-up care instructions. I complimented her on her practice, as I have seen quite a few in my day. Her whole clinic philosophy (I think owned by another veterinarian with the same values) flowed from their attitude that things happen at any time of day and night, and since she cared about animals, she had to offer help whenever asked. Being in a fairly remote area, there was no 24-hour clinic she could refer her patients to. Her clinic had the basics covered, and if I lived there, she'd be my veterinarian.

Similarly, in Ohio we had an excellent veterinarian at Suburban Veterinary Clinic in Dayton. We knew Brian when he started veterinarian school and ended up at his clinic where, for years, he took excellent care of our dogs and cats. His was at that time a mid-sized clinic, now grown still larger. We currently go to a very large clinic in the Twin Cities, Inver Grove Heights Animal Hospital with all of the specialized testing equipment in house, with experts on staff in nutrition, chiropractic, surgery, allergies, you name it. We don't go there for the clinic or the equipment. We go there because the team of veterinarians, including Jim and Heidi, is almost all the type we have come to appreciate. Clear, willing to say they don't know when they don't, with the detailed science explanations I demand combined with the good diagnostics our dogs need. Choose wisely, and stick with your veterinary choice.

Symptoms

While no book can substitute for veterinary advice, let's review those main categories of symptoms for visits, with a mind to the biology that causes them. Throughout this book, I have recommended consulting with a veterinarian for several reasons, here more than ever. Symptoms are a sign of a problem, not typically the problem itself. A loss of appetite can have many, many causes. You note the change, the veterinarian will work to figure out the cause. You simply cannot diagnose most issues with the tools you have at home, unless you are a veterinarian working out of your house. Veterinarians go to school for years to learn far more biological details than I cover in this book. They continue learning for a lifetime. We are on a first name basis with our veterinarians and our veterinarian techs, not because we pull the trigger and go in all the time, but with up to four dogs at once, some old, all active, sooner or later they all get SBI or show ADR. ADR, so you know, is "ain't doing right." SBI is the common diagnosis "something bad inside." The average (typical, or modal, not average as in mean) dog in the United States sees a veterinarian once a year. Most veterinarians I know think that without other causes, an annual visit is about right. It lets you get to know your vet, and your veterinarian to get to know you and your dog, to see what is baseline, and to catch slow changes early.

Veterinarian visits are not cheap, depending on what the problem is. A simple physical without tests will likely be less in cost than a really fancy leash and collar; blood tests and other diagnostics could double that. These yearly visits are great for keeping current on disease prevention through vaccines and medicines that prevent heartworm and fleas. Most years, our dogs see the veterinarian for an annual physical. Once every few years one of them develops ADR, and we are back to the veterinarian for some tests. With four dogs, that is a veterinarian visit about every six months. I think they named their new building wing after us.

About those symptoms. Look for unusual changes in the digestive system; metabolic waste system like peeing; respiratory and circulatory systems; skin, skeletal, and muscular systems, sensory systems; and mental health from the central processing in the brain. You know the biological foundations of each of these by now, unless you started the book with the last chapter. Knowing how systems look when they work well will help identify changes that need attention. You can expect any or all of these over your lifetime with dogs.

Internal parasites

We learned of parasites first with Beaker. He developed painful, explosive diarrhea. Obviously that was not normal, and over-the-counter medications to slow the digestive system down did not help. I still remember taking him outside in the middle of the night and him howling in pain loud enough that it woke up my wife inside the house. Clearly he needed medical attention, and a simple drug we have come to love took care of the giardia he had. Beaker came to us with tapeworms, noticeable from the sesame-seed-looking progloittids in his feces.

Vomiting

Every one of our dogs has vomited and/or had liquid stools at some point. OK, every dog on the planet has, right? Dog digestive systems evolved to be sensitive. One needs this when one is eating raw, sometimes decomposing food, itself of uncertain health, which makes it more likely to be chosen as food in the first place. You have to note the contents and color. Is this material from the stomach or the small intestines (recall that part of the digestion chapter)? Was this a one-time deal or does it happen under predictable circumstances?

Teeth

Gromit lost a few teeth to chewing or tugging, we don't know which. Otherwise we have been largely free of dental issues, but we do get our dogs' teeth cleaned every few years to protect the gums. Some breeds, and many (most?) individuals from any breed type benefit from daily tooth cleaning. Bacteria make a biofilm on teeth, digesting the food that did not get swallowed. Over time, that biofilm thickens in to a whiteish mineral-like deposit leading to tooth decay and gum disease. Many veterinarians recommend tooth brushing, and there is canine toothpaste out there. My friend Sarah swears a bit of gauze rolled around your finger, and gently rubbed across the teeth will do the trick. Diet matters: More carbohydrates leads to more sugars in the mouth (thank you, amylase) and so more decay. What, your dog won't tolerate your finger in their mouth? Do your fingers taste like soap or perfume? Is it because your dog does not trust you? Maybe your dog does not like to have their teeth rubbed because there is a problem, a mouth sore or a broken tooth. Look around in there. Oh, your dog is a biter? Frankly, for me, that would be a deal-breaker. If I can't trust my dog with my hands, and I feed them and care for them, how can I trust them around children or the rare (in our house anyway) non-dog-familiar person?

I also smell my dogs' breath. As Gromit ages, his shows the most change, likely due to changes in his gut flora and fauna. We check his mouth to make sure there is no decay or inflamed gums. Get to know normal so you can know abnormal. A wolf should have horrible breath, look what it eats. My dogs eat much better, their breath should not stop a train in its tracks. Severe halitosis should be discussed with your veterinarian. It could be an important symptom of something besides bad breath.

Why it helps to know a bit of biology

Cricket developed what appeared to be a urinary problem her first week with us. Naturally, the problem became apparent to us on a Friday, and we did not really figure out the issue until late on Saturday. She was suffering, which most certainly was not the way we wanted to start out our relationship, so we took her to the 24-hour clinic for a more expensive version of a routine check-up to confirm that it was just a bladder infection and not some neonatal crisis. Gromit's increase in urination signaled his kidney failure, itself a symptom of leptospirosis. Wish gets occasional bouts of coughing caused by pulling too hard on her leash and collar, thankfully not caused by respiratory infection or smoking. We generally use a chest harness for that, and to reduce potential neck problems. Beaker died of a cancer of the blood. Each of our dogs has had cuts and scrapes; every active dog gets those.

Wish is the only one with stitches to show for it, two big cuts on her face and a cut on her leg a week before competing in Nationals. She is a rough and tumble girl, and has broken a toe a few times and now torn her CCL. Beaker cracked the top of his nose, his nasal bone, turning his head rapidly while too near a doorway when he heard treats being pulled out. He was a big, strong dog and could crank his head around pretty fast. All of our older dogs have arthritis. Wish and Gromit have enlarged feet from it. Gromit's hips aren't what they used to be. Tattoo had severe hip dysplasia. At age 3 an X-ray showed that he shouldn't be able to walk, but he was competing in agility quite successfully. Our veterinarian said we treat the patient, not the X-ray. At 11 he had to retire, and at 13 the pain became unmanageable.

All but Cricket have had skin lumps. Typically, we get those aspirated and the veterinarian checks for cancer; so far all have been basic fatty lumps. Blizzard got a large lump on his chest. It did not move like a fatty lump and it was clearly deeper. It grew fast and an X-ray showed a cancerous growth on his ribs that had already spread to his spine.

Mostly our dogs have been free of ear issues, although Gromit has deafness. Beaker got ear mites. One morning Tattoo was walking in circles: vestibular disease, balance problems, self-correcting over time. Gromit is losing his vision. In every one of these situations, knowing a little biology helped us understand the problem, panic less, and feel better equipped to choose treatments in consultation with the veterinarian.

Behavioral health dog professionals

Don't think that licensed veterinarians are your only arrows in the quiver. There are specialists to help with all kinds of issues. In all cases, check certifications, as many states allow just about anyone to call themselves a dog specialist.

There are dog trainers with little real-world experience, some who apprenticed with dog trainers, some with specializations. I have seen examples of truth stretching, such as "I am a board-certified dog trainer," only to find out the certification was for a very specific subset of largely unrelated dog training, in this case canine massage, but the person was marketing dog behavior problem solutions. On the other hand, some of the most experienced dog behaviorists I know have no certification. A few sled dog handlers come to mind. Brilliant. Observant. Savant-like, even. Let the buyer beware.

Certified Professional Dog Trainers (CPDTs)

The Certification Council for Professional Dog Trainers (CCPDT) was created by the Association of Professional Dog Trainers (APDT), to independently certify dog trainers. Those with certification have had organized training, passed exams, and must abide by a professional code of ethics. (Declaration of conflict of interest: I have done programs for the APDT and am no-doubt a bit biased toward them or I wouldn't work with them.)

Behaviorists

Behaviorists come in many flavors, including academic degrees at the master's or PhD level.

Applied animal behaviorists, certified applied animal behaviorists (CAABs) and associate certified applied animal behaviorists (ACAABs) are applied animal behaviorists who have earned an MS, MA (these are the associate certified bunch) or PhD in animal behavior from accredited universities. Behaviorists study "normal" in dogs, as you should, so they can recognize "abnormal" and treat it. They know behavior modification, the latest and the best (not always the same) techniques, and they know people-training, so you can learn to manage or improve your dog.

Surprisingly, or maybe not given everything else they need to know, veterinarians usually get precious little time in vet school learning behavior. Even for most simple training matters, they will often recommend a behavior expert or a dog trainer. Like human doctors, veterinarians can specialize and get board certifications including in behavior. There are canine psychologists and psychiatrists. Any certified and licensed veterinarian knows enough when to prescribe basic medicines for behavioral issues like thunder phobia, and most know when they are in over their heads and will recommend an expert. Sometimes they can't do that either because none is available in the area, your pocket book has plumbed its depths, or the symptoms are not yet clear enough.

Behaviorists are a kind of dog trainer who can help solve or just manage problems. I know a suite of fabulous folks who get called in to help with barking, biting, and other issues. Blizzard was fear-reactive his whole life after puppyhood, and that took proactive management every day of his entire life, taught to us by a wonderful behaviorist named Leslie. She is as tough as an army drill sergeant with a soft spot in her heart the size of Texas that she won't admit is present. She taught me training skills like understanding "what are your criteria for that behavior?" She worked with me on timing of rewards. She taught me how to manage that which I could not control, such as dealing with all the people who want their dog to greet mine, when mine is scared to death of theirs. We called her classes "Tortures and Miracles." Give your dog a fair shake and get a professional when you cannot get the results you need. Any change in behavior in our dogs sends up warning flags, and we watch to see what more is at stake. All this is to say that things go wrong with our dogs, mostly they are fixable or manageable, and when they aren't, life sucks.

There are dog masseuses, nutritionists, physical therapists, sitters, walkers, you name it. Do you need them? Sometimes, yes you will. At other times, they can add enormous value to your relationship.

Other activity trainers

Get involved in some dog activities so your dog is mentally stimulated. Remember how complex the dog brain is? For most dogs, just watching you walk about the house is not good enough. We know that physical activities with your dog increases the addictive drug chemicals that help you bond to your dog and your dog to you. These activities are not just healthy habits to keep you and your dog moving; they make for great, socially acceptable addictions.

There are scores of recognized sports and activities, from dog freestyle dance to fly ball, to…OK, here comes a list I developed for a talk I gave a few years ago. There are more, many more, just not ones I know anything more about than you can find out by googling the name. Each has a very active following only too eager to convince you that theirs is the most fun you can have with your dog. Each is actually right, too!

- Agility: running a dog partner on an obstacle course designed by the judge with standard equipment
- Barn Hunt: teaching your dog to find and signal a rat in a cage hidden among piles of straw bales
- Bikejoring: your dog pulling you on a bike, often through the woods
- Carting: like dog sledding on wheels, pulling a cart with people or other items
- Conformation showing: judged display of dogs whose coats and body shape best match breed standards
- Disc dog: disc competitions for distance and accuracy
- Dock jumping: dogs leaping for distance over water, often in a pool
- Dog hiking, pack hiking: taking a dog on a hike, sometimes for time, sometimes with gear
- Field trials: hunting skill-related competitions such as finding birds or retrieving them
- Flyball: races where dogs clear some jumps, grab a ball from a dispenser, and bring it back — fast and furious
- Herding: working a group of ducks, cattle, sheep, or goats with your dog on organized tasks
- Hunting: using your dog to partner in identifying, flushing, or locating game
- Lure coursing: using a fixed line and pulley system on the ground to drag a sight-bait at high speeds with your dog chasing
- Mushing: sled dog work with teams of highly trained dogs, over snow
- Musical canine freestyle: dog and human partner choreographed dances set to music
- Nose work: tracking odor or scent boxes in well-hidden locations
- Obedience trial: precise execution of very specific standardized tasks
- Dog parkour: Agility using locally found obstacles for the dog and handler (think tables, low walls, etc.)
- Protection sports: a series of sports that teach a dog to protect the handler and be safe around others, including Schutzhund
- Rally obedience: dog obedience over a course

- Sighthound racing: classic dog racing (for breeds such as Greyhounds) around a fixed oval course
- Skijoring: your dog pulling you on skis
- Tracking trials: seeing how well your dog follows a scent laid down by course evaluators
- Treibball: dog soccer with an exercise ball, the dog moves the ball into a goal
- Weight pulling: dog pull competitions where the winner pulls the most weight on a cart

All of these are on top of the things you do at home, like walks and playing fetch. A good dog activity trainer for any of these sports can also be a gateway into the world of dog specialists who deal with management and health issues. No, you do not need a paid trainer for each of these. They help a lot, but you can have fun with your dog for free. Ignoring food costs. Vet bills. Collars. Specialized equipment. Prices may vary. So a great obedience trainer can usually direct you to a great animal behaviorist or a great veterinarian, for example.

End of life issues

I will end this chapter with how we decide when to wrap up a life. Sometimes there is no choice. When we lived in Ohio, our neighbors had an Akita who would come over and join us when we had a bonfire. He loved to lie by the fire. One morning when I went out for a walk, there he was, dead by our fire pit. No choices to make. He was a good and old dog, and his time had come. Sometimes you have no choice, but you still have to choose. When Beaker got cancer, we were told what to watch for and what could go wrong. Cancer spread to his spleen and that ruptured one morning while we are out having our normal game of fetch. He was suddenly in immense pain, quivering, and off to the clinic in minutes. We held him as the veterinarian permanently relieved his intense pain. With Blizzard, he was also in great pain and quickly succumbing to effects of the toxins his cancer was releasing into his body. We spoiled him rotten for a few days, letting him have all kinds of treats the dogs do not get at our house: ice cream and smoked beef brisket and eating at the table with us. We took him on a solo boat ride. We cried a lot, had our veterinarian come out to the house, and we held him while the veterinarian released him from his pain. Likewise with Tattoo. His pain gradually increased from chronic in the background to an inability to do what he normally could. There was no "one day you are fine, and one day you are gone." We had to make some decisions that were far harder, picking the day and time for the veterinarian to come out to our house. Death is a family affair in our home, not something avoided, with all dogs present. We held him tight while he died. Our cat, who loved to sleep on Tattoo, riding the deep breaths up and down, was never the same after Tattoo left us.

This week, we changed Gromit's diet to ice cream and smoked beef brisket after he started having seizures and his blood profile showed increasing kidney damage. He is eating at the table with us, too. I even grilled him some venison steaks. We have spoiled him with short walks to his favorite places. Minor spasms shake his body almost every minute, starting to deny him balance and sleep. His pain seems low, but he is well medicated. His apprehension seems high. We cannot let this continue, and it is incumbent on us to act now that he is suffering so greatly. Tomorrow morning, the veterinarian will come to our house. We will hold Gromit. We will weep. We will reminisce. I am already crying, no need to wait on that for death. Gromit made us dog people. His may be the hardest passing of all.

How do you decide when you have to decide? Notice that I did not ask that in a way that leaves room to say it is always up to the dog to die, not me to decide. I do not believe that. There are no easy, clear-cut answers in most cases. Modern veterinarian care and dogs living in the house with us instead of out in the barn with the cattle has led to a lot of early diagnosis and more aware dog partners. Veterinarians have checklists and websites that ask questions to help you decide if it is time. They all come down to a balance that you have to weigh. Is the dog able to participate in activities that they used to? Gromit demanded Frisbee until a week ago. I had previously written this chapter with "When he stops, I will worry. It clearly hurts him, but not so much that he defers." He stopped. I worried. Is your dog in pain? How much? How can you tell? Can they take care of basic needs like eating and eliminating without help and excessive pain? What is excessive?

Many of my dog friends use "when the bad days outnumber the good" as their measure of when it is time to say goodbye. What constitutes a bad day? Why is 50% the cut off, why not 75% or 33%? Someone has to decide, and there is no way around it; that will be on you. We set criteria well in advance, but then we question them and we circle around the issues of how bad is it? Is today worse than yesterday and last month? Are we stretching this out for us or for our dog? Wait too long for the inevitable, and my dearest friend will suffer (that can be my wife or the dog, take it either way you like). Too soon, and we deprive us all of a life no one wanted ended. The best I can say here is what my dear friend Sue says. "If you are a real lover of dogs, and truly know your dog, if you are seriously asking if now the time, it is most likely well past the time."

Right now, Gromit is asleep on a dog bed next to my desk in my office. He came over again today, as he has through much of my writing. I am watching him breathe, twitch in his dreams, and I wonder about my friend. I do not wonder if it is time. It is. He gets every pain management technique there is from acupuncture to Adequan injections that I administer, and daily pain meds. Most of the time he appears pain free, but he walks with a limp and does pant at times that show his pain is not completely managed all the time. When I am done writing this morning, he will not hear me get up. When he awakes, he will realize I have gone and come looking for me, barking all the while like a submarine using sonar. A ping every few seconds, searching. If we meet at the top of the stairs and the lights for the stairs are not on, he will turn his head and look up at me over his right shoulder as if to say I need some more light here. If the light is on, down he goes with no pause. He navigates stairs slowly now, they hurt him. But he still chooses to take them, so the pain can't be too bad. Tattoo gave up on stairs, gave up on running, eventually gave up on most walking. Maybe we waited too long with Tattoo, but his whole life had pain and he had the most life-loving spirit. Same with Gromit. He was transformational for us. His loss will go deep, we will never completely heal. We will not forget. We do not shirk our responsibility to decide, either. Not in life where we chose to give him care and food and fun activities and decide his healthy weight. Not in death, unless nature graciously chooses for us before we have to intervene in the morning.

TOUR 14

BALANCE

And the pandemic came.

That line is a direct theft from Lincoln's second inaugural address, converted for my purposes. The Civil War itself was just weeks from ending. For Lincoln, this great storm that had torn the country apart was finally drawing to a close, and he was already looking down the road toward the needed healing, to the future. We do not live in the past. No matter how hard we try, our only time travel is forward. We cannot even sit still in the present and savor it. The mathematics and science around time work both directions, but we live in only one direction. Sometimes science runs into reality and we see a mismatch.

The Covid-19 pandemic, or The Pandemic, the greatest biological invasion of aliens since the Spanish Flu of 1918 a century before it. A few weeks after Gromit died, with Wish just starting out after her surgery to repair her torn CCL, a week or so after a friend died from complications coming from the virus, my school — like just about every university in the country — did the math and announced major cuts. The university was hemorrhaging money trying to meet student needs while unemployment skyrocketed. I think with some understanding you can see that one might reasonably despair, not that despair — or its buddy, desperation — ever need a rational cause. The past was tragic, the present unbearable, and the future looked pretty bleak.

As she does every day, rain or shine, pandemic or not, Cricket out of nowhere flew up into my lap and licked my face. She did not do this to help my condition; at that time she did not care. She wanted to go outside. She needed to go outside. As long as we were going out, maybe I'd like to bring the Frisbee? Wish needed 15-minute slow walks during her first four weeks of knee recovery. Bones heal slowly. Not just slow walks, s-l-o-w walks. Despite all of what was going on, the birds still sang. The dogs demanded their walks, their play, and their meals. They still provided companionship. What I heard them saying — while fully acknowledging that they were not the ones talking, I was — what I heard over and over was, "Yes, sure, all that is bad, but we are here. Now." Time moves along, and Wish and Cricket, for now, are our future.

Wish's knee therapy required twice-daily range of motion exercises to stretch muscles and keep scar tissue from interfering with the joint. OK, see that? There is basic biology at work. The vet prescribed range of motion work. Most people, based on postings in dog recovery chat rooms, skip this and other steps "because my dog did not need it." The dogs did need it, the humans just did not know the "why" of the task, so they did not do it. Wish needed heat on the leg, to increase blood flow. The injured tissues need lots of the body's anti-inflammatents and infection fighters. Those slow walks stressed the bone that had been surgically modified, the tibia (and thank you for asking), so that new bone would grow. With no stress, there would be no new bone in the needed places, or much less dense bone, which would therefore be weaker and likely to be damaged later in life. Did knowing the biology of what was going on help us? Sure did. We knew why the veterinarian demanded the care, why it was important to Wish, and therefore what would happen if we skipped it. At four weeks, Wish showed more healing than most dogs at eight because, as the certified canine physical therapist said, we did all the exercises that most people skip.

Prior to the injury, Wish was fit, as in not overweight, so her knee was not carrying undue stress. She was cardiovascularly fit, meaning the blood already had a good network of vessels to bring healing cells, the needed immune factors to fight invasion. It also brought the medicines the doctor gave, including antibiotics to fight infection and pain medication. She was well used to being handled all the time, so we could easily get her to participate in range of motion, heat and cold therapy, and to check the incision. The best healing we did took place before the injury. Not a typo. Before. Wish was fit and used to being manipulated and had a healthy diet. That did far more for her healing than the meds afterward. Want to live with your dog longer and have them be healthier? Start now. Today. And every day from here forward, with the occasional day off when it is really yucky outside. Prevention is a much cheaper cure than fixing a later problem. Also more fun for you and the dog.

By the way, our surgeon was an artist (say that with the French accent I am using in my head). We saw incision horror pictures on the web. People only post the worst. Wish has healed up beautifully. The only scar you can find on her is on her face from that herding accident in Vermont.

Don't think post-surgery with a Border Collie is all fun and games. Wish is of a breed selected to work. Surgery made her unemployed, unemployable, in all of the tasks that mattered to her. When the surgeon told us we would have to keep her controlled, no stairs and no jumping, for eight weeks, we laughed. Impossible. But we knew with unhealed bones, to ignore that was certain to lead to malformed bones and a wasted surgery. Dogs are smart, and we could not engage the body beyond a very strict regime of methodical exercise and stretches. So we employed Wish with new a new job, and she had to learn. Brain work is great exercise.

Feeding. The simple act of putting down a bowl of food changed overnight. Ever heard of snuffle mats? I had not but my wife knew them well. It sure does help to be married to a dog trainer. These are devious feeding devices invented by some disciple of the Marquis de Sade. They have flaps and layers of overlapping washable cloth. One spreads the meal out amongst the layers into nooks and crannies and the dog, after a few dog-head looks, starts sniffing around to find the food. Meals stretched out with Wish working the mat. We bought silicon rubber place mats designed kind of like a waffle with squares. You spread cheese or peanut butter into them and freeze them. Takes the dog 10 times longer to get the food. There are puzzles that you hide food in and the dog works the puzzle to find the meal. Or just sprinkle food over a towel and roll it up so the dog has to unroll it, working the folds for food.

Before you know it, the pandemic seems normal and your slow walks reveal the spring migration of warblers is passing through. We move forward. My dogs give a wonderful future to look forward to because they are unfazed by the chaos around us. Stability and fun in the same furry package.

I have two dear friends who foster dogs. To me, that seems crazy. You get a dog, scared, lonely, pulled from what is too often a horrible or tragic life, fall in love, and then give them away. A death each time. They remind me, no, we go forward. Those dogs go on to great lives in loving families and they get to see many of those lives unfold, and know that they played a part in it. This helps keep one's eyes on the horizon when the sea is full of waves.

Do I miss Gromit, who died just as the pandemic matured into the horrid beast that it became? With every bone in my body, even though emotion is all in my brain. Do I miss Beaker, who died two days before my mom did and left me with no companion to mourn with (besides my wife, but you know what I really mean here)? Every day. Each of these dear friends, including Tattoo and Blizzard, gave me great joy, something to look forward to every single day, and reminded me that most of my cares were not really that important so long as we had each other. In fact, those now-departed friends still give me great joy and satisfaction.

Cricket and Wish, they carry that torch for us. Will we ever replace them? No. None of our dogs replaced a previous one. Each is their own bundle of mystery and joy. Most certainly not a bag of enzymes. A product of millions of years of natural selection that shaped the dog, tens of millennia of humans selecting for certain traits, that reached ultimate perfection to lie on the dog bed next to my desk and interrupt my labors for play or their own work.

Dogs give balance to our lives. We give them lives. We share lives. Take a minute and ponder the blood flowing to every part of your dog (or picture my dog if yours is currently unavailable). Air moving in and out of the lungs. How often? Is that the normal amount for this situation? I check my notes, relieved. Food slowly working its way through the digestive tract while organ after organ secretes chemicals or mechanically mixes the hot mess into a digestible soup that will wondrously come out the other side a solid lump. If not, what is the color? Does it seem normally shaped? Is its smell normal? What thoughts are racing through my dog's mind as its neurons fire? Does Cricket count my breaths? She certainly enters the bathroom as if she intends to check out my, uh, droppings. I look out the open window. What scents about to hit sensors in Cricket's nose are invisible to mine? Some sound draws her attention. I do not hear it. Is it a high-pitched sound just for her? Some squirrel in a tree? Yes, that's the cause this time.

Enjoy the journey.

My wife took a picture of me walking in the woods with Blizzard. I am looking down at him and he is looking up at me. She added a caption to the picture, a line that she read somewhere, attributed to Roger Caras, "Some of our treasures we place in museums. Others we take for walks."

I need to go for a walk now.

About the Author

Tim Lewis, Ph.D., approaches canine research through the lens of an evolutionary ecologist. Born in Colorado in sight of the Rocky Mountains and raised near Chicago, mostly he has lived his adult life in the woods surrounded by wildlife, and surrounded by dogs. Like many of us, his first dog found him, greeting the Lewises as they returned from a friend's wedding. Beaker lived outside almost a full week before he owned the house. Wild at heart, he would roam the countryside anytime he could slip his leash or  dart out the door. So much of what he did appeared natural, and clearly had not been taught to this puppy. Beaker showed Tim how to see the world through a dog's eyes.

Tim's formal, non-canine education began at Augustana College in Illinois, where he received his bachelor's degree in biology, followed by a master's and doctorate in wildlife ecology from the University of Wisconsin-Madison. Tim taught for two decades at Wittenberg University in Ohio where he was an award-winning professor of biology; now he is a professor of biology at the University of St. Thomas in St. Paul, Minnesota. His classes include ecology, evolution, mammalian ecology, forest biology, tropical ecology, and general biology survey. He frequently uses dogs to illustrate biological ideas, and even taught a class built around dog biology for university students and friends of dogs. His research ranges across many species, including wolves, deer, squirrels, turtles and, of course, dogs. He has presented findings of his research in journals, at conferences, and as an invited speaker for more than 30 years. He currently cohabitates with two Border Collies, prefers herding with his dogs to most other activities beside walks, and hovers on the edges of the dog agility and canine freestyle worlds with his wife, who competes in those sports and teaches others to do so.

Cited Works

Adams, V.J. et al. (2010). Methods and mortality results of a health survey of purebred dogs in the UK. *Journal of Small Animal Practice* 51(10):512-524.

Arendt, M. et al. (2016). Diet adaptation in dog reflects spread of prehistoric agriculture. *Heredity* 117:301–306.

Bonnett, B.N. et al. (1997). Mortality in insured Swedish dogs: rates and diagnostic category of death in various breeds. *The Veterinary Record* 141:40-44.

Dawkins, R. (1976). *The Selfish Gene.* Oxford, U.K. Oxford University Press.

Dobson, J.M. (2013). Breed-predispositions to cancer in pedigree dogs. I*SRN Veterinary Science* 2013(11):941275.

Dreger, D.L. et al. (2016). Whole-genome sequence, SNP chips and pedigree structure: building demographic profiles in domestic dog breeds to optimize genetic-trait mapping. *Disease Models & Mechanisms* 9:1445-1460.

Dreher, J.C. et al. (2016). Testosterone causes both prosocial and antisocial status-enhancing behaviors in human males. *Proceedings of the National Academy of Science* 113(41):11633-11638.

Egenvall, A., et al. (2005). Mortality in over 350,000 Insured Swedish dogs from 1995–2000: II. Breed-specific age and survival patterns and relative risk for causes of death. *Acta Veterinaria Scandinavica* 46(3):121-36.

Gatti, R.C. (2016). Self-consciousness: beyond the looking-glass and what dogs found there. *Ethology Ecology & Evolution* 28:232-240.

Horowitz, A. (2017). Smelling themselves: Dogs investigate their own odours longer when modified in an "olfactory mirror" test. *Behavioural Processes* 143:17-24.

Jia, H. et al. (2015). Functional MRI of the olfactory system in conscious dogs. *PLOS One* 9(1):e86362.

Miller, P.E., and Murphy, C.J. (1995). Vision in dogs. *Journal of the American Veterinary Medical Association*, 207(12):1623-1634.

Pilley, J.W. (2014). *Chaser: Unlocking the Genius of the Dog Who Knows a Thousand Words*. Boston, MA, Mariner Books.

Stahler, D.R. et al. (2006). Foraging and feeding ecology of the gray wolf (Canis lupus): lessons from Yellowstone National Park, Wyoming, USA. *The Journal of Nutrition*, 136(7):1923S–1926S.

Sternberg, S. (2016). *Assessing Aggression Thresholds in Dogs: Using the Assess-A-Pet Protocol to Better Understand Aggression*. Wenatchee, WA, Dogwise Publishing.

Theurl, I. et al. (2016). On-demand erythrocyte disposal and iron recycling requires transient macrophages in the liver. *Nature Medicine* 22:945–951.

Vilar, J.M. et al. (2016). Biomechanic characteristics of gait of four breeds of dogs with different conformations at walk on a treadmill. *Journal of Applied Animal Research*, 44(1):252-257.

Index

A

B

Also available from Dogwise Publishing

Go to www.dogwise.com for more books and ebooks.

Aggression in Dogs
PRACTICAL MANAGEMENT, PREVENTION AND
BEHAVIOR MODIFICATION

Brenda Aloff

Brenda Aloff's book has become the bible for identifying, understanding, and resolving aggression problems in dogs. Contains detailed training protocols to use in specific types of aggression situations and how to manage the aggressive dog for his safety and the community's.

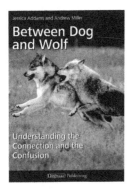

Between Dog and Wolf
UNDERSTANDING THE CONNECTION AND THE
CONFUSION

Jessica Addams and Andrew Miller

Is a dog a wolf? Yes and no. Get beyond stereotypes and learn what science and research can teach us about the differences as well as similarities between the domestic dog and its wild and hybrid wolf relations.

The Wild Canids

THEIR SYSTEMATICS, BEHAVIORAL ECOLOGY AND EVOLUTION

Michael W. Fox, PhD, Editor

Edited by one of the premier researchers in the field, these 30 scholarly studies from around the world is still important today.

Encyclopedia of K-9 Terminology

Edward M. Gilbert Jr. and Patricia H. Gilbert

Learn the language of purebred dogs from veteran AKC judges and breeders. Every page is filled with terminology and images that are essential to understanding breed standards and the sport of dogs. Well organized, illustrated and indexed for ease of use.

Dogwise.com is your source for quality books, ebooks, DVDs, training tools and treats.

We've been selling to the dog fancier for more than 25 years and we carefully screen our products for quality information, safety, durability and FUN! You'll find something for every level of dog enthusiast on our website dogwise.com or drop by our store in Wenatchee, Washington.